INTERMEDIATE CHINESE:
A GRAMMAR AND WORKBOOK

'No existing book of its kind can compete with this one.'
(Dr Qian Kan, Cambridge University)

Intermediate Chinese is designed for students who have some knowledge of the language. Each of the 25 units deals with a particular grammatical point and provides associated exercises. Features include:

* clear, accessible format
* many useful language examples
* jargon-free grammar explanations
* ample drills and exercises
* full key to exercises

All Chinese entries are presented in both *pinyin* romanisation and Chinese characters. They are accompanied, in most cases, by English translations to facilitate self-tuition in both the spoken and written language. *Intermediate Chinese* is also ideal for classroom use.

Intermediate Chinese, together with its sister volume, *Basic Chinese*, forms a compendium of the essentials of Chinese syntax. The two books form an integrated set but both may be regarded as self-contained.

Yip Po-Ching is Lecturer in Chinese Studies and **Don Rimmington** is Professor of East Asian Studies, both at the University of Leeds. They are the authors of *Chinese: An Essential Grammar* (1996).

Titles of related interest published by Routledge:

Basic Chinese: A Grammar and Workbook
by Yip Po-Ching and Don Rimmington

Chinese: An Essential Grammar
by Yip Po-Ching and Don Rimmington

Colloquial Chinese
by Qian Kan

Colloquial Chinese (Reprint of the first edition)
by Ping-Cheng T'ung and David E. Pollard

Colloquial Chinese CD Rom
by Qian Kan

Colloquial Cantonese
by Gregory James and Keith S. T. Tong

Cantonese: A Comprehensive Grammar
by Steven Matthews and Virginia Yip

INTERMEDIATE CHINESE: A GRAMMAR AND WORKBOOK

Yip Po-Ching and Don Rimmington
with Zhang Xiaoming and Rachel Henson

London and New York

First published 1998 by Routledge
11 New Fetter Lane, London EC4P 4EE

Simultaneously published in the USA and Canada
by Routledge
29 West 35th Street, New York, NY 10001

© 1998 Yip Po-Ching and Don Rimmington

Typeset in Times by Graphicraft Limited, Hong Kong
Printed and bound in Great Britain by TJ International Ltd, Padstow, Cornwall

British Library Cataloguing in Publication Data
A catalogue record for this book is available from the British Library

Library of Congress Cataloguing in Publication Data
Yip, Po-Ching, 1935–
   Intermediate Chinese: a grammar and workbook / Yip Po-Ching and
Don Rimmington.
     p.   cm. — (Routledge grammars)
   Includes index.
   ISBN 0–415–16038–3 (alk. paper). — ISBN 0–415–16039–1 (pbk. :
alk. paper)
   1. Chinese language—Grammar. 2. Chinese language—Syntax.
3. Chinese language—Textbooks for foreign speakers—English.
I. Rimmington, Don. II. Title. III. Series.
PL1111. Y564 1998
495.1′82421—dc21
                                                  97–49486
                                                    CIP

ISBN 0–415–16038–3 (hbk)
ISBN 0–415–16039–1 (pbk)

CONTENTS

15 Adverbials (summary) 96

16 的 **de**, 得 **de**, 地 **de** (summary) 103

17 'Every', 'each' – 每 **měi**, 各 **gè** and indefinite pronouns 111

18 Comparisons with 比 **bǐ** and 没有 **méiyǒu** (summary) 118

19 Various uses of 有 **yǒu** (summary) 127

20 Idiomatic uses of 是 **shì** (summary) 134

21 The aspect marker 了 **le** (summary) 144

22 The aspect markers 着 **zhe**, (正) 在 (**zhèng**)**zài** and 过 **guo** (summary) 152

23 The idiomatic uses of 来着 **lái zhe**, 呗 **bei**, 嘛 **ma**, 罢了 **bà le**, 么 **me** and 吧 **ba** 160

24 The idiomatic uses of 呢 **ne** 165

25 Onomatopoeia and interjection 170

Key to exercises 176

INTRODUCTION

This book is a sequel to its companion volume *Basic Chinese: A Grammar and Workbook* and is likewise designed to assist learners of Mandarin or Modern Standard Chinese, which is the language spoken by close on 70 per cent of the people in China. It presents the more complex features of Chinese syntax in an easily accessible reference-and-practice format. We hope it will be of help to students of the Chinese language at intermediate and advanced levels, and we envisage that it will be suitable for classroom use and, in particular, for independent study, as well as for reference purposes.

The book is divided into 25 units. Firstly it introduces a number of intricate linguistic structures, which are characteristic elements in the Chinese language, and then it goes on to provide in-depth reviews and analyses of basic grammatical patterns in variant and more complex forms.

Each unit deals with an individual language category or structure, and provides follow-up exercises for immediate reinforcement. A key to the exercises is given at the end of the book. Readers may wish to consult the units separately or work progressively through the book, but we suggest that, when going through a particular unit, they attempt all the exercises in it, before consulting the key.

Practical, functional vocabulary is used in the grammatical explanations and exercises, and overall provides an extensive range of frequently occurring terms and expressions. All illustrative examples throughout the book are given in Chinese script and *pinyin* romanisation* with English translations.

Students looking for guidance on more elementary grammatical structures should refer to *Basic Chinese: A Grammar and Workbook*.

The preparation of the book received financial assistance from the University of Leeds Academic Development Fund. Two Research Assistants, Ms Zhang Xiaoming and Ms Rachel Henson carried out much of the important work of assembling the illustrative material. The project could also not have been completed without the painstaking efforts of Ms Li Quzhen, who closely monitored the vocabulary progression and proof-read the text. Any errors or omissions are, of course, the fault of the authors.

* Note: We have used 'a' rather than 'ɑ', which is the standard form in *pinyin* romanisation.

L.Chia - 07/03/02 - 把 a) Post Verbal
hikes Clutter avoided
b) Definite Reference
c) Disposal element
(ie dol verbs of speaking)
(doing s/t to object-needed)

UNIT ONE
The 把 **bǎ** structure

A The 把 **bǎ** structure, which is unique to the Chinese language, has the effect of shifting the object of the verb in the sentence to a pre-verbal position. It is used most often with action verbs. The sentence: 他打破了那个杯子。 **tā dǎ pò le nà/nèi gè bēizi** 'He broke that cup.', for example, may also be expressed as: 他把那个杯子打破了。 **tā bǎ nà/nèi gè bēizi dǎ pò le**. There are two important rules concerning the use of 把 **bǎ**:

(1) The object must be of definite reference. In our example, the object 那个杯子 **nà/nèi gè bēizi** is of definite reference.

   One cannot say:

   > *他把一个杯子打破了。 **tā bǎ yī gè bēizi dǎ pò le**
   > because 一个杯子 **yī gè bēizi** is of indefinite reference.

(2) The verb must incorporate a complement. In our example, the verb 打 **dǎ** is complemented by 破 **pò**, without which the sentence would sound incomplete.

   One cannot say:

   > *他把那个杯子打。 **tā bǎ nà/nèi gè bēizi dǎ**

B There are various kinds of complements. In the examples given below, the complement in each case is shown in round brackets:

(1) Result complements. These are either adjectives or verbs, which indicate the outcome of an action. 破 **pò** above is an example of a verbal result complement. (See also *Basic Chinese*, Unit 22.)

   > 司机把汽车修好了。 **sījī bǎ qìchē xiū hǎo le** (好 **hǎo**)
   > The driver repaired his car.

学生把黑板擦干净了。 **xuésheng bǎ hēibǎn cā gānjìng le** (干净 **gānjìng**)
The student cleaned the blackboard.

他把那篇文章写完了。
tā bǎ nà/nèi piān wénzhāng xiě wán le (完 **wán**)
He has finished writing that essay.

她把窗户都打开了。 **tā bǎ chuānghu dōu dǎ kāi le** (开 **kāi**)
She opened all the windows.

弟弟把电视机弄坏了。 **dìdi bǎ diànshìjī nòng huài le** (坏 **huài**)
My younger brother broke the television set.

小猫把地毯弄脏了。 **xiǎo māo bǎ dìtǎn nòng zāng le** (脏 **zāng**)
The kitten has made the carpet dirty.

Note: It can be seen from the above examples that the particle 了 **le**, which usually signifies a changed state, is naturally associated with these result complements. If the verb used in the 把 **bǎ** structure, apart from indicating an action, also possesses an inherent notion of result, 了 **le** by itself may be sufficient to function as the complement:

她把窗户都开了。 **tā bǎ chuānghu dōu kāi le**
She opened all the windows.

他们把门关了。 **tāmen bǎ mén guān le**
They closed the door.

(2) Location complements using 在 **zài** phrases. (See *Basic Chinese*, Unit 21.)

我把画儿挂在墙上。
wǒ bǎ huàr guà zài qiáng shang (在 . . . 上 **zài . . . shang**)
I hung the picture on the wall.

妈妈把花儿插在花瓶里。
māma bǎ huār chā zài huāpíng li (在 . . . 里 **zài . . . li**)
Mother put the flowers in the vase.

妹妹把压岁钱放在枕头下。
mèimei bǎ yāsuìqián fàng zài zhěntou xià (在 . . . 下 **zài . . . xià**)
(My) younger sister put her new-year lucky money under (her) pillow.

(3) Direction indicators as complements. (See *Basic Chinese*, Unit 21.)

我把衣服放回衣柜里去了。
wǒ bǎ yīfu fàng huí yīguì li qù le (回 . . . 去 **huí . . . qù**)
I put the clothes back into the wardrobe.

爸爸把钱存进银行里去了。
bàba bǎ qián cún jìn yínháng li qù le (进 . . . 去 **jìn . . . qù**)
Father put the money in the bank.

她把茶端上楼来了。
tā bǎ chá duān shàng lóu lái le (上 . . . 来 **shàng . . . lái**)
She carried the tea upstairs.

(4) Duration and frequency complements. (See *Basic Chinese*, Unit 14.)

我把课文复习了两遍。
wǒ bǎ kèwén fùxí le liǎng biàn (两遍 **liǎng biàn** frequency complement)
I revised the text twice.

厨师把鸡烤了一个小时。
chúshī bǎ jī kǎo le yī gè xiǎoshí (一个小时 **yī gè xiǎoshí** duration complement)
The cook roasted the chicken for an hour.

我把头发梳了一下。
wǒ bǎ tóufa shū le yīxià (一下 **yīxià** brief duration complement)
I gave my hair a brush.

Note: Brief duration may also be expressed by repeating the verb:

我把头发梳了梳。 **wǒ bǎ tóufa shū le shū**
I gave my hair a brush.

(5) 成 **chéng**/作 **zuò** 'treat . . . as', 'regard . . . as' as complements.

他把学生当成自己的孩子。
tā bǎ xuésheng dàng chéng zìjǐ de háizi (成 **chéng** . . .)
He treated his students as his own children.

他们把这种酒叫作'茅台酒'。
tāmen bǎ zhè/zhèi zhǒng jiǔ jiào zuò máotái jiǔ (作 **zuò** . . .)
They call this kind of liquor 'Maotai'.

作家把自己的作品翻译成英文。
zuòjiā bǎ zìjǐ de zuòpǐn fānyì chéng yīngwén (成 **chéng** . . .)
The author translated his/her own works into English.

(6) 给 **gěi** 'give to' as complement:

阿姨把那瓶香水送给我。
āyí bǎ nà/nèi píng xiāngshuǐ sòng gěi wǒ (给 **gěi** . . .)
(My) aunt gave me that bottle of perfume.

请你把这封信交给你爸爸。
qǐng nǐ bǎ zhè/zhèi fēng xìn jiāo gěi nǐ bàba (给 **gěi** . . .)
Please pass this letter to your father.

(7) The manner/resultant state 得 **de** phrase/clause as a complement. (See also *Basic Chinese*, Unit 22.)

    (a) Phrase:

理发师把弟弟的头发剪得太短了。
lǐfàshī bǎ dìdi de tóufa jiǎn de tài duǎn le (得 **de** . . .)
The barber cut (my) younger brother's hair too short.

他把这个问题解释得清清楚楚。
tā bǎ zhè/zhèi gè wèntí jiěshì de qīngqīngchǔchu (得 **de** . . .)
He explained this problem extremely clearly.

    (b) Clause:

她把这件事情办得大家都满意。
tā bǎ zhè/zhèi jiàn shìqing bàn de dàjiā dōu mǎnyì (得 **de** . . .)
She dealt with the problem to the satisfaction of everybody.

C   In imperative sentences, 了 **le** and 着 **zhe** may sometimes be used as complements for a 把 **bǎ** structure to indicate completion or continuation of the verb in question:

请把蛋糕吃了。 **qǐng bǎ dàngāo chī le**
Please finish the cake.

请把我的大衣拿着。 **qǐng bǎ wǒ de dàyī ná zhe**
Please hold my coat.

D   When the negators 没 (有) **méi(yǒu)** 'did not', 'have not' (used in statements) and 别 **bié** or 不要 **bù yào** 'do not' (used in imperatives) occur with 把 **bǎ**, they are always placed before 把 **bǎ** in the sentence:

他没有把帽子戴上。 **tā méiyǒu bǎ màozi dài shàng**
He didn't put his hat on.

别把我的东西搞乱了。 **bié bǎ wǒ de dōngxi gǎo luàn le**
Don't mess up my things.

The 把 **bǎ** structure usually expresses an action which has already been realised, and the negator (as above) is likely to be 没 (有) **méi(yǒu)**. However, 不 **bù** may be used with it, where a condition is stated:

母亲对孩子说：你不把甲克穿上，别出去玩儿。

mǔqīn duì háizi shuō: nǐ bù bǎ jiǎkè chuān shàng, bié chū qù wánr

Mother said to her child: 'If you don't put on your jacket, you mustn't (*lit.* don't) go out and play.'

E Modal verbs always precede the 把 **bǎ** structure:

你必须把屋子收拾干净。 **nǐ bìxū bǎ wūzi shōushi gānjìng**

You must tidy up the room.

妹妹不肯把玩具还给姐姐。 **mèimei bù kěn bǎ wánjù huán gěi jiějie**

The younger sister was not willing to return the toy to the elder sister.

F Coverbal phrases and adverbials of manner generally precede 把 **bǎ**. They may, however, follow the 把 **bǎ** phrase, where emphasis is on them:

她用刀子把柠檬切成一片片。

tā yòng dāozi bǎ níngméng qiē chéng yī piàn piàn

She cut the lemon into slices with a knife.

less usual:

她把柠檬用刀子切成一片片。

tā bǎ níngméng yòng dāozi qiē chéng yī piàn piàn

She cut the lemon into slices <u>with a knife</u>.

Similarly:

他轻轻地把东西放下。 **tā qīngqīng de bǎ dōngxi fàng xià**

He put the things down quietly.

less usual:

他把东西轻轻地放下。 **tā bǎ dōngxi qīngqīng de fàng xià**

He put the things down <u>quietly</u>.

G Generally speaking, 把 **bǎ** constructions indicate 'intentional manipulation' as most of the above examples show. Occasionally, however, a 把 **bǎ** construction may also indicate 'unintentional intervention' or the result of it. For example:

妹妹把裙子弄脏了。 **mèimei bǎ qúnzi nòng zāng le**

My younger sister dirtied her skirt.

弟弟没 (有) 把电脑搞坏。 **dìdi méi(yǒu) bǎ diànnǎo gǎo huài**

My younger brother did not break the computer.

Note: 搞 **gǎo** and 弄 **nòng** both meaning 'handle' are often used in association with complements indicating undesirable results.

Exercise 1.1

Rewrite the following sentences using the 把 **bǎ** structure:

1 小孩儿打破了玻璃窗。 **xiǎoháir dǎ pò le bōlichuāng**
  The child broke the window.
2 小红梳了一下头发。 **xiǎo hóng shū le yīxià tóufa**
  Xiao Hong gave his hair a brush.
3 请吃这些药。 **qǐng chī zhè/zhèi xiē yào**
  Please take this medicine.
4 她从银行里取出了那笔钱来。 **tā cóng yínháng li qǔ chū le nà/nèi bǐ qián lái**
  She took the money out of the bank.
5 这个问题老师解释得很清楚。 **zhè/zhèi gè wèntí lǎoshī jiěshì de hěn qīngchu**
  The teacher explained the problem very clearly.
6 你的衣服我放在衣柜里了。 **nǐ de yīfu wǒ fàng zài yīguì li le**
  I put your clothes in the wardrobe.

Exercise 1.2

Make 把 **bǎ** sentences using the words and phrases below and translate the resulting sentences into English:

1 讲义 **jiǎngyì** 发给 **fā gěi** 老师 **lǎoshī** 学生 **xuésheng**
2 洗了 **xǐ le** 衣服 **yīfu** 他 **tā**
3 护士 **hùshi** 递给 **dì gěi** 药片 **yàopiàn** 病人 **bìngrén**
4 留在家里了 **liú zài jiā li le** 我 **wǒ** 钥匙 **yàoshi**
5 小偷 **xiǎotōu** 警察 **jǐngchá** 抓住了 **zhuā zhù le**
6 修好了 **xiū hǎo le** 司机 **sījī** 汽车 **qìché**

Exercise 1.3

The following Chinese sentences all contain errors. Make the necessary correction in each case:

1 小孩把杯子打。 **xiǎohái bǎ bēizi dǎ**
  The child broke the cup.
2 老师把书在桌子上。 **lǎoshī bǎ shū zài zhuōzi shang**
  The teacher put the books on the table.
3 我把信必须写完。 **wǒ bǎ xìn bìxū xiě wán**
  I must finish writing the letter.

4 她把石头到海里去扔了。 **tā bǎ shítou dào hǎi li qù rēng le**
   She threw the stone into the sea.

5 厨师把鸡熟了。 **chúshī bǎ jī shú/shóu le**
   The cook roasted the chicken.

6 请把拿好火车票。 **qǐng bǎ ná hǎo huǒchēpiào**
   Please keep your train ticket safe. (*lit.* Please hold on to your train ticket.)

7 小李把一个苹果吃了。 **xiǎo lǐ bǎ yī gè píngguǒ chī le**
   Xiao Li has eaten an apple.

8 她把生词记了。 **tā bǎ shēngcí jì le**
   She remembered all the new words.

9 护士把门没关上。 **hùshi bǎ mén méi guān shàng**
   The nurse didn't shut the door.

10 请把这件事不要告诉他。 **qǐng bǎ zhè/zhèi jiàn shì bù yào gàosu tā**
   Please don't tell him about this.

Exercise 1.4

Complete the Chinese sentences below with the appropriate complement in each case:

1 她把汽车停 _____ 车库 _____。
   tā bǎ qìchē tíng _____ **chēkù** _____ (location)
   She parked the car in the garage.

2 花匠把花儿浇了 _____ _____/_____ _____。
   huājiàng bǎ huār jiāo le _____ _____/_____ _____ (frequency)
   The gardener watered the flowers twice.

3 老大爷把茶都喝 _____ 了。 **lǎodàyé bǎ chá dōu hē** _____ **le** (result)
   The old man drank all the tea.

4 小伙子替朋友把菜买 _____ 了。
   xiǎohuǒzi tì péngyou bǎ cài mǎi _____ **le** (direction)
   The young man came back with the food he had bought for his friend.

5 男孩儿把小弟弟背 _____ 背 _____。
   nánháir bǎ xiǎo dìdi bēi _____ **bèi** _____ (location)
   The boy carried his little brother on his back.

6 老大娘把小姑娘当 _____ _____ _____ _____。
   lǎodàniáng bǎ xiǎo gūniang dàng _____ _____ _____ _____ (result)
   The old woman treated the little girl as her own daughter.

7 会计把钱数了 _____ _____/_____。
   kuàijì bǎ qián shǔ le _____/_____ (brief duration)
   The cashier counted the money.

8 厨师把菜煮了 _____ (_____) _____ _____。
   chúshī bǎ cài zhǔ le _____ (_____) _____ _____ (duration)
   It took the chef half an hour to prepare the dish.

Exercise 1.5

Translate the following into Chinese, using the 把 **bǎ** construction:

1 Don't forget (your) keys.
2 He put the book back on the shelf.
3 I don't want to mix up my things with yours.
4 He also looked on me as a friend.
5 They made (弄 **nòng**) me furious.
6 I read her application five times.
7 He wrote the letter very long.
8 Would you like to leave your bag here?

Exercise 1.6

Rewrite the following Chinese sentences as 把 **bǎ** constructions, adding an appropriate adjective or verb complement (together with 了 **le** in each case) to match the English:

EXAMPLE:
清洁工抹窗户。 **qīngjiégōng mā chuānghu**
The cleaners wiped the windows (clean).

Answer: 清洁工把窗户抹干净了。 **qīngjiégōng bǎ chuānghu mā gānjìng le**

1 爸爸洗汽车。 **bàba xǐ qìchē**
  Father washed the car.
2 妈妈晾衣服。 **māma liàng yīfu**
  Mother hung out the clothes to dry.
3 医生医病人。 **yīshēng yī bìngrén**
  The doctor cured the patient.
4 小猫抓/逮老鼠。 **xiǎo māo zhuā/dǎi lǎoshǔ**
  The kitten caught the mouse.
5 我朋友煮饭。 **wǒ péngyou zhǔ fàn**
  My friend cooked the meal.
6 妹妹借书。 **mèimei jiè shū**
  (My) younger sister borrowed the books.
7 秘书寄信。 **mìshū jì xìn**
  The secretary posted the letter.
8 小男孩擦皮鞋。 **xiǎo nánhái cā píxié**
  The little boy brushed (his) leather shoes.

UNIT TWO
The 被 **bèi** structure

A The 被 **bèi** structure in Chinese is similar to the passive voice in English. However, English passive voice sentences are commonly rendered in Chinese as topic–comment sentences. (For further discussion of topic–comment structures, see Unit 7.):

菜吃完了。 **cài chī wán le**
The food has been eaten.

教室打扫干净了。 **jiàoshì dǎsǎo gānjìng le**
The classroom has been swept clean.

Note: As a general rule, verbs followed by complements of result (e.g. 吃 **chī** 'eat' + 完 **wán** 'to a finish', 打扫 **dǎsǎo** 'sweep' + 干净 **gānjìng** 'till clean', etc.) tend to be associated with the sentence particle 了 **le**. (See Units 1 and 8.)

The 被 **bèi** structure comes into play (1) when an 'agent' is introduced into the sentence or (2) the speaker adopts a narrative stance and describes how something has happened:

(1) 被 **bèi** with an agent:

菜被我吃完了。 **cài bèi wǒ chī wán le**
The food was finished by me. (我 **wǒ** – the 'agent')

教室被学生们打扫干净了。 **jiàoshì bèi xuéshengmen dǎsǎo gānjìng le**
The classroom was swept clean by the students. (学生 **xuésheng** – the 'agent')

(2) 被 **bèi** in a narrative sentence:

菜被吃完了。 **cài bèi chī wán le**
The food was eaten (by someone).

教室被打扫干净了。 **jiàoshì bèi dǎsǎo gānjìng le**
The classroom was swept clean (by someone).

Note: In the sentence 菜吃完了 **cài chī wán le**, the speaker takes a commentative stance, observing that the food has been finished and there is none left. By contrast, in the sentence 菜被吃完了 **cài bèi chī wán le**, the speaker adopts a narrative stance, and is saying what has happened to the food, i.e. it has been eaten by somebody.

B   The verb in a 被 **bèi** sentence, as in a 把 **bǎ** sentence (see Unit 1), should always be followed by a complement:

电视机被弟弟弄坏了。
diànshìjī bèi dìdi nòng huài le (坏 **huài** result complement)
The TV set was damaged by (my) younger brother.

窗户都被打开了。 **chuānghu dōu bèi dǎ kāi le** (开 **kāi** result complement)
All the windows had been opened.

钱被藏在抽屉里。
qián bèi cáng zài chōuti li (在 . . . 里 **zài . . . li** location complement)
The money was kept in a drawer.

小猫被爸爸抱在怀里。
xiǎo māo bèi bàba bào zài huái li (在 . . . 里 **zài . . . li** location complement)
Father held the kitten in his arms. (*lit.* The kitten was held in his arms by Father.)

礼物被装进一个漂亮的盒子里去了。
lǐwù bèi zhuāng jìn yī gè piàoliang de hézi li qù le (进 . . . 去 **jìn . . . qù** direction complement)
The gift was put into an attractive box.

狼被赶出村子去。
láng bèi gǎn chū cūnzi qù (出 . . . 去 **chū . . . qù** direction complement)
The wolf was driven away from the village.

她被爸爸批评了几次。
tā bèi bàba pīpíng le jǐ cì (几次 **jǐ cì** frequency complement)
She was reprimanded several times by her father.

犯人被关了三年。
fànrén bèi guān le sān nián (三年 **sān nián** duration complement)
The criminal was imprisoned for three years.

这种画儿被叫作现代画。

zhè/zhèi zhǒng huàr bèi jiào zuò xiàndài huà (作 **zuò** . . . as complement)
This style of painting is called Modern Art.

这个骗子被我当成好人。

zhè/zhèi gè piànzi bèi wǒ dàng chéng hǎo rén (成 **chéng** . . . as complement)
This cheat was taken by me to be an honest person.

头发被剪得太短了。

tóufa bèi jiǎn de tài duǎn le (manner/resultant state 得 **de** phrase as complement)
His/her hair was (cut) too short.

她被雨淋得衣服都湿透了。

tā bèi yǔ lín de yīfu dōu shī tòu le (得 **de** clause as complement)
She was soaked to the skin by the rain.
(*lit.* She was drenched so much by the rain that her clothes were all soaked.)

Note: It can be seen from the last two examples that adjectival complements modified by degree adverbs 太 **tài** 'too' or degree complement 透 **tòu** 'through and through', etc. generally require the use of sentence particle 了 **le**.

C   In spoken Chinese or in colloquial writing, 被 **bèi** is often replaced by 让 **ràng** or 叫 **jiào**, but only if an agent is involved. In these cases 给 **gěi** may also be used directly before the verb:

衣服让孩子 (给) 弄脏了。 **yīfu ràng háizi (gěi) nòng zāng le**
The child made his/her clothes dirty.

强盗叫警察 (给) 抓住了。 **qiángdào jiào jǐngchá (gěi) zhuā zhù le**
The robber was arrested by the police.

Note that 被 **bèi** does not usually go with 给 **gěi**:

One does not say:

*强盗被警察 (给) 抓住了。
qiángdào bèi jǐngchá (gěi) zhuā zhù le to translate 'The robber was arrested by the police'.

In addition, in colloquial speech, 给 **gěi** itself may be used to replace 被 **bèi** in sentences where the agent is not specified:

强盗给抓住了。 **qiángdào gěi zhuā zhù le**
The robber was caught.

D   It should also be noted that the 被 **bèi** structure is often used to narrate an unpleasant event:

他被爸爸骂了一顿。 **tā bèi bàba mà le yī dùn**
He was told off by his father.

她让老师批评得哭了起来。 **tā ràng lǎoshī pīpíng de kū le qǐlái**
She was criticised so much by the teacher that she began to cry.

花瓶叫小吴 (给) 打破了。 **huāpíng jiào xiǎo wú (gěi) dǎ pò le**
The vase was broken by Xiao Wu.

E The 被 **bèi** construction, being a narrative sentence about something that has happened, is always negated by 没 (有) **méi(yǒu)**, which is placed immediately before 被 **bèi**. In a negative 被 **bèi** sentence, 了 **le**, of course, is not present after the complement:

衣服没 (有) 被雨淋湿。 **yīfu méi(yǒu) bèi yǔ lín shī**
The clothes were not (made) wet by the rain.

小女孩没 (有) 被火烧伤。 **xiǎo nǚhái méi(yǒu) bèi huǒ shāo shāng**
The little girl was not burnt by the fire.

F Adverbials of manner or location in 被 **bèi** sentences may precede either 被 **bèi** or the verb. In the latter case, the adverbial becomes more emphatic:

月亮慢慢地被一片乌云遮住了。
yuèliang mànmàn de bèi yī piàn wūyún zhē zhù le
The moon was slowly covered by a patch of black clouds.

那些调皮的孩子让校长 (给) 狠狠地批评了一顿。
nà/nèi xiē tiáopí de háizi ràng xiàozhǎng (gěi) hěnhěn de pīpíng le yī dùn
Those naughty children were severely criticised by the head teacher.

小女孩被消防队员从屋子里救了出来。
xiǎo nǚhái bèi xiāofáng duìyuán cóng wūzi li jiù le chūlái
The little girl was rescued from the house by the firemen.

Note 1: However, monosyllabic referential adverbs like 都 **dōu** 'all', 'both', 就 **jiù** 'then', 'soon', 才 **cái** 'only', 'then', etc. must always precede 被 **bèi**:

剩下的饭菜都被 (厨师) 倒掉了。
shèng xià de fàncài dōu bèi (chúshī) dào diào le
All the food that was left over was thrown away (by the cook).

Note 2: A number of examples given in this unit show that complements of direction, frequency and duration can in a narrative tone follow verbs marked by the aspect marker 了 **le** (e.g. 哭了起来 **kū le qǐlái** 'started to cry'/'weep', 救了出来 **jiù le chūlái** 'be rescued from (the house)', 骂了一顿 **mà le yī dùn** 'told (somebody) off severely', 批评了几次 **pīpíng le jǐ cì** 'reprimanded several times', 关了三年 **guān le sān nián** 'imprisoned for three years'). However, verbs taking complements of result cannot be interrupted by the aspect marker 了 **le**, which has to come after the complement. In this situation it therefore often coincides with the sentence particle 了 **le** at the end of the sentence (e.g. 打破了 **dǎ pò le** 'be broken', 倒掉了 **dào diào le** 'be thrown away', etc.).

Exercise 2.1

Rewrite the following Chinese sentences using the 被 **bèi** structure:

1 小孩儿把窗户打破了。 **xiǎoháir bǎ chuānghu dǎ pò le**
  The child broke the window.
2 她从银行里把钱取了出来。 **tā cóng yínháng li bǎ qián qǔ le chūlái**
  She took the money out of the bank.
3 警察当场把小偷抓住了。 **jǐngchá dāngchǎng bǎ xiǎotōu zhuā zhù le**
  The police caught the thief on the spot.
4 司机把汽车修好了。 **sījī bǎ qìchē xiū hǎo le**
  The driver mended the car.
5 厨师把鸡烤熟了。 **chúshī bǎ jī kǎo shú/shóu le**
  The cook roasted the chicken.
6 理发师把他的头发剪得太短了。 **lǐfàshī bǎ tā de tóufa jiǎn de tài duǎn le**
  The barber cut his hair too short.

Exercise 2.2

Form 被 **bèi** sentences using the words and phrases given below and then translate the sentences into English:

1 她 **tā** 吃了 **chī le** 那个苹果 **nà/nèi gè píngguǒ**
2 我 **wǒ** 钥匙 **yàoshi** 找到了 **zhǎo dào le**
3 批评了 **pīpíng le** 我女儿 **wǒ nǚ'ér** 老师 **lǎoshī** 一顿 **yī dùn**
4 他 **tā** 撞倒了 **zhuàng dǎo le** 卡车 **kǎchē**
5 老板 **lǎobǎn** 撤了职 **chè le zhí** 工人 **gōngrén**
6 小偷 **xiǎotōu** 监狱 **jiānyù** 关进 **guān jìn**

Exercise 2.3

There are mistakes in all the Chinese sentences below. Supply the correct version in each case:

1 我要的书被人借。 **wǒ yào de shū bèi rén jiè**
  The book I wanted has been borrowed by someone else.
2 蛋糕叫小李吃。 **dàngāo jiào xiǎo lǐ chī**
  The cake was eaten by Xiao Li.
3 大家被她说得笑。 **dàjiā bèi tā shuō de xiào**
  She made everybody laugh with what she said.
4 老鼠让猫给逮。 **lǎoshǔ ràng māo gěi dǎi**
  The mouse was caught by the cat.

5 她叫自行车给撞。 **tā jiào zìxíngchē gěi zhuàng**
She was knocked over by a bike.

6 这个计划大家给取消了。 **zhè/zhèi gè jìhuà dàjiā gěi qǔxiāo le**
Everyone decided we should cancel this plan. (*lit.* This plan was cancelled
by everyone.)

7 她被孙老师当自己的女儿。 **tā bèi sūn lǎoshī dàng zìjǐ de nǚ'ér**
She was treated by Sun the teacher as his/her own daughter.

8 这个问题被老师解释。 **zhè/zhèi gè wèntí bèi lǎoshī jiěshì**
The problem was explained very clearly by the teacher.

9 花儿被插花瓶里了。 **huār bèi chā huāpíng li le**
The flowers were put in a vase.

10 行李都让火车给运。 **xíngli dōu ràng huǒchē gěi yùn**
The luggage was all taken by train.

Exercise 2.4

Translate the following into Chinese, using the 被 **bèi** structure:

1 Our supper was eaten by the cat.
2 The keys were forgotten by the driver.
3 I was told off by the teacher.
4 The child was knocked down by a bus.
5 I was treated by him like his own son.
6 The door was kicked open by the police.
7 The bicycle was damaged by the thief.
8 Her book was hidden behind the cupboard.
9 The fence was blown over by the wind.
10 I was made so angry by him that I could not speak. (气 **qì** 'make angry')

UNIT THREE
Dative constructions with direct and indirect objects

A In Chinese, verbs like 给 **gěi** 'give', 送 **sòng** 'give as a present', 借 **jiè** 'borrow'/'lend', 还 **huán** 'give back'/'return' and 赔 **péi** 'compensate'/'pay for' entail the use of a direct and an indirect object, thereby forming a dative sentence:

他给她一束花。 **tā gěi tā yī shù huā**
(一束花 **yī shù huā** direct object, 她 **tā** indirect object)
He gave her a bunch of flowers.

朋友送我一瓶酒。 **péngyou sòng wǒ yī píng jiǔ**
(一瓶酒 **yī píng jiǔ** direct object, 我 **wǒ** indirect object)
My friend gave me a bottle of wine as a present.

他借了图书馆一批书。 **tā jiè le túshūguǎn yī pī shū**
(一批书 **yī pī shū** direct object, 图书馆 **túshūguǎn** indirect object)
He borrowed a number of books from the library.

她还了我们一张邮票。 **tā huán le wǒmen yī zhāng yóupiào**
(一张邮票 **yī zhāng yóupiào** direct object, 我们 **wǒmen** indirect object)
She returned a stamp to us.

保险公司赔了他们一笔钱吗？ **bǎoxiǎn gōngsī péi le tāmen yī bǐ qián ma**
(一笔钱 **yī bǐ qián** direct object, 他们 **tāmen** indirect object)
Did the insurance company give them a sum of money in compensation?

我没 (有) 欠他什么东西。 **wǒ méi(yǒu) qiàn tā shénme dōngxi**
I did not owe him anything.

Note: The verbs 送 **sòng**, 还 **huán** and 赔 **péi** may be suffixed by 给 **gěi** without any change in meaning:

朋友送给我一瓶酒。 **péngyou sòng gěi wǒ yī píng jiǔ**
My friend gave me a bottle of wine as a present.

她还给我们一张邮票。 **tā huán gěi wǒmen yī zhāng yóupiào**
She returned a stamp to us.

保险公司赔给他们一笔钱吗？ **bǎoxiǎn gōngsī péi gěi tāmen yī bǐ qián ma**
Did the insurance company give them a sum of money in compensation?

Note: The verb 借 **jiè** usually means 'to borrow', but when suffixed with 给 **gěi**, it means 'to lend':

他借我两镑钱。 **tā jiè wǒ liǎng bàng qián**
He borrowed two pounds from me.

他借给我两镑钱。 **tā jiè gěi wǒ liǎng bàng qián**
He lent me two pounds.

B   Many verbs may be suffixed by 给 **gěi** to produce dative (two-object) constructions:

邮递员递给我一封信。 **yóudìyuán dì gěi wǒ yī fēng xìn**
The post(wo)man handed me a letter.

她寄给你一张明信片。 **tā jì gěi nǐ yī zhāng míngxìnpiàn**
She sent you a postcard.

房东租给我一套房间。 **fángdōng zū gěi wǒ yī tào fángjiān**
The landlady let a flat to me.

小贩卖给我半斤李子。 **xiǎofàn mài gěi wǒ bàn jīn lǐzi**
The pedlar sold me half a catty of plums.

她交给李老师一张条子。 **tā jiāo gěi lǐ lǎoshī yī zhāng tiáozi**
She handed a note to teacher Li.

爷爷买给孩子们几盒录像带。 **yéye mǎi gěi háizimen jǐ hé lùxiàngdài**
Grandfather bought the children several video tapes.

张小姐转给我好几盒录音带。 **zhāng xiǎojie zhuǎn gěi wǒ hǎo jǐ hé lùyīndài**
Miss Zhang passed quite a few cassette tapes on to me.

陈叔叔带给我弟弟一本中文字典。
chén shūshu dài gěi wǒ dìdi yī běn zhōngwén zìdiǎn
Uncle Chen brought my younger brother a Chinese dictionary.

C   A dative construction with 给 **gěi** may be expressed as a serial construction (see Unit 5), with the first verb governing the direct object, and the second verb, 给 **gěi**, relating to the indirect object:

观众献了一束花给演员。 **guānzhòng xiàn le yī shù huā gěi yǎnyuán**
The audience presented a bouquet of flowers to the actor.

领事馆发签证给他。 **lǐngshìguǎn fā qiānzhèng gěi tā**
The consulate issued him with a visa.

D   Dative constructions generally involve verbs of physical action, like 给 **gěi** 'give to', 递 **dì** 'hand to', 交 **jiāo** 'hand to'/'submit to', 还 **huán** 'return to', etc. However, verbs like 告诉 **gàosu** 'tell', 通知 **tōngzhī** 'inform'/'notify', 教 **jiāo** 'teach' and 叫 **jiào** 'call'/'address as', all of which involve some form of communication, can also form dative sentences:

我朋友告诉我一个秘密。 **wǒ péngyou gàosu wǒ yī gè mìmì**
(秘密 **mìmì** direct object, 我 **wǒ** indirect object)
My friend told me a secret.

秘书通知他一件事。 **mìshū tōngzhī tā yī jiàn shì**
(一件事 **yī jiàn shì** direct object, 他 **tā** indirect object)
The secretary notified him about something.

她教她女儿英语。 **tā jiāo tā nǚ'ér yīngyǔ**
(英语 **yīngyǔ** direct object, 她女儿 **tā nǚ'ér** indirect object)
She taught her daughter English.

大家叫我老王。 **dàjiā jiào wǒ lǎo wáng**
(老王 **lǎo wáng** direct object, 我 **wǒ** indirect object)
Everybody calls me Lao Wang.

Note: This kind of dative construction cannot incorporate 给 **gěi**:

One cannot say:

*她告诉给我一个秘密。 **tā gàosu gěi wǒ yī gè mìmì**
*她告诉一个秘密给我。 **tā gàosu yī gè mìmì gěi wǒ**
(*lit.* in both sentences: She told me a secret.)

E   Dative constructions may be used in both 把 **bǎ** and 被 **bèi** sentences:

邮递员把那封信递给我。 **yóudìyuán bǎ nà/nèi fēng xìn dì gěi wǒ**
The post(wo)man gave me the letter.

别把那个秘密告诉他。 **bié bǎ nà/nèi gè mìmì gàosu tā**
Don't tell him that secret.

那瓶酒被她送给一个朋友了。
nà/nèi píng jiǔ bèi tā sòng gěi yī gè péngyou le
That bottle of wine was given by her to a friend.

Exercise 3.1

Identify the direct and indirect objects in the sentences below:

1 我送朋友一只手表。 **wǒ sòng péngyou yī zhī shǒubiǎo**
   I gave my friend a watch.
2 他递给同学一杯牛奶。 **tā dì gěi tóngxué yī bēi niúnǎi**
   He passed his coursemate a glass of milk.
3 经理交给秘书一批文件。 **jīnglǐ jiāo gěi mìshū yī pī wénjiàn**
   The manager gave the secretary a stack of documents.
4 病人借了医生一本杂志。 **bìngrén jiè le yīshēng yī běn zázhì**
   The patient borrowed a magazine from the doctor.
5 他把那把(雨)伞还给他的邻居。 **tā bǎ nà/nèi bǎ (yǔ)sǎn huán gěi tā de línjū**
   He returned the umbrella to his neighbour.
6 老师借给我一本书。 **lǎoshī jiè gěi wǒ yī běn shū**
   The teacher lent me a book.
7 我的一个朋友告诉我一个秘密。 **wǒ de yī gè péngyou gàosu wǒ yī gè mìmì**
   One of my friends told me a secret.
8 学生问老师一些问题。 **xuésheng wèn lǎoshī yīxiē wèntí**
   The student asked the teacher some questions.

Exercise 3.2

Form dative sentences with the Chinese words and phrases given below:

1 The consulate issued me with a visa.
   领事馆 **lǐngshìguǎn** 一张签证 **yī zhāng qiānzhèng** 给我 **gěi wǒ** 发 **fā** issue
2 My friend lent me a video tape.
   朋友 **péngyou** 借给 **jiè gěi** 一盘录像带 **yī pán lùxiàngdài** 我 **wǒ**
3 I borrowed an umbrella from him.
   一把(雨)伞 **yī bǎ (yǔ)sǎn** 我 **wǒ** 他 **tā** 借了 **jiè le**
4 She brought a pair of shoes for her friend.
   朋友 **péngyou** 带给 **dài gěi** 一双鞋 **yī shuāng xié** 她 **tā**
5 The driver handed me a ticket.
   我 **wǒ** 司机 **sījī** 递给 **dì gěi** 一张票 **yī zhāng piào**
6 The children gave the queen a bouquet of flowers.
   女王 **nǚwáng** 孩子们 **háizimen** 一束花 **yī shù huā** 献给 **xiàn gěi**

Exercise 3.3

Complete the Chinese sentences below with 'verb + 给 **gěi**' as appropriate in
each case:

1 我 ＿＿＿ ＿＿＿ 朋友一张圣诞卡。
 wǒ ＿＿＿ ＿＿＿ péngyou yī zhāng shèngdànkǎ
 I sent my friend a Christmas card.
2 爸爸 ＿＿＿ ＿＿＿ 孩子一个玩具。
 bàba ＿＿＿ ＿＿＿ háizi yī gè wánjù
 The father bought a toy for his child.
3 邻居 ＿＿＿ ＿＿＿ 我们一只小狗。
 línjū ＿＿＿ ＿＿＿ wǒmen yī zhī xiǎo gǒu
 The neighbour gave us a puppy.
4 小李 ＿＿＿ ＿＿＿ 她的同学一本杂志。
 xiǎo lǐ ＿＿＿ ＿＿＿ tā de tóngxué yī běn zázhì
 Xiao Li passed a magazine to her classmate.
5 小贩 ＿＿＿ ＿＿＿ 我一瓶酒。 **xiǎofàn ＿＿＿ ＿＿＿ wǒ yī píng jiǔ**
 The pedlar sold me a bottle of wine.
6 姐姐 ＿＿＿ ＿＿＿ 客人一杯茶。 **jiějie ＿＿＿ ＿＿＿ kèrén yī bēi chá**
 My elder sister poured out a cup of tea for the guest.
7 王女士 ＿＿＿ ＿＿＿ 我们一间办公室。
 wáng nǚshì ＿＿＿ ＿＿＿ wǒmen yī jiān bàngōngshì
 Miss Wang let an office to us.
8 秘书 ＿＿＿ ＿＿＿ 每个人一张通知。
 mìshū ＿＿＿ ＿＿＿ měi gè rén yī zhāng tōngzhī
 The secretary handed out a notice to everybody.
9 我同事 ＿＿＿ ＿＿＿ 我一封信。
 wǒ tóngshì ＿＿＿ ＿＿＿ wǒ yī fēng xìn
 My colleague passed a letter on to me.
10 姐姐 ＿＿＿ ＿＿＿ 妹妹两镑钱。
 jiějie ＿＿＿ ＿＿＿ mèimei liǎng bàng qián
 (The) elder sister lent two pounds to (the) younger sister.

Exercise 3.4

Translate the following into Chinese:

1 Please lend me two yuan/dollars.
2 My friend borrowed a sweater from me.
3 The students gave a present to the teacher.
4 Don't call me Old Zhang.
5 I'll give that pen back to you tomorrow.
6 What shall we buy him?
7 Did you pass the dictionary on to him?
8 I didn't tell them that secret.

UNIT FOUR
Causative constructions

A In Chinese, verbs such as 使 **shǐ** 'cause'/'make' and 让 **ràng** 'let'/'permit' are used to form causative constructions, in which the object of the first verb (e.g. 使 **shǐ** or 让 **ràng**) becomes the notional subject of a second verb:

> 她让我休几天假。 **tā ràng wǒ xiū jǐ tiān jià**
> (我 **wǒ** is the object of 让 **ràng** and the subject of 休假 **xiūjià**)
> She let me have a few days off.

> '砰' 的一声，使她吓了一跳。 **pēng de yī shēng | shǐ tā xiā le yī tiào**
> (她 **tā** is the object of 使 **shǐ** and the subject of 吓 **xiā**)
> A crashing noise made her jump.

B As well as 使 **shǐ** and 让 **ràng**, other verbs, ranging in meaning from request to coercion, also produce causative constructions:

> 请 **qǐng** 'ask someone to do something':
> 我请她看电影。 **wǒ qǐng tā kàn diànyǐng**
> I asked her to go to the cinema with me.

> 叫 **jiào** 'tell'/'get someone to do something':
> 她没(有) 叫我去照看孩子。 **tā méi(yǒu) jiào wǒ qù zhàokàn háizi**
> She didn't tell me to look after the child(ren)/babysit for her.

> 要 **yào** 'want'/'require someone to do something':
> 护士要病人吃药。 **hùshi yào bìngrén chī yào**
> The nurse required the patient to take some medicine.

> 劝 **quàn** 'try to persuade':
> 大家劝他戒烟。 **dàjiā quàn tā jiè yān**
> Everybody tried to persuade him to give up smoking.

> 催 **cuī** 'urge':
> 妈妈催她快点儿起床吗？ **māma cuī tā kuài diǎnr qǐchuáng ma**
> Did mother urge her to get up quickly?

命令 **mìnglìng** 'order':

排长命令士兵冲锋。 **páizhǎng mìnglìng shìbīng chōngfēng**
The platoon leader ordered the soldiers/troops to charge.

逼 **bī** 'force':

强盗逼银行经理交出钥匙。 **qiángdào bī yínháng jīnglǐ jiāo chū yàoshi**
The robber forced the bank manager to hand over the keys.

禁止 **jìnzhǐ** 'forbid':

学校禁止学生打架。 **xuéxiào jìnzhǐ xuésheng dǎjià**
The school forbids the pupils to fight (with one another).

允许 **yǔnxǔ** 'permit':

父母允许孩子周末看电视。 **fùmǔ yǔnxǔ háizi zhōumò kàn diànshì**
The parents gave the children permission to watch television at weekends.

C   The verb 使 **shǐ** or 让 **ràng** (and sometimes more colloquially, 叫 **jiào** or its variant 教 **jiào**) may also be used with a second verb which is derived from an adjective:

这个消息使我很高兴。 **zhè/zhèi gè xiāoxi shǐ wǒ hěn gāoxìng**
This piece of news made me very happy.

她的话使他很难过。 **tā de huà shǐ tā hěn nánguò**
Her words made him sad.

儿子的行为让父亲着急。 **érzi de xíngwéi ràng fùqīn zhāojí**
The son's behaviour made the father worried.

这件事叫 (or 教) 我不安。 **zhè/zhèi jiàn shì jiào wǒ bù ān**
This matter made me feel uneasy/anxious.

Note: 令 **lìng** may be used in a similar way but has a more formal tone, particularly when used with 人 **rén** 'people/one':

这个消息令人高兴。 **zhè/zhèi gè xiāoxi lìng rén gāoxìng**
This news was encouraging. (*lit.* This news made people/one happy.)

她的话令人失望。 **tā de huà lìng rén shīwàng**
Her words were disappointing. (*lit.* Her words caused people/one to be disappointed.)

D   To negate a causative construction one may make either the first or the second verb negative, depending on the meaning required:

(1) Negating the first verb:

他没叫你去游泳。 **tā méi jiào nǐ qù yóuyǒng**
He didn't tell you to go swimming.

小李不准我去参加这次活动。
xiǎo lǐ bù zhǔn wǒ qù cānjiā zhè/zhèi cì huódòng
Xiao Li will not allow me to take part in these activities.

她不让我把门打开。 **tā bù ràng wǒ bǎ mén dǎ kāi**
She didn't let me open the door.

(2) Negating the second verb:

他叫你别去游泳。 **tā jiào nǐ bié qù yóuyǒng**
He told you not to go swimming.

小李准我不参加这次活动。
xiǎo lǐ zhǔn wǒ bù cānjiā zhè/zhèi cì huódòng
Xiao Li allowed me not to take part in these activities.

她让我别把门打开。 **tā ràng wǒ bié bǎ mén dǎ kāi**
She told me not to open the door.

E 有 **yǒu** (see *Basic Chinese*, Unit 11) is often used in a pattern similar to the causative structure. Sentences of this type begin either with 有 **yǒu** or with a time or location phrase followed by 有 **yǒu**:

有人找你。 **yǒu rén zhǎo nǐ**
There is someone looking for you.

这儿有火车去伦敦。 **zhèr yǒu huǒchē qù lúndūn**
There are trains to London from here.

早上有个朋友给你打电话。 **zǎoshang yǒu gè péngyou gěi nǐ dǎ diànhuà**
A friend phoned you this morning.

Exercise 4.1

Complete the Chinese sentences below selecting an appropriate verb from the list given:

让 **ràng**	使 **shǐ**	请 **qǐng**	叫 **jiào**
劝 **quàn**	催 **cuī**	逼 **bī**	命令 **mìnglìng**
禁止 **jìnzhǐ**	允许 **yǔnxǔ**	吩咐 **fēnfù**	要 **yào**

1 他 _____ 我坐在他旁边。 **tā** _____ **wǒ zuò zài tā pángbiān**
He told me to sit beside him.
2 我女朋友 _____ 我吸烟。 **wǒ nǚ péngyou** _____ **wǒ xīyān**
My girlfriend won't allow me to smoke.

3 朋友 ——— 我去吃饭。 **péngyou ——— wǒ qù chīfàn**
A friend invited me to dinner.

4 医生 ——— 病人好好休息。 **yīshēng ——— bìngrén hǎohǎo xiūxi**
The doctor advised the patient to have a good rest.

5 经理 ——— 秘书打一封信。 **jīnglǐ ——— mìshū dǎ yī fēng xìn**
The manager requested the secretary to type a letter.

6 政府 ——— 捕杀大熊猫。
zhèngfǔ ——— bǔshā dà xióngmāo
The government forbids the capture and killing of giant pandas.

7 老朋友 ——— 我忘了那些不愉快的时间。
lǎo péngyou ——— wǒ wàng le nà/nèi xiē bù yúkuài de shíjiān
My old friend persuaded me to forget those sad times.

8 王老师 ——— 我们赶快交作业。
wáng lǎoshī ——— wǒmen gǎnkuài jiāo zuòyè
Wang the teacher urged us to hurry up and hand in our homework.

9 房东 ——— 他今天交出房租。 **fángdōng ——— tā jīntiān jiāo chū fángzū**
The landlord forced him to pay the rent today.

10 警察 ——— 强盗放下枪。
jǐngchá ——— qiángdào fàng xià qiāng
The police ordered the robber to put down the gun.

11 请 ——— 我说一下我的意见。
qǐng ——— wǒ shūo yīxià wǒ de yìjian
Please allow me to state my opinion.

12 工程师 ——— 我帮她一下儿忙。
gōngchéngshī ——— wǒ bāng tā yīxiàr máng
The engineer wanted me to give her a hand.

13 爷爷的病 ——— 他很担心。 **yéye de bìng ——— tā hěn dānxīn**
His grandfather's illness worried him a lot.

14 她 ——— 妹妹去洗手。 **tā ——— mèimei qù xǐ shǒu**
She instructed her younger sister to wash her hands.

15 他的话 ——— 我们都笑了。 **tā de huà ——— wǒmen dōu xiào le**
What he said made us all laugh.

16 她真 ——— 我生气！ **tā zhēn ——— wǒ shēngqì**
She really makes me angry!

Exercise 4.2

Rewrite the Chinese sentences below in the negative to match the second English translation or translations:

1 父母允许孩子吃巧克力。 **fùmǔ yǔnxǔ háizi chī qiǎokèlì**
The parents allow their children to eat chocolate.
The parents don't allow their children to eat chocolate.

2 这个消息使我很难过。 **zhè/zhèi gè xiāoxi shǐ wǒ hěn nánguò**
This piece of news made me very sad.
This piece of news didn't make me sad at all.

3 他劝我买这双鞋。 **tā quàn wǒ mǎi zhè/zhèi shuāng xié**
He urged me to buy this pair of shoes.
He urged me not to buy this pair of shoes.

4 经理准我出席这次会议。 **jīnglǐ zhǔn wǒ chūxí zhè/zhèi cì huìyì**
The manager allowed me to attend the meeting.
The manager allowed me not to attend the meeting.
and
The manager didn't allow me to attend the meeting.

5 她叫我开灯。 **tā jiào wǒ kāi dēng**
She told me to turn the light on.
She didn't tell me to turn the light on.
and
She told me not to turn the light on.

6 我让儿子学汉语。 **wǒ ràng érzi xué hànyǔ**
I got my son to learn Chinese.
I didn't let my son learn Chinese.

Exercise 4.3

Translate the sentences below into Chinese using 有 **yǒu**.

1 There was once a child who lost her way in the forest.
   (曾经 **céngjīng** 'once', 迷路 **mílù** 'lose one's way')
2 Who knows you here?
3 Some friends are coming to my place tonight.
4 There is a bus to London going at six o'clock.
5 Someone is waiting for you outside.
6 Is there anyone here who can speak Chinese?

Exercise 4.4

Translate the following sentences into Chinese using an appropriate causative verb in each case:

1 The mother told her child to tidy his clothes.
2 My elder sister urged me to get out of bed quickly.
3 My younger brother wanted me to help him repair his computer.
4 I didn't dare to persuade her not to smoke.
5 She is unwilling to let me go with her.
6 The teacher would not allow the pupils to climb the trees.
7 The coach ordered the players to assemble on the playing field.
8 My elder brother forced me to give him my best toy.

UNIT FIVE
Serial constructions

A   A serial construction consists of two or more verbs used in a series, often without any conjunctional devices. The second verb may follow the first verb directly, or the first verb may take an intervening object:

我去买报纸。 **wǒ qù mǎi bàozhǐ**
I'm going to buy a newspaper.

你找他要什么？ **nǐ zhǎo tā yào shénme**
Why are you looking for him? (*lit.* You look for him want what.)

There are various kinds of serial construction, some of which are discussed below.

B   **Sequence**. One action is completed before the next one takes place:

孩子吃了饭回家去了。 **háizi chī le fàn huí jiā qù le**
After eating, the child went home.
(The actions 吃饭 **chīfàn** 'eat' and 回家 **huí jiā** 'go home' happen one after the other.)

他把信封好，贴上邮票，投进邮筒。
tā bǎ xìn fēng hǎo | tiē shàng yóupiào | tóu jìn yóutǒng
He sealed the envelope, stuck a stamp on (it) and dropped (it) into the letter box.

C   **Purpose**. The second action explains the purpose of the first action. The verb expressing the first action is usually either 来 **lái** 'come' or 去 **qù** 'go' (as in the first example under **A**):

朋友们来我家看望我。 **péngyoumen lái wǒ jiā kànwàng wǒ**
My friends came to my house to visit me.
(The second action, 看望 **kànwàng** 'visit', explains the purpose of the first action: 来我家 **lái wǒ jiā** 'came to my place'.)

我们全家去海边度假。 **wǒmen quán jiā qù hǎi biān dùjià**
The whole family went to the seaside on holiday/to take a holiday.

More colloquially, 来 **lái** 'come' and 去 **qù** 'go' may be placed at the end of the sentence:

他上街去买菜了。 **tā shàng jiē qù mǎi cài le**
他上街买菜去了。 **tā shàng jiē mǎi cài qù le**
He has gone out to buy some food.

她到图书馆去还书了。 **tā dào túshūguǎn qù huán shū le**
她到图书馆还书去了。 **tā dào túshūguǎn huán shū qù le**
She has gone to the library to return her books.

工人来修理水龙头了。 **gōngrén lái xiūlǐ shuǐlóngtóu le**
工人修理水龙头来了。 **gōngrén xiūlǐ shuǐlóngtóu lái le**
The plumber has come to mend the tap.

Note: (没)有 (**méi**)**yǒu** + noun may be used as the first action in a serial construction where the second action expresses purpose:

我有机会学汉语。 **wǒ yǒu jīhuì xué hànyǔ**
I have the opportunity to learn Chinese.

你有时间教我开车吗? **nǐ yǒu shíjiān jiāo wǒ kāichē ma**
Have you got time to teach me to drive?

你没有理由这么说。 **nǐ méi yǒu lǐyóu zhème shuō**
You have no reason to say that/talk like that.

我没有钱买香烟。 **wǒ méi yǒu qián mǎi xiāngyān**
I have no money to buy cigarettes.

D   Instrument or vehicle. The first action explains the means (the instrument or vehicle) by which the second action is carried out:

中国人用筷子吃饭。 **zhōngguó rén yòng kuàizi chīfàn** (instrument)
Chinese people eat with chopsticks.
(The first action, 用筷子 **yòng kuàizi** 'using chopsticks', indicates the instrument with which the second action, 吃饭 **chīfàn** 'eat', is carried out.)

他坐火车上班。 **tā zuò huǒchē shàngbān** (vehicle)
He goes to work by train.
(The first action, 坐火车 **zuò huǒchē** 'by train' (*lit.* sit on train), indicates the means by which the second action, 上班 **shàngbān** 'go to work', takes place.)

Note: This construction is similar to the coverb structure.

In a 把 **bǎ** construction (see Unit 1), the verbal phrase expressing the instrument or vehicle should come before the 把 **bǎ** phrase.

我用吸尘器把地毯吸干净了。 **wǒ yòng xīchénqì bǎ dìtǎn xī gānjìng le**
I vacuumed the carpet. (*lit.* I cleaned the carpet with the vacuum cleaner.)

One does not usually say:

*我把地毯用吸尘器吸干净了。 **wǒ bǎ dìtǎn yòng xīchénqì xī gānjìng le**
to translate, 'I cleaned the carpet with the vacuum cleaner'.

E   Accompanying circumstances. The first action is marked with 着 **zhe** indicating that it takes place at the same time as the second action (see *Basic Chinese*, Unit 15):

她握着我的手说：'谢谢' **tā wò zhe wǒ de shǒu shuō xièxie**
Holding my hand, she said, 'Thank you.'
(The first action, 握着我的手 **wō zhe wǒ de shǒu** 'holding my hand', takes place at the same time as the second action, 说 **shuō** 'said'.)

他微笑着回答我的问题。 **tā wēixiào zhe huídá wǒ de wèntí**
He smiled as he answered my questions. (*lit.* He smiling answered . . .)

孩子抱着玩具熊睡着了。 **háizi bào zhe wánjùxióng shuì zháo le**
The child went to sleep holding the teddy bear in his/her arms.

F   Negative reinforcement. The second action is a negative expression reinforcing the meaning expressed by the first action, which is usually marked with 着 **zhe**:

爷爷坐着不动。 **yéye zuò zhe bù dòng**
Grandpa sat completely still/motionless. (*lit.* Grandpa was sitting and did not move.)
(The first action, 坐着 **zuò zhe** 'sat'/'sitting', is reinforced by the second action, 不动 **bù dòng** 'not moving'.)

奶奶握着我的手不放。 **nǎinai wò zhe wǒ de shǒu bù fàng**
Grandma held my hand firmly in hers. (*lit.* Grandma was holding my hand and did not let go.)

Exercise 5.1

Form serial construction sentences in Chinese with the words and phrases given in each case below and then translate the sentences into English:

1 他 **tā** 给 **gěi** 拿出 **ná chū** 打开 **dǎ kāi** 衣柜 **yīguì** 我 **wǒ** 一件衬衫 **yī jiàn chènshān**
2 去 **qù** 看望 **kànwàng** 买了 **mǎi le** 医院 **yīyuàn** 我 **wǒ** 我的朋友 **wǒ de péngyou** 一束花 **yī shù huā**
3 戴上 **dài shàng** 她 **tā** 眼镜 **yǎnjìng** 文件 **wénjiàn** 看 **kàn**

4 门 **mén** 病人 **bìngrén** 打针 **dǎzhēn** 护士 **hùshi** 病房 **bìngfáng** 走进 **zǒu jìn** 给 **gěi** 推开 **tuī kāi**

5 问题 **wèntí** 问 **wèn** 老师 **lǎoshī** 学生 **xuésheng** 有 **yǒu** 几个 **jǐ gè**

6 需要 **xūyào** 房租 **fángzū** 我 **wǒ** 一些钱 **yīxiē qián** 付 **fù**

Exercise 5.2

Complete the following Chinese sentences to match the English translations:

1 经理 ＿＿＿＿＿＿ 去上海开会。 **jīnglǐ** ＿＿＿＿＿＿ **qù shànghǎi kāihuì**
The manager went to Shanghai by plane to attend a meeting.

2 他们 ＿＿＿＿＿＿ 谈话。 **tāmen** ＿＿＿＿＿＿ **tánhuà**
They chatted in Chinese.

3 小猫 ＿＿＿＿＿＿ 洗脸。 **xiǎo māo** ＿＿＿＿＿＿ **xǐ liǎn**
The kitten washed its face with its paws (爪子 **zhuǎzi**).

4 我们 ＿＿＿＿＿＿ 渡过黄河。 **wǒmen** ＿＿＿＿＿＿ **dù guò huánghé**
We crossed the Yellow River by boat.

5 孩子们 ＿＿＿＿＿＿ 说话。 **háizimen** ＿＿＿＿＿＿ **shuōhuà**
The children stood talking.

6 妹妹 ＿＿＿＿＿＿ 上学。 **mèimei** ＿＿＿＿＿＿ **shàngxué**
My younger sister goes to school by bicycle.

Exercise 5.3

Translate the following sentences into Chinese using the colloquial format with 来 **lái** or 去 **qù** at the end of the sentence (in some cases followed by 了 **le**):

1 He goes to work by train.
2 We returned home to see our grandma.
3 He will set out for Spain tomorrow.
4 All my friends came to my birthday party.
5 She went off to work.
6 Xiao Liu has come to baby-sit for me.

Exercise 5.4

Complete the Chinese sentences below with 不 **bù** + verb, to match the English translation:

1 士兵们站着 ＿＿＿ ＿＿＿。 **shìbīngmen zhàn zhe** ＿＿＿ ＿＿＿
The soldiers stood completely still.

2 孩子睁着眼睛 ＿＿＿ ＿＿＿。 **háizi zhēng zhe yǎnjing** ＿＿＿ ＿＿＿
The child kept his eyes wide open and refused to go to sleep.

3 小狗咬着骨头 _____ _____。 **xiǎo gǒu yǎo zhe gútou** _____ _____
The puppy gripped the bone firmly in its mouth.

4 他留着一双新鞋 _____ _____。
tā liú zhe yī shuāng xīn xié _____ _____
He keeps a pair of new shoes he never wears.

5 她只顾说话拿着一杯咖啡 _____ _____。
tā zhǐ gù shuōhuà ná zhe yī bēi kāfēi _____ _____
She was so involved in what she was saying that she didn't drink any of the
(cup of) coffee she was holding. (*lit.* She only paid attention to talking,
holding a cup of coffee without drinking.)

6 病人躺着 _____ _____ _____。 **bìngrén tǎng zhe** _____ _____ _____
The invalid lay there without getting up.

Exercise 5.5

The Chinese sentences below all contain errors. Rewrite each one to make it a
correct translation of the English:

1 我把地毯用吸尘器吸干净了。 **wǒ bǎ dìtǎn yòng xīchénqì xī gānjìng le**
I vacuumed the carpet. (*lit.* I vacuumed the carpet with a vacuum cleaner.)

2 我说英语没有机会。 **wǒ shuō yīngyǔ méi yǒu jīhuì**
I have no opportunity to speak English.

3 孩子们看电影去电影院买票。
háizimen kàn diànyǐng qù diànyǐngyuàn mǎi piào
The children went to the cinema to buy tickets for the film.

4 我把门用白油漆漆了一下。 **wǒ bǎ mén yòng bái yóuqī qī le yīxià**
I gave the door a coat of white paint.

5 船卸货靠码头。 **chuán xièhuò kào mǎtóu**
The ship docked to unload its cargo.

6 叔叔来拜年到我家带着他的孩子。
shūshu lái bàinián dào wǒ jiā dài zhe tā de háizi
Bringing his children with him, uncle came to our place to wish us a happy
new year.

UNIT SIX
Existence sentences

A   Sentences expressing existence normally begin with a time or location word (or expression). The most common involve the verb 有 **yǒu** (see *Basic Chinese*, Unit 11), which follows the time/location word (or expression) and is then itself followed by the relevant noun:

昨天有一场足球赛。 **zuótiān yǒu yī chǎng zúqiúsài**
There was a football match yesterday./Yesterday, there was a football match.

大学对面有一家书店。 **dàxué duìmiàn yǒu yī jiā shūdiàn**
There is a bookshop opposite the university./Opposite the university there is a bookshop.

这儿没有人。 **zhèr méi yǒu rén**
There is no one here. (*lit.* Here there are no people.)

B   Existence is also conveyed: (1) by verbs marked with 着 **zhe** to express an observable or describable situation or (2) by verbs (usually followed by direction indicators) marked by 了 **le** to indicate a completed action which has brought about the appearance (i.e. coming into existence) or disappearance (i.e. going out of existence) of something or somebody. These sentences follow the pattern of time or location word (or expression) + verb + noun (see **A** above), though location rather than time is the more common reference with verbs marked by 着 **zhe**.

(1) Verbs with 着 **zhe**:

花园里开着玫瑰花。 **huāyuán li kāi zhe méiguìhuā**
There are roses blooming/flowering in the garden.
(*lit.* In the garden are blooming/flowering roses.)

墙上挂着一张地图。 **qiáng shang guà zhe yī zhāng dìtú**
There is a map hanging on the wall.
(*lit.* On the wall is hanging a map.)

床下放着一双拖鞋。 **chuáng xià fàng zhe yī shuāng tuōxié**
There is a pair of slippers under the bed.
(*lit.* Under the bed is placed a pair of slippers.)

老太太面前搁着一篮鸡蛋。 **lǎotàitai miànqián gē zhe yī lán jīdàn**
There is a basket of eggs in front of the old lady.
(*lit.* In front of the old lady is placed a basket of eggs.)

屋顶上停着一只鸟。 **wūdǐng shang tíng zhe yī zhī niǎo**
There is a bird on the roof. (*lit.* On the roof is resting a bird.)

(2) Verbs indicating direction or incorporating direction markers followed by
了 **le**:

昨天来了两个朋友。 **zuótiān lái le liǎng gè péngyou**
Two friends came yesterday. (*lit.* Yesterday came two friends.)

家里走了三个客人。 **jiā li zǒu le sān gè kèren**
Three visitors/guests left my house. (*lit.* House left three visitors/guests.)

空中飞来了一群鸟。 **kōngzhōng fēi lái le yī qún niǎo**
A flock of birds came flying over. (*lit.* In the sky flew over a flock of birds.)

水面上游来了一只天鹅。 **shuǐmiàn shang yóu lái le yī zhī tiān'é**
A swan came gliding over the water. (*lit.* On water came swimming a
swan.)

上个星期搬走了两家人。 **shàng gè xīngqī bān zǒu le liǎng jiā rén**
Two families moved away last week. (*lit.* Last week moved away two
families.)

图书馆借走了一万册书。 **túshūguǎn jiè zǒu le yī wàn cè shū**
Ten thousand volumes have been borrowed from the library.
(*lit.* Library have been borrowed ten thousand volumes.)

树篱下钻出了一只松鼠来。 **shùlí xià zuān chū le yī zhī sōngshǔ lái**
A squirrel emerged from under the hedge. (*lit.* (From) under the hedge
came/burrowed out a squirrel.)

广场上聚集了数千人。 **guǎngchǎng shang jùjí le shù qiān rén**
A few thousand people gathered at the square.

突然开来了一辆大坦克车。 **tūrán kāi lái le yī liàng dà tǎnkèchē**
Suddenly there came a big tank.

(3) A common complement for verbs marked by 了 **le** is 满 **mǎn** 'full of', 'filled with', 'packed with':

箱子里塞满了衣服。 **xiāngzi li sāi mǎn le yīfu**
The box was (packed) full of clothes.

桌子上堆满了书。 **zhuōzi shang duī mǎn le shū**
The table was piled high with books.

礼堂里挤满了人。 **lǐtáng li jǐ mǎn le rén**
The hall was packed with people.

圣诞树下放满了礼物。 **shèngdànshù xià fàng mǎn le lǐwù**
There were lots of presents under the Christmas tree.

(4) Verbs such as 生 **shēng** 'to be born', 死 **sǐ** 'to die', 增加 **zēngjiā** 'to increase', 减少 **jiǎnshǎo** 'to decrease', etc. which have the inherent meaning of coming into or going out of existence also follow this pattern:

他们家生了个胖娃娃。 **tāmen jiā shēng le gè pàng wáwa**
Their family has a new baby. (*lit.* In their family has been born a chubby baby.)

动物园里死了一头大象。 **dòngwùyuán li sǐ le yī tóu dàxiàng**
An elephant died in the zoo. (*lit.* In the zoo died an elephant.)

董事会增加了两个成员。 **dǒngshìhuì zēngjiā le liǎng gè chéngyuán**
There were two new directors on the board (of directors).
(*lit.* On the board of directors were added two members.)

上海减少了交通事故。 **shànghǎi jiǎnshǎo le jiāotōng shìgù**
There has been a reduction of traffic accidents in Shanghai.
(*lit.* Shanghai reduced traffic accidents.)

我们办公室(里)裁减了人员。 **wǒmen bàngōngshì (li) cáijiǎn le rényuán**
There has been a reduction of staff in our office. (*lit.* (In) our office reduced staff.)

(5) Similarly the adjectives 多 **duō** 'many' and 少 **shǎo** 'few' can be used as verbs in this construction:

果盘里少了一只苹果。 **guǒpán li shǎo le yī zhī píngguǒ**
An apple was missing from the fruit bowl.

家里多了一条狗。 **jiā li duō le yī tiáo gǒu**
The family got a new dog. (*lit.* (In) the family was increased (by) a dog.)

C Existence may also be expressed with the verb 是 **shì**. While 有 **yǒu** indicates that something exists among other things, 是 **shì** indicates that something(s) is/are the sole occupant(s) of the place indicated. 是 **shì** is often accompanied by 都 **dōu**:

地上都是水。 **dì shang dōu shì shuǐ**
The ground is covered with water. (*lit.* On the ground all is water.)

商店里都是人。 **shāngdiàn li dōu shì rén**
The shop is/was crowded with people. (*lit.* In the shop all is people.)

她身上都是泥。 **tā shēn shang dōu shì ní**
She was covered in mud. (*lit.* She on body all was mud.)

是 **shì** also implies that something is permanently associated with a location, with the emphasis being on the location rather than the fact of existence:

足球场对面是饭馆。 **zúqiúchǎng duìmiàn shì fànguǎn**
There is a restaurant opposite the football ground. (*lit.* Opposite the football ground is a restaurant.)

饭店下面是酒吧间。 **fàndiàn xiàmian shì jiǔbājiān**
There is a bar below the restaurant. (*lit.* Below the restaurant is a bar.)

This in some contexts may therefore mean that the thing that exists has definite reference:

宿舍后边是图书馆。 **sùshè hòubian shì túshūguǎn**
Behind the dormitory is the library.

卧室旁边是洗澡间。 **wòshì pángbiān shì xǐzǎojiān**
Next to the bedroom is the bathroom.

Exercise 6.1

Complete the following Chinese sentences with 是 **shì**, 都是 **dōu shì** or 有 **yǒu**:

1 今天上午 _____ 汉语考试。 **jīntiān shàngwǔ** _____ **hànyǔ kǎoshì**
There is a Chinese examination this morning.
2 明天 _____ 一个音乐会。 **míngtiān** _____ **yī gè yīnyuèhuì**
There will be a concert tomorrow.
3 箱子里 _____ _____ 衣服。 **xiāngzi li** _____ _____ **yīfu**
The box was full of clothes.
4 八点半 _____ 一班火车。 **bā diǎn bàn** _____ **yī bān huǒchē**
There's a train at half past eight.
5 广场上 _____ _____ 鸽子。 **guǎngchǎng shang** _____ _____ **gézi**
The square is full of pigeons.

6 银行前面 ———— 汽车站。 **yínháng qiánmian** ———— **qìchēzhàn**
There's a bus stop in front of the bank.

7 门前 ———— ———— 玫瑰花。 **mén qián** ———— ———— **méiguīhuā**
There are roses everywhere in front of the door.

8 我家对面 ———— 小李的家。 **wǒ jiā duìmiàn** ———— **xiǎo lǐ de jiā**
Xiao Li's house is opposite my house.

Exercise 6.2

Replace 有 **yǒu** in the Chinese sentences below with the appropriate verb + 着 **zhe** phrase chosen from the list below:

游着 **yóu zhe**	放着 **fàng zhe**	亮着 **liàng zhe**	拿着 **ná zhe**
站着 **zhàn zhe**	挂着 **guà zhe**	长着 **zhǎng zhe**	藏着 **cáng zhe**

1 湖面上有一只天鹅。 **húmiàn shang yǒu yī zhī tiān'é**
There is a swan on the lake.

2 山下有一个小伙子。 **shān xià yǒu yī gè xiǎohuǒzi**
There is a young man at the foot of the hill.

3 柜子里有一盒非常贵重的首饰。 **guìzi li yǒu yī hé fēicháng guìzhòng de shǒushi**
There is a box of extremely valuable jewellery in the cabinet.

4 教室墙上有一块黑板。 **jiàoshì qiáng shang yǒu yī kuài hēibǎn**
There is a blackboard on the classroom wall.

5 果盘里有很多水果。 **guǒpán li yǒu hěn duō shuǐguǒ**
There (is/are) a lot of fruit(s) in the fruit bowl.

6 学校东面有一棵大树。 **xuéxiào dōngmiàn yǒu yī kē dà shù**
There is a large tree on the east side of the school.

7 屋子里有灯光。 **wūzi li yǒu dēngguāng**
There is a light on in the room.

8 他手里有一封信。 **tā shǒu li yǒu yī fēng xìn**
He has a letter (in his hand).

Exercise 6.3

Complete the following Chinese sentences with the appropriate verb + 满 **mǎn** phrase chosen from the list below:

装满 **zhuāng mǎn**	坐满 **zuò mǎn**	塞满 **sāi mǎn**
长满 **zhǎng mǎn**	挤满 **jǐ mǎn**	充满 **chōng mǎn**

1 The bus is packed with passengers.
公共汽车上 ———— ———— 了乘客。
gōnggòng qìchē shang ———— ———— **le chéngkè**

2 The hall is full of people.
礼堂里 ———— ———— 了人。 **lǐtáng li** ———— ———— **le rén**

3 The bottle is full of wine.

瓶子里 _____ _____ 了酒。 **píngzi li** _____ _____ **le jiǔ**

4 The garden is full of flowers.

花园里 _____ _____ 了花。 **huāyuán li** _____ _____ **le huā**

5 The air is full of smoke.

空气里 _____ _____ 了烟雾。 **kōngqì li** _____ _____ **le yānwù**

6 The fridge is full of food.

冰箱里 _____ _____ 了食物。 **bīngxiāng li** _____ _____ **le shíwù**

Exercise 6.4

Complete the Chinese sentences below with a verb + 来 **lái**/走 **zǒu** complement phrase to match the English translation:

1 The museum has bought a lot of cultural relics.

博物馆 _____ _____ 了很多文物。

bówùguǎn _____ _____ **le hěn duō wénwù**

2 Dark clouds filled the sky.

空中 _____ _____ 了一大片乌云。

kōngzhōng _____ _____ **le yī dà piàn wūyún**

3 Two parcels were sent off this morning.

今天早上 _____ _____ 了两个包裹。

jīntiān zǎoshang _____ _____ **le liǎng gè bāoguǒ**

4 A criminal escaped (逃 **táo**) from the prison.

监狱里 _____ _____ 了一个犯人。 **jiānyù li** _____ _____ **le yī gè fànrén**

5 The shop sold over a hundred computers this month.

这个月店里 _____ _____ 了一百多台电脑。

zhè/zhèi gè yuè diàn li _____ _____ **le yī bǎi duō tái diànnǎo**

6 Two families moved into the village.

村子里 _____ _____ 了两户人家。

cūnzi li _____ _____ **le liǎng hù rénjiā**

Exercise 6.5

Translate the following sentences into Chinese, using an existence construction:

1 The tree is laden with pears.
2 A flock of seagulls flew over the surface of the sea.
3 There are green fields (田野 **tiányě**) all along the road.
4 A lot of fresh vegetables have been delivered to the market.
5 There is dirt all over his trousers.
6 The station is crowded with passengers.
7 A great deal of furniture was taken away last week.
8 There isn't a drop of wine in the bottle.

UNIT SEVEN
Subject–predicate and topic–comment sentences

A Sentences in Chinese may be divided into two basic categories: subject–predicate and topic–comment. Subject–predicate sentences are generally used for narrative purposes, whereas topic–comment sentences provide description or comment. The former essentially express an action, while the latter express a state:

他们昨天去钓鱼。 **tāmen zuótiān qù diàoyú**
They went fishing yesterday.
(他们 **tāmen** subject, 去钓鱼 **qù diàoyú** predicate)

他们的爱好是钓鱼。 **tāmen de àihào shì diàoyú**
Their hobby is fishing.
(他们的爱好 **tāmen de àihào** topic, 是钓鱼 **shì diàoyú** comment)

B The subject in a subject–predicate sentence must always be of definite reference:

火车到达终点站。 **huǒchē dàodá zhōngdiǎnzhàn**
The train arrived at the terminal station.

孩子今天过生日。 **háizi jīntiān guò shēngrì**
It is the child's birthday today. (*lit.* The child today has/passes birthday.)

One cannot normally say:

*一辆火车到达终点站。 **yī liàng huǒchē dàodá zhōngdiǎnzhàn**
(*lit.* A train arrived at the terminal station.)

C In subject–predicate sentences, the subject may act as either initiator or recipient of an action:

(1) The subject as initiator:

我去年学驾驶。 **wǒ qùnián xué jiàshǐ**
I took driving lessons last year.

他在打扫房间。 **tā zài dǎsǎo fángjiān**
He is tidying the room.

小红写了两封信。 **xiǎo hóng xiě le liǎng fēng xìn**
Xiao Hong wrote two letters.

她天天拉小提琴。 **tā tiāntiān lā xiǎotíqín**
She plays the violin every day.

(2) The subject as recipient:

When the subject is a recipient, verbs such as 受到 **shòudào** 'be a bene-
ficiary or target of', 遭到 **zāodào** 'suffer from', 遇到 **yùdào** 'meet with',
得到 **dédào** 'gain', 'be a winner of', are used:

学生受到老师的表扬。 **xuésheng shòudào lǎoshī de biǎoyáng**
The students were commended by the teacher. (*lit.* The students received
the teacher's praise.)

她家遭到盗窃。 **tā jiā zāodào dàoqiè**
Her house was burgled. (*lit.* Her house suffered a burglary.)

运动员得到一千镑奖金。 **yùndòngyuán dédào yī qiān bàng jiǎngjīn**
The athlete received a prize of one thousand pounds.

中国遭到特大洪水。 **zhōngguó zāodào tè dà hóngshuǐ**
China suffered a huge flood.

Note: The 被 **bèi** structure (see Unit 2) naturally falls into this category:

孩子被爸爸骂了一顿。 **háizi bèi bàba mà le yī dùn**
The child was told off/rebuked by his/her father.

鱼被小猫叼走了。 **yú bèi xiǎo māo diāo zǒu le**
The fish was taken/carried off by the kitten.

D   In a topic–comment sentence the topic may be a noun, pronoun, verb, phrase
or clause. The comment usually consists of either a 是 **shì** phrase, a 有 **yǒu**
phrase, an adjective or adjectival phrase:

他们是运动员。 **tāmen shì yùndòngyuán**
They are athletes.
(他们 **tāmen** pronoun topic, 是 **shì** phrase as comment)

我有一个弟弟。 **wǒ yǒu yī gè dìdi**
I have a younger brother.
(我 **wǒ** pronoun topic, 有 **yǒu** phrase as comment)

这儿的空气很新鲜。 **zhèr de kōngqì hěn xīnxiān**
The air here is fresh.
(空气 **kōngqì** noun as topic, 很新鲜 **hěn xīnxiān** adjectival phrase as comment)

抽烟对健康有害。 **chōuyān duì jiànkāng yǒuhài**
Smoking is bad for health.
(抽烟 **chōuyān** verb as topic, 有害 **yǒuhài** adjective as comment)

他迟到是不对的。 **tā chídào shì bù duì de**
He shouldn't have been late. (*lit.* He arrive late was wrong.)
(他迟到 **tā chídào** clause as topic, 是 **shì** phrase as comment)

Note: The topic may be of definite or indefinite reference:

这个小女孩是我妹妹。 **zhè/zhèi gè xiǎo nǚhái shì wǒ mèimei**
This little girl is my younger sister.

蜘蛛有八只脚。 **zhīzhū yǒu bā zhī jiǎo**
A spider has eight legs.

E Sentences may also be identified as topic–comment structures in the following situations:

(1) When a modal verb is present:

一个人应该学一门外语。 **yī gè rén yīnggāi xué yī mén wàiyǔ**
One should learn a foreign language.

锻炼能增强人的体质。 **duànliàn néng zēngqiáng rén de tǐzhì**
Exercise can improve one's physique.

(2) When the sentence particle 了 **le** is incorporated (see Unit 8):

孩子上学去了。 **háizi shàngxué qù le**
The child has gone to school.

太阳出来了。 **tàiyáng chū lái le**
The sun has come out.

(3) When a passive notion is implied (without the use of 被 **bèi** structure):

衣服都洗干净了。 **yīfu dōu xǐ gānjìng le**
The clothes have all been washed.

饭煮好了。 **fàn zhǔ hǎo le**
The meal is ready. (*lit.* The food has been cooked.)

Note: In these 'passive' sentences, the topic is usually of definite reference and the sentence particle 了 **le** is always present.

(4) When a verb is unmodified or unmarked for aspect and indicates a permanent characteristic:

猫吃鱼。 **māo chī yú**
Cats eat fish.
铁爱生锈。 **tiě ài shēngxiù**
Iron rusts easily. (*lit.* Iron is apt to rust.)
旅游增进见闻。 **lǚyóu zēngjìn jiànwén**
Travelling broadens knowledge.
他喜欢打篮球。 **tā xǐhuan dǎ lánqiú**
He likes playing basketball.

F Subject and topic, however, may be seen to coexist in the following types of constructions:

(1) Topic | subject–predicate:

牛奶我已经喝了。 **niúnǎi | wǒ yǐjing hē le**
I have drunk the milk.

In this case, the subject–predicate structure 我已经喝了 **wǒ yǐjing hē le** serves as a comment to the topic 牛奶 **niúnǎi**. This kind of construction can be viewed as a 'notional passive' with the original object 牛奶 **niúnǎi** of the transitive verb 喝 **hē** being moved to the beginning of the sentence.

However, in some cases the verb in a construction like this may take an object which has a part and whole relationship with the topic. For example:

马铃薯我削了皮了。 **mǎlíngshǔ | wǒ xiāo le pí le**
I have peeled the potatoes. (*lit.* Potatoes I have peeled the skins.)

Sometimes a complement (of location, duration, etc.) may be found after the verb in such constructions.

花儿妈妈插在花瓶里了。 **huār | māma chā zài huāpíng li le**
Mother has put the flowers in the vase.
(*lit.* Flowers mother has put in the vase.)

那个地方我们去过好几次了。
nà/nèi gè dìfang | wǒmen qù guo hǎo jǐ cì le
We have been to that place quite a number of times.
(*lit.* That place we have been to quite a number of times.)

(2)　Subject | topic–comment:

　　　这个孩子中文说得不错。 **zhè/zhèi gè háizi | zhōngwén shuō de bùcuò**
　　　This child speaks very good Chinese.

This construction is in most cases the reverse of the previous topic | subject–predicate format. The sentence, for example, may be reworded thus, posing 中文 **zhōngwén** 'the Chinese language' as the topic:

　　　中文这个孩子说得不错。 **zhōngwén zhè/zhèi gè háizi shuō de bùcuò**
　　　This child speaks very good Chinese.

From this point of view, the two types of sentences: topic | subject–predicate, and subject | topic–comment are in fact similar in meaning and may both be counted as belonging to the topic–comment category, their only difference being in their word order and emphasis.

The above sentence can also be reworded thus:

　　　这个孩子说中文说得不错。
　　　zhè/zhèi gè háizi | shuō zhōngwén shuō de bùcuò
　　　This child speaks very good Chinese.

In this reworded sentence 孩子 **háizi** 'the child' remains the subject (i.e. the initiator) of the verb (i.e. the action) 说 **shuō** 'speak' (here the second 说 **shuō**, in 说得不错 **shuō de bùcuò**). However, 说中文 **shuō zhōngwén** 'speaking Chinese' has now become the topic of the sentence rather than simply 中文 **zhōngwén** 'Chinese', and, as with the previous two examples, the sentence is obviously a topic and comment construction. The sentence could be further reformulated as 这个孩子的中文说得不错 **zhè/zhèi gè háizi de zhōngwén shuō de bùcuò**, which is clearly a simple topic–comment sentence.

(3)　Topic | topic–comment:

　　　那个人年纪不小了。 **nà/nèi gè rén | niánjì bù xiǎo le**
　　　That person isn't young any more. (*lit.* That person age not small.)

　　　我哥哥身体很好。 **wǒ gēge | shēntǐ hěn hǎo**
　　　My elder brother is in good shape. (*lit.* Elder brother physique very good.)

　　　中亚国家经济发展很快。 **zhōngyà guójiā | jīngjì fāzhǎn hěn kuài**
　　　The economic growth of central Asian countries is very fast.

Note: The second topic in the above constructions usually has a part and whole relationship with the first topic. In the first example, 'age' is related to 'that person'; in the second, 'physique' is part of 'elder brother', and in the third, 'economic development' is an observable feature of 'central Asian countries'.

Exercise 7.1

Indicate which of the following Chinese sentences are subject–predicate sentences and which are topic–comment structures:

1 我在研究中国历史。 **wǒ zài yánjiū zhōngguó lìshǐ**
   I'm researching Chinese history.
2 这双皮鞋太大。 **zhè/zhèi shuāng píxié tài dà**
   This pair of shoes is too big.
3 现在是两点半。 **xiànzài shì liǎng diǎn bàn**
   It's half past two now.
4 这列火车有八节车厢。 **zhè/zhèi liè huǒchē yǒu bā jié chēxiāng**
   This train has eight carriages.
5 我们遇到很大的困难。 **wǒmen yùdào hěn dà de kùnnan**
   We came up against huge problems.
6 汽车修好了。 **qìchē xiū hǎo le**
   The car has been repaired.
7 飞机准时起飞。 **fēijī zhǔnshí qǐfēi**
   The plane departed on time.
8 喝茶对健康有益。 **hē chá duì jiànkāng yǒuyì**
   Drinking tea is good for your health.
9 警察穿制服。 **jǐngchá chuān zhìfú**
   Policemen wear uniform.
10 小李得到了一份好工作。 **xiǎo lǐ dédào le yī fèn hǎo gōngzuò**
   Xiao Li got a good job.

Exercise 7.2

Rewrite the Chinese sentences below adding the subject given in the round brackets to the topic–comment structure and translate the resulting sentence into English:

1 药已经吃了。 **yào yǐjing chī le**
   The medicine was taken. (病人 **bìngrén** patients)
2 衣服都晾出去了。 **yīfu dōu liàng chūqù le**
   All the washing has been hung out to dry. (我 **wǒ** I)
3 割草机借走了。 **gēcǎojī jiè zǒu le**
   Somebody borrowed the lawnmower. (邻居 **línjū** neighbour)
4 那个问题讨论过没有 **nà/nèi gè wèntí tǎolùn guo méiyǒu**
   Has that question been discussed? (大家 **dàjiā** everybody)
5 第二篇文章写好了吗? **dì èr piān wénzhāng xiě hǎo le ma**
   Has the second essay been written? (你 **nǐ** you)
6 妈妈要的东西昨天买回来了。 **māma yào de dōngxi zuótiān mǎi huílái le**
   What mother wanted was bought yesterday. (爸爸 **bàba** father)

Exercise 7.3

Change the following 把 **bǎ** and 被 **bèi** constructions into topic–comment sentences, omitting the subject or adding the sentence particle 了 **le** where appropriate:

1 弟弟把积蓄都存进银行里去了。 **dìdi bǎ jīxù dōu cún jìn yínháng li qù le**
  Younger brother has put all his savings into the bank.
2 他已经把房间收拾好了。 **tā yǐjing bǎ fángjiān shōushi hǎo le**
  He has tidied the room.
3 爸爸把那笔奖金捐给学校了。 **bàba bǎ nà/nèi bǐ jiǎngjīn juān gěi xuéxiào le**
  Father has donated the prize money to the school.
4 我已经把这件事告诉他了。 **wǒ yǐjing bǎ zhè/zhèi jiàn shì gàosu tā le**
  I've already told him about this.
5 昨天买的香蕉全被他吃完了。
  zuótiān mǎi de xiāngjiāo quán bèi tā chī wán le
  The bananas which were bought yesterday were all eaten up by him.
6 剩下的饭菜被妈妈倒在阴沟里。
  shèng xià de fàncài bèi māma dào zài yīngōu li
  All the leftovers were tipped down the drain by mother.

Exercise 7.4

Translate the following into Chinese, making the underlined elements the topics of the sentences:

1 I have cleaned <u>the room</u>.
2 She has posted <u>the two letters</u>.
3 I have cooked <u>the rice</u>.
4 My younger brother has borrowed <u>my father's car</u>.
5 I have been to <u>the Great Wall</u> twice already.
6 Mother has given <u>that box of chocolates</u> to a friend.

UNIT EIGHT
Sentence particle 了 le

Sentence particle 了 le is a common and important feature of Chinese, in particular spoken Chinese. We saw in Unit 7 section **E** that the presence of 了 le at the end of a sentence converted the sentence into a topic–comment structure. This is because the speaker, in adding 了 le, is providing a personal gloss in reaction to a statement just made or to circumstances that may have become apparent. This gloss invariably introduces some expression of change which the speaker wishes *see Li,* to convey. This change may indicate that things have taken a turn or that they *Thampson* are not what one would have expected, or that they are about to be different. Sentence particle 了 le therefore often occurs naturally with verbs or adjectives *p. 244* that pose contrasts and possess an inherent implication of change.

A As 了 le is often used to indicate a change from one state to another, it naturally occurs with adjectival predicates:

天黑了。 **tiān hēi le**
It's getting dark./It's gone dark.

天气暖和起来了。 **tiānqì nuǎnhuo qǐlái le**
It's getting warmer./It's got warmer.

妈妈老了。 **māma lǎo le**
Mother is getting older./Mother is old now.

他的病好了。 **tā de bìng hǎo le**
He's better./He has got better. (*lit.* His illness is better.)

B As 了 le is also used to indicate the completion of an action, it readily combines the aspectual use of 了 le with the sentential particle 了 le following a verb at the end of a statement:

春天到了。 **chūntiān dào le**
Spring has arrived.

冬天过去了。 **dōngtiān guò qù le**
Winter is over.

车来了。 **chē lái le**
Here comes the bus.

车走了。 **chē zǒu le**
The bus has gone.

花开了。 **huā kāi le**
The flowers have opened/are in bloom.

花谢了。 **huā xiè le**
The flowers have withered/fallen.

我的表停了。 **wǒ de biǎo tíng le**
My watch has stopped.

邻居的狗死了。 **línjū de gǒu sǐ le**
The neighbour's dog has died.

C From the discussion in **A** and **B**, it logically follows that 了 **le** is generally used after an adjective or a verb (or verb phrase) at the end of a sentence when the speaker sees a situation as having come to a stage which requires comment or summing up:

好了。 **hǎo le**
That's it. (e.g. Some job has been done; some discussion should end, etc.)

(我的话) 完了。 **(wǒ de huà) wán le**
That's all. (*lit.* My words are finished. (e.g. at the end of a speech or talk))

时间到了。 **shíjiān dào le**
Time's up. (*lit.* The time has come.)

算了，算了。 **suàn le | suàn le**
Okay, okay. (e.g. It's no longer worth making a fuss about.)

别生气了。 **bié shēngqì le**
Don't you fret/be angry any more.

不要说话了。 **bù yào shuōhuà le**
Please be quiet. (*lit.* Don't talk any more.)

This usage leads on to the speaker's call for the beginning of a new action:

起床了。 **qǐchuáng le**
Get up, please.

咱们开始了。 **zánmen kāishǐ le**
Let's get started./Let's begin.

D   了 **le** is therefore seen to be frequently used with expressions of imminent action, intention or change, often with adverbs such as 快 **kuài** 'soon', (就) 要 (**jiù**) **yào** 'just about to', etc.:

我走了。 **wǒ zǒu le**
I'm off now.

来了。 **lái le**
I'm coming. (*lit.* come)

(天) 要下雨了。(**tiān**) **yào xià yǔ le**
It looks like rain.

飞机快起飞了。 **fēijī kuài qǐfēi le**
The plane is about to take off.

火车马上就要开了。 **huǒchē mǎshàng jiù yào kāi le**
The train is just about to start/leave.

E   To indicate the end state or result of an action, 了 **le** is commonly used in sentences where the verb incorporates a result complement and once again combines the aspectual use with the sentence particle function (see *Basic Chinese*, Unit 22):

汽车修好了。 **qìchē xiū hǎo le**
The car has been repaired.

衣服烫/熨好了。 **yīfu tàng/yùn hǎo le**
The clothes have been ironed.

一切都准备好了。 **yīqiè dōu zhǔnbèi hǎo le**
Everything is ready.

牛奶喝完了。 **niúnǎi hē wán le**
The milk is finished.

弟弟长高了。 **dìdi zhǎng gāo le**
My younger brother has grown taller.

爷爷病倒了。 **yéye bìng dǎo le**
Grandpa has fallen ill.

婴儿睡着了。 **yīng'ér shuì zháo le**
The baby has gone to sleep.

他喝醉了吗？ **tā hē zuì le ma**
Is he drunk?

这个字写错了吧？ **zhè/zhèi gè zì xiě cuò le ba**
I suspect this character has been written wrongly.

Similarly, the direction marker 起来 **qǐlái**, signalling the beginning of a new stage, and potential complements expressing probability or particularly non-probability also require 了 **le**:

那两个喝醉酒的人打起来了。 **nà/nèi liǎng gè hē zuì jiǔ de rén dǎ qǐlái le**
The two people who were drunk came to blows.

我今天走不了了。 **wǒ jīntiān zǒu bu liǎo le**
I can't leave today. (e.g. It's too late and the last train is gone, etc.)

妈妈伤心得说不下去了。 **māma shāngxīn de shuō bu xiàqù le**
Mother was so sad that she could not go on. (*lit.* could not go on talking)

这件事我记不起来了。 **zhè/zhèi jiàn shì wǒ jì bu qǐlái le**
I can't recall this incident. (*lit.* This matter I can't remember.)

F   As an indicator of change, 了 **le** may also be used to express the emergence of a situation (present, past or future) which the speaker has not expected or is very much concerned about:

你怎么了？ **nǐ zěnme le**
What's wrong with you? (Has anything (unusual) happened?)

你去哪儿了？ **nǐ qù nǎr le**
Where did you go? (I could not find you anywhere.)

太好了。 **tài hǎo le**
Terrific! (It's much better than I expected.)

你孩子今年几岁了？ **nǐ háizi jīnnián jǐ suì le**
How old is your child? (I would really like to know.)

G   Sentence 了 **le** naturally often occurs in sentences which include a verb–object or verb–complement phrase marked by aspect 了 **le**. In these cases the speaker, by using sentence 了 **le**, is adding his or her gloss to the statement or question. Consider the following pairs of examples in which the first is a statement of fact and the second adds the speaker's comment:

我们等了两个钟头。 **wǒmen děng le liǎng gě zhōngtóu**
We waited two hours.
我们等了两个钟头了。 **wǒmen děng le liǎng gè zhōngtóu le**
We have been waiting/have waited for two hours.

她去了三次。 **tā qù le sān cì**
She went three times.
她去了三次了。 **tā qù le sān cì le**
She's been there three times.

我们看了那个电影。 **wǒmen kàn le nà/nèi gè diànyǐng**
We saw that film.
我们看了那个电影了。 **wǒmen kàn le nà/nèi gè diànyǐng le**
We've seen that film.

他喝了十杯啤酒。 **tā hē le shí bēi píjiǔ**
He drank ten glasses of beer.
他喝了十杯啤酒了。 **tā hē le shí bēi píjiǔ le**
He's had ten glasses of beer (and that's why he can't stand up).

H   了 **le** is not generally used in the following situations:

(1) In sentences which express processes (past, present or future):

我昨天去看电影。 **wǒ zuótiān qù kàn diànyǐng**
I went to the cinema yesterday.

她正在接电话。 **tā zhèngzài jiē diànhuà**
She is on the phone at the moment. (*lit.* She is receiving a phone call right now.)

我明天去探望他。 **wǒ míngtiān qù tànwàng tā**
I am going to pay him a visit tomorrow.

(2) In sentences expressing habitual actions:

我常常打高尔夫球。 **wǒ chángcháng dǎ gāo'ěrfū qiú**
I often play golf.

我天天坐火车上班。 **wǒ tiāntiān zuò huǒchē shàngbān**
I go to work by train every day.

(3) In negative sentences indicating that something did not, does not or will not take place:

那天晚上我没有喝酒。 **nà/nèi tiān wǎnshang wǒ méiyǒu hē jiǔ**
I didn't drink that evening.

我不抽烟。 **wǒ bù chōuyān**
I don't smoke.

我不去。 **wǒ bù qù**
I won't go.

Note: However, 了 **le** can be used in any situation listed under **F**, if the speaker is expressing an assertion, contradiction or change of mind, etc.:

我没有再喝酒了。 **wǒ méiyǒu zài hē jiǔ le**
I never drank again (after that).

See also Henne (Hdbk Ch) p121

我不抽烟了。 **wǒ bù chōuyān le**
I've given up smoking./I don't smoke any more.

我不去了。 **wǒ bù qù le**
I'm not going any more.

我天天坐火车上班了。 **wǒ tiāntiān zuò huǒchē shàngbān le**
Nowadays I go to work by train every day.
(I didn't use to.)

我昨天去看电影了。 **wǒ zuótiān qù kàn diànyǐng le**
I went to the cinema yesterday.
(I hadn't intended to; I hadn't been before; that's why I was not somewhere else, etc.)

Exercise 8.1

Identify which Chinese sentence in the pairs below is a more accurate translation of the English in each case:

1 I can speak Chinese now.
   我会说汉语。 **wǒ huì shuō hànyǔ**/我会说汉语了。 **wǒ huì shuō hànyǔ le**
2 He doesn't smoke.
   他不抽烟。 **tā bù chōuyān**/他不抽烟了。 **tā bù chōuyān le**
3 The leaves are going yellow.
   树叶黄了。 **shùyè huáng le**/树叶很黄。 **shùyè hěn huáng**
4 The shop is closed.
   商店关了门。 **shāngdiàn guān le mén**/商店关门了。 **shāngdiàn guān mén le**
5 It was cold.
   天气很冷。 **tiānqì hěn lěng**/天气冷了。 **tiānqì lěng le**

6 He won't go to the library any more.
他不去图书馆了。 **tā bù qù túshūguǎn le**/他不去图书馆。 **tā bù qù túshūguǎn**

7 This place has become a supermarket.
这儿是超级市场了。 **zhèr shì chāojí shìchǎng le**/
这儿是超级市场。 **zhèr shì chāojí shìchǎng**

8 The kitten has grown very big.
小猫很大。 **xiǎo māo hěn dà**/小猫大了。 **xiǎo māo dà le**

Exercise 8.2

Translate the following sentences into Chinese:

1 Here comes the train.
2 I have grown taller.
3 The watch has been mended.
4 The dog is getting old.
5 The picture has fallen down. (掉 **diào** 'fall')
6 The clock has stopped.
7 The fish died.
8 The work is finished.
9 He is drunk.
10 The child is asleep.

Exercise 8.3

Make adjustments to the Chinese sentences below to make them appropriate representations of the English in each case:

1 鞋子太大。 **xiézi tài dà**
   The shoes are too big.
2 我天天喝牛奶了。 **wǒ tiāntiān hē niúnǎi le**
   I drink milk every day.
3 我们快到山顶。 **wǒmen kuài dào shāndǐng**
   We're nearly at the top of the mountain.
4 哥哥经常喝酒了。 **gēge jīngcháng hē jiǔ le**
   My elder brother often drinks.
5 会议就要结束。 **huìyì jiù yào jiéshù**
   The meeting will finish in a minute.
6 他喜欢跳舞了。 **tā xǐhuan tiàowǔ le**
   He likes dancing.
7 我每晚都读报了。 **wǒ měi wǎn dōu dú bào le**
   I read the newspaper every evening.

8 新房子快造好。 **xīn fángzi kuài zào hǎo**
   The new house will be finished very soon.
9 水马上就开。 **shuǐ mǎshàng jiù kāi**
   The water will boil in a second.
10 弟弟是医生了。 **dìdi shì yīshēng le**
   My younger brother is a doctor.

Exercise 8.4

Translate the following into Chinese:

1 Last year things were very expensive here, but now they are much cheaper.
2 We are just off.
3 Where have they gone to now?
4 I'll be back in a moment.
5 I don't like eating meat any more.
6 His hair has gone grey.
7 She is not here any more.
8 It's going to snow.
9 I don't have any more money.
10 My Chinese is a bit better than it used to be.

UNIT NINE
Abbreviated sentences

A Sentences in Chinese are often dependent on the context for meaning, and abbreviated sentences are therefore extremely common, particularly in speech, since in clearly contextualised utterances some language features can become redundant. Take the following examples:

我买了一个橘子，太酸，没吃。 **wǒ mǎi le yī gè júzi | tài suān | méi chī**
I bought a tangerine, (but it) was too sour, (and I) didn't eat (it).

那家商店还有雨伞卖，这儿卖完了。
nà/nèi jiā shāngdiàn hái yǒu yǔsǎn mài | zhèr mài wán le
There are umbrellas for sale in that shop, (but they) are sold out here.

It will be seen from the above that context in Chinese allows for omissions and that conjunctions and pronouns in particular, especially the third person neuter, are often omitted.

B In answer to questions, abbreviated forms of the initial questions are normally used rather than 'yes' or 'no' (see *Basic Chinese*, Unit 18):

你喝酒吗？ **nǐ hē jiǔ ma**
Do you drink?
喝。 **hē**
Yes. (*lit.* drink)

你抽烟吗？ **nǐ chōuyān ma**
Do you smoke?
不抽。 **bù chōu**
No. (*lit.* don't smoke)

他来了没有？ **tā lái le méiyǒu**
Has he turned up?
来了。 **lái le**
Yes. (*lit.* has come)

你明天去不去游泳？ **nǐ míngtiān qù bù qù yóuyǒng**
Are you going swimming tomorrow?
去。 **qù**
Yes. (*lit.* go)

你是不是这儿的服务员？ **nǐ shì bù shì zhèr de fúwùyuán**
Are you a waiter here?
是。 **shì**
Yes. (*lit.* am)

你有没有手电筒？ **nǐ yǒu méi yǒu shǒudiàntǒng**
Have you got a torch?
对不起，没有。 **duìbuqǐ | méi yǒu**
Sorry, no. (*lit.* sorry, haven't got)

If a modal verb is present it should be used in the answer:

你想不想去看电影？ **nǐ xiǎng bù xiǎng qù kàn diànyǐng**
Do you want to go to the cinema?
想。 **xiǎng**
Yes. (*lit.* want)

你要上市场买东西吗？ **nǐ yào shàng shìchǎng mǎi dōngxi ma**
Would you like to go shopping in the market?
不要。 **bù yào**
No. (*lit.* not want)

我能借一下你的打火机吗？ **wǒ néng jiè yīxià nǐ de dǎhuǒjī ma**
May I borrow your lighter for a moment?
能。 **néng**
Yes. (*lit.* may)

In answer to question-word questions, as with most languages it is possible to supply an abbreviated response containing only what is relevant to the question being asked:

她是谁？ **tā shì shéi/shuí**
Who is she?
我的朋友。 **wǒ de péngyou**
My friend.

你有几个孩子？ **nǐ yǒu jǐ gè háizi**
How many children have you got?
两个。 **liǎng gè**
Two.

这是谁的钱包？ **zhè shì shéi/shuí de qiánbāo**
Whose purse is this?
我的。 **wǒ de**
Mine.

火车什么时候到？ **huǒchē shénme shíhou dào**
What time is the train due?
下午三点半。 **xiàwǔ sān diǎn bàn**
Half past three in the afternoon.

C   In everyday idioms the subject or topic may be omitted:

(1) Everyday expressions:

> 谢谢！ **xièxie**
> Thank you!
> 对不起！ **duìbuqǐ**
> (I'm) sorry!/Excuse me!
> 再见！ **zàijiàn**
> Good-bye!/See you later!
> 当然喽！ **dāngrán lou**
> Of course!
> 没关系！ **méi guānxi**
> It doesn't matter!/Never mind!
> 行！/好！ **xíng/hǎo**
> All right!
> 找你两毛。 **zhǎo nǐ liǎng máo**
> Here's your change of twenty cents. (*lit.* return you two mao)

(2) Expressions about the weather:

> 下雨了！ **xià yǔ le**
> It's raining!
> 起雾了！ **qǐ wù le**
> It's foggy!
> 下雪了！ **xià xuě le**
> It's snowing!
> 刮风了！ **guā fēng le**
> It's windy!
> 打雷了！ **dǎ léi le**
> It's thundering!
> 闪电了！ **shǎn diàn le**
> It's lightning!
> 下霜了！ **xià shuāng le**
> It's frosty!

出太阳了！ **chū tàiyáng le**
The sun has come out!/It's sunny!

Note the use of sentence particle 了 **le** indicating change of state.

(3) Requests or instructions:

过来！ **guò lái**
Come here!
开会了！ **kāihuì le**
Let's start!/We're starting (a meeting).
别动！ **bié dòng**
Don't move!
慢走！ **màn zǒu**
Take care!/Go carefully!
留步！ **liú bù**/不送！ **bù sòng**
Don't bother seeing me to the door!/No need to see me out!
请进！ **qǐng jìn**
Come in please!
请喝茶 **qǐng hē chá?**
Would you like a cup of tea?

(4) Military commands:

立正！ **lì zhèng**
Attention!
稍息！ **shàoxī**
Stand at ease!
齐步走！ **qíbù zǒu**
Quick march!
向右转！ **xiàng yòu zhuǎn**
Right turn!

Note: In these commands the first (or first two) words are often pronounced with a level tone, and the last word always assumes a falling note, no matter what the original tone is.

(5) Public notices of instruction or prohibition:

禁止吸烟！ **jìnzhǐ xīyān**
No smoking!
不准入内！ **bù zhǔn rù nèi**
No entry!
在此排队！ **zài cǐ páiduì**
Queue here!

随手关门！**suíshǒu guān mén**
Close the door behind you!
不准乱扔果皮、纸屑！**bù zhǔn luàn rēng guǒpí | zhǐxiè**
Don't drop litter!/No litter!
(*lit.* dropping fruit skins and bits of paper not allowed)

拉 **lā**
Pull (notice/sign on door)
推 **tuī**
Push (notice/sign on door)

D   In exclamations or instructions a single word or a short phrase is often enough:

票！**piào**
Tickets, please!
火！**huǒ**
Fire!
救命！**jiùmìng**
Help!
注意！**zhùyì**/小心！**xiǎoxīn**
Look out!/Watch out!
蜘蛛！**zhīzhū**
A spider!/A daddy-longlegs!
天哪！**tiān na**
Heavens!/Good heavens!

E   Exclamations also often omit the subject or topic and, therefore, consist simply of a qualifying adjective preceded by a degree adverb like 多 (么) **duō (me)** 'how', 这么 **zhème** 'so', 真 **zhēn** 'truly', etc.:

多么幸运哪！**duōme xìngyùn na**
How lucky (we are)!
多巧哇！**duō qiǎo wa**
What a coincidence!
这么漂亮啊！**zhème piàoliang à**
How pretty!
真热呀！**zhēn rè ya**
How hot it is!

Sometimes a qualified headword or topic suffices:

多可爱的孩子啊！**duō kě'ài de háizi a**
What a lovely child!

多凶的狗哇！**duō xiōng de gǒu wa**
What a fierce dog!
多好的天气呀！**duō hǎo de tiānqì ya**
What lovely weather!
多高的山哪！**duō gāo de shān na**
What a high mountain!

Exercise 9.1

Translate the following into Chinese:

1　I'm sorry!
2　It doesn't matter!
3　It's lightning!
4　It's thundering!
5　Sign here, please!
6　Fire!
7　What a clever person!
8　Sit down, please!
9　Be quiet, please!
10　No parking!
11　Turn off the light as you go out!
12　Don't cry!
13　Your receipt!
14　What heavy rain!

Exercise 9.2

Provide positive and negative answers in Chinese for each of the questions below using abbreviated forms:

1　昨晚你洗澡了吗？**zuó wǎn nǐ xǐzǎo le ma**
　　Did you have a shower/bath last night?
2　你想买杂志吗？**nǐ xiǎng mǎi zázhì ma**
　　Do you want to buy a magazine?
3　她是不是你的牙医？**tā shì bù shì nǐ de yáyī**
　　Is she your dentist?
4　你有没有擦手纸？**nǐ yǒu méi yǒu cāshǒuzhǐ**
　　Have you got any tissues?
5　你写不写回信？**nǐ xiě bù xiě huíxìn**
　　Are you going to write back?
6　我可以坐在这儿吗？**wǒ kěyǐ zuò zài zhèr ma**
　　May I sit here?
7　你的孩子会走路了吗？**nǐ de háizi huì zǒulù le ma**
　　Can your child walk now?
8　我能请你帮个忙吗？**wǒ néng qǐng nǐ bāng gè máng ma**
　　May I ask a favour?
9　你们去过大英博物馆吗？**nǐmen qù guo dàyīng bówùguǎn ma**
　　Have you been to the British Museum?
10　男厕在楼上吗？**náncè zài lóushang ma**
　　Is the Gents upstairs?

Exercise 9.3

Translate the Chinese sentences or expressions below into English:

1 随手关门！ **suìshǒu guān mén**
2 下课了！ **xiàkè le**
3 赶快！ **gǎnkuài**
4 别说话！ **bié shuōhuà**
5 滚蛋！ **gǔndàn**

6 睡觉了！ **shuìjiào le**
7 拉 **lā**
8 推 **tuī**
9 出太阳了！ **chū tàiyáng le**
10 小心！ **xiǎoxīn**

Exercise 9.4

Translate the following into Chinese, using abbreviations where appropriate:

1 That case is very heavy. I don't want to buy it.
2 It's raining.
3 It's Sunday today.
4 Those flowers are beautiful. Can I buy them for you?
5 Have you been to Japan? No.
6 Are you coming to play football tonight? Yes.
7 Our house is on this map, but I can't see it.
8 Do you like it here?
9 Fancy seeing you here. What a coincidence!
10 What beautiful music! (好听 **hǎotīng** pleasant to listen to)
11 Do you recognise that man? No.
12 I'm looking for my key, but I can't find it.
13 The blue one is very attractive, but I can't afford it.
14 Can you smoke here? No.
15 It's really easy to speak Chinese.

UNIT TEN
Rhetorical questions

A   Rhetorical questions by definition are not neutral enquiries and they always carry some degree of assumption on the part of the speaker. In their mildest form they simply repeat the previous statement with a quizzical tone (with or without the interrogative particle 吗 **ma**), implying that the speaker is questioning or expressing doubts about the validity of the statement. This quizzical tone is introduced (1) by stressing particular elements in the question or (2) by adding a qualifying phrase like 真的 **zhēn de**, 确实 **quèshí**, etc. meaning 'Is it true that . . .':

他们同意了 (吗)？(with stress on 同意 **tóngyì**)
tāmen tóngyì le (ma)
Have they <u>agreed</u>?

or

他们真的同意了 (吗)？
tāmen <u>zhēn de</u> tóngyì le (ma)
Have they really agreed?

你喜欢喝茅台 (吗)？(with stress on 茅台 **máotái** – a strong Chinese liquor)
nǐ xǐhuan hē máotái (ma)
You like (drinking) <u>Maotai</u>?

or

你确实喜欢喝茅台 (吗)？
nǐ <u>quèshí</u> xǐhuan hē máotái (ma)
Do you really like (drinking) Maotai?

Note: More simply, the speaker may of course just use the simple idiom 是吗？**shì ma** 'Is that so?' to the same effect:

他们同意了，是吗？**tāmen tóngyì le | shì ma**
They have agreed, haven't they? (*lit.* They have agreed, is that so?)

A stronger form of rhetorical question is couched in the negative where the speaker is actually inviting a positive answer. The interrogative particle 吗 **ma** may be added, but the question can sound even more rhetorical without it:

你不知道 (吗)？ **nǐ bù zhīdao (ma)**
Didn't/Don't you know?

他没有告诉你 (吗)？ **tā méiyǒu gàosu nǐ (ma)**
Hasn't he told you?

你不喜欢跳舞 (吗)？ **nǐ bù xǐhuan tiàowǔ (ma)**
Don't you like dancing?

你不是大夫 (吗)？ **nǐ bù shì dàifu (ma)**
Aren't you a doctor?

The negator 不 **bù** can also be followed by the intensifier 是 **shì** before the verb to highlight the whole predicate or comment. Under such circumstances, 吗 **ma** is more often included:

你不是去过美国吗？ **nǐ bù shì qù guo měiguó ma**
Haven't you been to America?

你不是说她是俄国人吗？ **nǐ bù shì shuō tā shì éguó rén ma**
Didn't you say that she was Russian?

中国话不是有很多不同的方言吗？
zhōngguóhuà bù shì yǒu hěn duō bù tóng de fāngyán ma
Doesn't Chinese have very many different dialects?

他不是把那本小说翻译成英文了吗？
tā bù shì bǎ nà/nèi běn xiǎoshuō fānyì chéng yīngwén le ma
Hasn't he translated that novel into English?

Note: The rhetorical tone may be further strengthened by placing the phrase 难道 **nándào** 'Is it possible/true that . . .' at the beginning of the question or immediately after the subject:

难道你不知道吗？ **nándào nǐ bù zhīdao ma**
Do/Did you really not know?

你难道真的不懂中文吗？ **nǐ nándào zhēn de bù dǒng zhōngwén ma**
Do you mean to say that you really don't understand Chinese?

B   The sentence particle 吧 **ba** also occurs in rhetorical questions. It makes an enquiry which itself suggests the answer:

她是老师吧？ **tā shì lǎoshī ba**
She is a teacher, isn't she?

她不是老师吧？ **tā bù shì lǎoshī ba**
She isn't a teacher, is she?

他们会溜冰吧？ **tāmen huì liūbīng ba**
They know how to skate, don't they?

我们不是明天去见经理吧？ **wǒmen bù shì míngtiān qù jiàn jīnglǐ ba**
We aren't going to see the manager tomorrow, are we?

C Interrogative pronouns like 什么 **shénme**, 哪儿 **nǎr** or 怎么 **zénme** are used in rhetorical questions to convey a more contentious enquiry:

(1) 什么 **shénme**:

   (a) Following an adjective:

   你忙什么？ **nǐ máng shénme**
   What are you so busy with?

   你急什么？ **nǐ jí shénme**
   What are you so worried about?/There is no hurry./There's nothing to worry about.

   这道题难什么？ **zhè/zhèi dào tí nán shénme**
   What's so difficult about this question?

   (b) Preceding a noun:

   吃什么鱼！ **chī shénme yú**
   What do you mean (eat) fish?/What fish?
   (implies 'There isn't any fish.')

   看什么电影！ **kàn shénme diànyǐng**
   There is no way you are going to the cinema!

   摆什么架子！ **bǎi shénme jiàzi**
   You've got nothing to be proud of!/Don't give yourself airs!

   (c) After a verb:

   你哭什么？ **nǐ kū shénme**
   What are you crying for?

你嚷什么？ **nǐ rǎng shénme**
What are you shouting for?/What's all the shouting about?

你埋怨什么？ **nǐ mányuàn shénme**
What are you complaining about?/Why are you making such a fuss?

(d) With the verb 有 **yǒu**:

这有什么用？ **zhè yǒu shénme yòng**
What's the use of (doing) this?

这些书有什么意思？ **zhè/zhèi xiē shū yǒu shénme yìsi**
What's so interesting about these books?

(2) 哪儿 **nǎr** before a noun (with 的 **de**), verb or adjective:

这是哪儿的话？ **zhè shì nǎr de huà**
What sort of talk is that/this? (derogatory)/Don't mention it. (polite)

我哪儿吃得下呢？ **wǒ nǎr chī de xià ne**
How (on earth) can I eat it/any more?

我的话哪儿错了？ **wǒ de huà nǎr cuò le**
What (on earth) is wrong with what I said?

(3) 怎么 **zénme** before a verb or modal verb, often followed by 呢 **ne**:

他怎么会不明白呢！ **tā zénme huì bù míngbai ne**
How (on earth) can/could he fail to understand?

你怎么能不去呢？ **nǐ zénme néng bù qù ne**
How can you not go?

你怎么可以怪她呢！ **nǐ zénme kěyǐ guài tā ne**
How can/could you blame her! (implies 'You can't blame her.')

(4) 谁 **shéi/shuí** also usually with 呢 **ne**:

谁知道呢？ **shéi/shuí zhīdao ne**
Who knows? (Nobody knows.)

谁不知道呢？ **shéi/shuí bù zhīdao ne**
Who doesn't know? (Everybody knows.)

谁猜得着呢？ **shéi/shuí cāi de zháo ne**
Who would have guessed it?

还能是谁呢？ **hái néng shì shéi/shuí ne**
Who else could it be (then)?

(5) 何必 **hébì**/何苦 **hékǔ** 'what need', 'why' or 何不 **hébù** 'why not' again often
with 呢 **ne**:

你何必当真呢？ **nǐ hébì dàngzhēn ne**
Why take it (so) seriously?/Why so serious?

你何苦跟自己过不去呢？ **nǐ hékǔ gēn zìjǐ guò bu qù ne**
Why be so hard on yourself?

你何不马上告诉他呢？ **nǐ hébù mǎshàng gàosu tā ne**
Why don't you tell him straightaway?

(6) 干吗 **gànmá**/干什么 **gàn shénme** 'what(ever) for', 'why (ever)' (colloquial):

你干吗这么客气？ **nǐ gànmá zhème kèqi**
Why are you being so polite?/Why all this formality?

你干什么生气？ **nǐ gàn shénme shēngqì**
Why are you so angry?/What are you so angry for?

你骂人干什么？ **nǐ mà rén gàn shénme**
Why are you being so insulting/abusive?

D Affirmative-negative questions are often used to introduce a rhetorical tone,
particularly when introduced by phrases like 你说 **nǐ shuō** (*lit.* 'What do you say
to that?'):

你说这件事怪不怪？ **nǐ shuō zhè/zhèi jiàn shì guài bù guài**
Don't you think this is strange?

你说她这个人厉害不厉害？ **nǐ shuō tā zhè/zhèi gè rén lìhài bù lìhài**
She is really tough/formidable isn't she?/Don't you think she is really
tough/formidable?

你说这种工作难不难？ **nǐ shuō zhè/zhèi zhǒng gōngzuò nán bù nán**
This is a difficult job isn't it?/Don't you think this is a difficult job?

Exercise 10.1

Rewrite the Chinese sentences below in the form of rhetorical questions using the phrases or structures given in the round brackets, and then translate the resulting question into English. (In some cases the negative may have to be dropped from the original statement.):

1 那位运动员很健康。 **nà/nèi wèi yùndòngyuán hěn jiànkāng**
  That athlete is very healthy. (. . . 不是 . . . 吗 . . . **bù shì . . . ma**)
2 他吃过西瓜了。 **tā chī guo xīguā le**
  He has eaten watermelon before. (. . . 没有 . . . 吗 . . . **méiyǒu . . . ma**)
3 那个孩子懂礼貌。 **nà/nèi gè háizi dǒng lǐmào**
  The child is very polite. (难道 . . . 不 . . . 吗 **nándào . . . bù . . . ma**)
4 我没有错。 **wǒ méiyǒu cuò**
  I'm not wrong. (. . . 哪儿 . . . 了 . . . **nǎr . . . le**)
5 他不可以说这样的话。 **tā bù kěyǐ shuō zhè/zhèi yàng de huà**
  He can't say things like that. (. . . 怎么 . . . . . . **zénme . . .**)
6 大家都知道这件事。 **dàjiā dōu zhīdao zhè/zhèi jiàn shì**
  Everyone knows about this. (谁不 . . . **shéi/shuí bù . . .**)
7 你可以跟他一起去美国。 **nǐ kěyǐ gēn tā yīqǐ qù měiguó**
  You can go to America with him. (. . . 何不 . . . 呢 . . . **hébù . . . ne**)
8 这件事情真复杂。 **zhè/zhèi jiàn shìqing zhēn fùzá**
  This matter is really complicated. (你说 . . . 不 . . . 吗 **nǐ shuō . . . bù . . . ma**)
9 她不应该生气。 **tā bù yīnggāi shēngqì**
  She shouldn't be angry. (. . . 干什么 . . . **gàn shénme**)
10 他是王工程师。 **tā shì wáng gōngchéngshī**
  He's Wang the engineer. (难道 . . . 不是 . . . **nándào . . . bù shì . . .**)

Exercise 10.2

Translate the following into English:

1 你不爱吃巧克力吗？ **nǐ bù ài chī qiǎokèlì ma**
2 你何苦住这样旧的房子呢？ **nǐ hékǔ zhù zhè/zhèi yàng jiù de fángzi ne**
3 谁买这么贵的汽车呢？ **shéi/shuí mǎi zhème guì de qìchē ne**
4 哭有什么用呢？ **kū yǒu shénme yòng ne**
5 你怎么做这样危险的事呢？
  nǐ zěnme zuò zhè/zhèi yàng wēixiǎn de shì ne
6 他难道不高兴吗？ **tā nándào bù gāoxìng ma**
7 这么说不对吗？ **zhème shuō bù duì ma**
8 你说这件事复杂不复杂？ **nǐ shuō zhè/zhèi jiàn shì fùzá bù fùzá**
9 还有什么比这个更便宜的吗？
  hái yǒu shénme bǐ zhè/zhèi gè gèng piányi de ma
10 你懂什么？ **nǐ dǒng shénme**

Exercise 10.3

Translate the following into Chinese:

(a) Using 不 **bù** . . . 吗 **ma**, 真的 **zhēn de**, etc.:

1 Don't you understand?
2 Do you really watch television every evening?
3 Have your friends really all arrived?
4 Do you really want to go?
5 Can't you use chopsticks?

(b) Using 不是 **bù shì** . . . 吗 **ma**:

6 Didn't you say they could all speak Chinese?
7 Haven't you seen that film?
8 Isn't she very like her mother?
9 Aren't you extremely busy on Saturdays?
10 Isn't Shanghai the biggest city in China?

(c) Using 难道 **nándào** . . . 吗 **ma**:

11 You haven't left your tickets at home, have you?
12 Do you mean to say you still can't write that (Chinese) character?
13 Didn't he even say 'thank you'?
14 Could it be possible that she doesn't eat tomatoes?

(d) Using the question word indicated:

15 What's the hurry? (什么 **shénme**)
16 How can she help you? (哪儿 **nǎr**)
17 How could he possibly agree with your opinions? (怎么 **zénme**)
18 Why won't she say anything? (干吗 **gànmá**)
19 Who would buy such expensive things? (谁 **shéi/shuí** . . . 呢 **ne**)
20 Why not go by train then? (何不 **hébù** . . . 呢 **ne**)

UNIT ELEVEN
Conjunctions and conjunctives linking clauses in compound sentences (1)

A   This unit and the next one deal with conjunctions (e.g. 因为 **yīnwèi** . . . 所以 **suǒyǐ**, 但是 **dànshì**) and conjunctives (e.g. 就 **jiù**, 才 **cái**, 却 **què**) which link clauses together in compound sentences. A conjunction may occur in the first or second clause and may be placed either before or immediately after the subject/ topic whereas a conjunctive, which is in fact a referential adverb functioning as a link word, may only occur in the second clause and it must be placed immediately before the predicate/comment:

因为昨天下雨，所以运动会暂停。
yīnwèi **zuótiān xià yǔ** | *suǒyǐ* **yùndònghuì zàntíng**
Because it rained yesterday, the sports meeting was (therefore) cancelled.
(因为 **yīnwèi** 'because' and 所以 **suǒyǐ** 'therefore' are both conjunctions.)

昨天下雨，运动会却照常举行。
zuótiān xià yǔ | **yùndònghuì** *què* **zhàocháng jǔxíng**
It rained yesterday but the sports meeting went ahead as planned.
(却 **què** 'on the other hand' is a conjunctive.)

Quite often a conjunction (in the first clause) and a conjunctive (in the second clause) work together for the linkage:

雨虽然很大，他却来了。 **yǔ** *suīrán* **hěn dà** | **tā** *què* **lái le**
He came in spite of the heavy rain./Although the rain was heavy, he did (however) come.
(虽然 **suīrán** '(al)though' is a conjunction and 却 **què** 'on the contrary' is a conjunctive.)

Note: By clauses we mean subject–predicate or topic–comment constructions which are part of a larger compound sentence. If the subjects/topics or the objects of the linked clauses are the same, they are usually omitted in the second clause:

(因为)她跑得很快，所以得了第一。 (*yīnwèi*) **tā pǎo de hěn kuài** | *suǒyǐ* **dé le dì yī**
Because she ran very fast, (therefore) she came first.

(因为)你不喜欢吃苹果，所以我没买。 (*yīnwèi*) **nǐ bù xǐhuan chī píngguǒ** | *suǒyǐ* **wǒ méi mǎi**
Because you don't like apples, (therefore) I didn't buy any.

B   The most commonly used conjunctions and conjunctives are:

(1) but, yet, however

> conjunctions: 可是 **kěshì**, 然而 **rán'ér**, 不过 **bùguò**
> conjunctive: 却 **què**

我想去参加音乐会，可是没有票。
wǒ xiǎng qù cānjiā yīnyuèhuì | *kěshì* **méi yǒu piào**
I wanted/want to go to the concert, but I didn't/don't have a ticket.

他失败多次，然而并不灰心。 **tā shībài duō cì** | *rán'ér* **bìng bù huīxīn**
He failed many times, yet he certainly did not lose hope.

我会说英文，不过我懂的词不多。
wǒ huì shuō yīngwén | *bùguò* **wǒ dǒng de cí bù duō**
I can speak English but I don't know many words.

这件事很重要，我却把它忘了。
zhè/zhèi jiàn shì hěn zhòngyào | **wǒ** *què* **bǎ tā wàng le**
This (matter) is really important, but I forgot all about it.

although . . . (yet) . . .

> paired conjunctions: 虽然 **suīrán** . . . 但是 **dànshì** . . .

虽然我学过俄语，但是全忘了。
suīrán **wǒ xué guo éyǔ** | *dànshì* **quán wàng le**
Even though I have studied Russian, I have forgotten it all.

(2) otherwise, or

> conjunctions: 否则 **fǒuzé**, 不然 **bùrán**

你得小心驾驶，否则会出事故。
nǐ děi xiǎoxīn jiàshǐ | *fǒuzé* **huì chū shìgù**
You should drive carefully, or you'll have an accident.

我年纪大了，不然我会去参加游泳比赛。
wǒ niánjì dà le | *bùrán* **wǒ huì qù cānjiā yóuyǒng bǐsài**
I am getting old, otherwise I would take/have taken part in the swimming competition.

(3) or

conjunction: 或者 **huòzhě**

这件事由你负责，或者由我负责。
zhè/zhèi jiàn shì yóu nǐ fùzé | *huòzhě* **yóu wǒ fùzé**
You or I should be responsible for this.
(*lit.* This business is either up to you to take responsibility or up to me to take responsibility.)

either . . . or

paired conjunctions: 要么 **yàome** . . . 要么 **yàome** . . . , 不是 **bùshì** . . . 就是 **jiùshì** . . .

今晚我要么去图书馆看书，要么去实验室做实验。
jīn wǎn wǒ *yàome* **qù túshūguǎn kànshū,** *yàome* **qù shíyànshì zuò shíyàn**
This evening I'll either be going to the library to do some reading or going to the laboratory to do some experiments.

在海边度假的时候，我们每天不是吃鱼，就是吃蟹。
zài hǎi biān dùjià de shíhou | wǒmen měi tiān *bùshì* **chī yú |** *jiùshì* **chī xiè**
When we were spending our holiday by the sea, we ate either fish or crabs every day.
(*lit.* . . . if we didn't eat fish, then (we) ate crab.)

Note: In alternative-questions, 还是 **háishi** rather than 或者 **huòzhě** should be used:

这件事你去办，还是我去办？
zhè/zhèi jiàn shì nǐ qù bàn | *háishi* **wǒ qù bàn**
Will you deal with this matter or shall I?

(4) moreover, also

conjunction: 而且 **érqiě**

这个学生很聪明，而且很勤奋。
zhè/zhèi gè xuésheng hěn cōngming | *érqiě* **hěn qínfèn**
This student is very intelligent and also very industrious.

not only . . . but also . . .   *see Ch. Feb. Words p4-21*

paired conjunctions: 不但 **bùdàn**/不仅 **bùjǐn** . . . 而且 **érqiě**/甚至 **shènzhì** . . .

她不但会说英文，而且会说德文。
tā *bùdàn* huì shuō yīngwén | *érqiě* huì shuō déwén
Not only can she speak English but she can speak German as well.

他不仅会种花，甚至会种菜。
tā *bùjǐn* huì zhòng huā | *shènzhì* huì zhòng cài
He can not only grow flowers but he can even grow vegetables as well.

(5) therefore

conjunction: 因此 **yīncǐ**

他经常撒谎，因此大家不相信他。
tā jīngcháng sāhuǎng | *yīncǐ* dàjiā bù xiāngxìn tā
He often tells lies so nobody believes him.

because . . . , (therefore)

paired conjunctions: 因为 **yīnwèi** . . . 所以 **suǒyǐ** . . .

因为她专心学习，所以进步很大。
yīnwèi tā zhuānxīn xuéxí | suǒyǐ jìnbù hěn dà
Because she has been concentrating on her studies, (therefore) she has
made great progress.

because (of)

conjunction: 由于 **yóuyú**

由于路太滑，他摔了一交。 **yóuyú lù tài huá | tā shuāi le yī jiāo**
Because the road was slippery, he fell over.

Note: 由于 **yóuyú** 'owing to', 'due to' may also function as a preposition. It is then followed
by a noun instead of a clause:

由于各种原因，他没有出席这次会议。
yóuyú gè zhǒng yuányīn | tā méiyǒu chūxí zhè/zhèi cì huìyì
Owing to various reasons, he did not attend this meeting.

(6) since . . . , (then) . . .

conjunction followed by conjunctive: 既然 **jìrán** . . . 那(么)就 **nà(me)
jiù** . . .

既然你没空，那就改日再谈吧。
jìrán nǐ méi kòng | nà jiù gǎi rì zài tán ba
Since you are busy, let's talk about it some other day.

既然他不愿意，那就算了。 **jìrán tā bù yuànyì** | *nà jiù* **suàn le**
Since he is not willing, let's leave it at that.

(7) as long as . . . , (then) . . .   (NB 要是 = "if" — no sense of requirement)

conjunction followed by conjunctive: 只要 **zhǐyào** . . . 就 **jiù** . . .

只要你愿意学，我就教你。 **zhǐyào nǐ yuànyì xué** | **wǒ** *jiù* **jiāo nǐ**
As long as you are willing to learn, (then) I'll teach you.

NB

only if/when . . .

conjunction followed by conjunctive: 只有 **zhǐyǒu** . . . 才 **cái** . . . (*lit.* and only then)

只有大家互相支持，才能完成这项任务。
zhǐyǒu **dàjiā hùxiāng zhīchí** | *cái* **néng wánchéng zhè/zhèi xiàng rènwu**
Only if we all support each other will we be able to complete this task.

unless

conjunction followed by conjunctive: 除非 **chúfēi** . . . 才 **cái** or by conjunction: 不然 **bùrán**/否则 **fǒuzé** . . .

除非交通阻塞，我才会迟到。 *chúfēi* **jiāotōng zǔsè** | **wǒ** *cái* **huì chídào**
I won't be late unless there is a traffic jam.

除非你每天吃药，不然/否则你的病好不了了。
chúfēi **nǐ měi tiān chī yào** | *bùrán/fǒuzé* **nǐ de bìng hǎo bu liǎo le**
Unless you take the medicine every day, you won't get well.

(8) no matter, regardless   despite, however

paired conjunctions: 不管 **bùguǎn** . . . 还是 **háishi** . . .
conjunction followed by conjunctive: 无论 **wúlùn**/不论 **bùlùn** . . . 也 **yě** 'still', 'in addition'/都 **dōu** 'all', 'in every case' . . .

不管风多大，飞机还是照常起飞。
bùguǎn **fēng duō dà** | **fēijī** *háishi* **zhàocháng qǐfēi**
No matter how strong the wind is, the plane will take off as usual.

无论/不论价钱多贵，她也要买。
wúlùn/bùlùn **jiàqian duō guì** | **tā** *yě* **yào mǎi**
No matter how expensive it is, she will still want to buy it.

无论/不论天多热，他都洗热水澡。
***wúlùn/bùlùn* tiān duō rè | tā *dōu* xǐ rèshuǐ zǎo**
No matter how hot it is, he always takes a hot bath.

(9) on the contrary

paired conjunctions: 不但 **bùdàn bù/méi** ... , 反而 **fǎn'ér** ...

雨不但不/没停，反而更大了。 **yǔ bùdàn bù/méi tíng | *fǎn'ér* gèng dà le**
Instead of letting up, the rain came down even harder.
(*lit.* Not only has the rain not stopped, but (on the contrary) it is even
heavier.)

The list of conjunctions and conjunctives continues in Unit 12.

Exercise 11.1

Complete the Chinese sentences below with appropriate conjunctions and/or
conjunctives to match the English:

1 ——— 天气多冷，我 ——— 洗冷水澡。
    ——— **tiānqì duō lěng | wǒ ——— xǐ lěngshuǐ zǎo**
    No matter how cold it is, I always take a cold shower.
2 你想要黑白胶卷 ——— 彩色胶卷？
    nǐ xiǎng yào hēibái jiāojuǎn | ——— cǎisè jiāojuǎn
    Did you want black and white or colour film?
3 她写了一本名著，——— 在历史上有了一席之地。
    tā xiě le yī běn míngzhù | ——— zài lìshǐ shang yǒu le yī xí zhī dì
    She wrote a famous book, and so won a place in history.
4 他这么一个人，你 ———爱他 ——— 恨他。
    tā zhème yī gè rén | nǐ ——— ài tā ——— hèn tā
    You can either love or hate someone like him.
5 ——— 雨下得多大，学校运动会 ——— 照常进行。
    ——— **yǔ xià de duō dà | xuéxiào yùndònghuì ——— zhàocháng jìnxíng**
    The school sports day will go ahead as planned no matter how heavy the rain is.
6 ——— 那个孩子变好了，我 ——— 放心。
    ——— **nà/nèi gè háizi biàn hǎo le | wǒ ——— fàngxīn**
    Only when that child is better will I stop worrying.
7 ——— 是成人，——— 学校的孩子也知道这一点。
    ——— **shì chéngrén | ——— xuéxiào de háizi yě zhīdao zhè/zhèi yī diǎn**
    It's not just adults, even schoolchildren would know that.
8 ——— 工作很辛苦，——— 我干得很高兴。
    ——— **gōngzuò hěn xīnkǔ | ——— wǒ gàn de hěn gāoxìng**
    It's hard work but I enjoy it.

9 她没有吃早饭 _____ (她) 饿了。 **tā méiyǒu chī zǎofàn | _____ (tā) è le**
She's hungry because she didn't have breakfast.

10 _____ 这间房间太热，_____ 我打开了窗户。
_____ zhè/zhèi jiān fángjiān tài rè | _____ wǒ dǎ kāi le chuānghu
I opened the window because it was very hot in the room.

11 她提醒了我，_____ 我就会把这件事忘了。
tā tíxǐng le wǒ | _____ wǒ jiù huì bǎ zhè/zhèi jiàn shì wàng le
She reminded me of what I would have otherwise forgotten.

12 _____ 你无法回答这个问题，_____ 我们去问别人。
_____ nǐ wúfǎ huídá zhè/zhèi gè wèntí | _____ wǒmen qù wèn biérén
If you can't answer the question, we'll ask someone else.

13 他仍然有点感冒，_____ 其他方面都正常。
tā réngrán yǒu diǎn gǎnmào | _____ qítā fāngmiàn dōu zhèngcháng
He's still got a bit of a cold, but otherwise he's all right.

14 _____你表示了决心，_____ 应该见之于行动。
_____ nǐ biǎoshì le juéxīn | _____ yīnggāi jiàn zhī yú xíngdòng
Since you have proved your determination, you should go ahead/take action.

15 赶快，_____ 你要迟到了。 **gǎnkuài | _____ nǐ yào chídào le**
Hurry up, or you'll be late.

16 我买了报纸，_____ 还没有读。
wǒ mǎi le bàozhǐ | _____ hái méiyǒu dú
I bought a newspaper but I haven't read it yet.

17 _____ 你问，我 _____ 回答你。 **_____ nǐ wèn | wǒ _____ huídá nǐ**
Since you asked me, I'll answer.

18 _____ 他先写信给我，我 _____ 写信给他。
_____ tā xiān xiě xìn gěi wǒ | wǒ _____ xiě xìn gěi tā
I won't write to him unless he writes to me first.

19 她 _____ 喜欢读诗，_____ 喜欢写诗。
tā _____ xǐhuan dú shī | _____ xǐhuan xiě shī
She likes reading poems, but she also likes writing them.

20 她这个人很怪，_____ 你禁不住会喜欢她。
tā zhè/zhèi gè rèn hěn guài | _____ nǐ jīn bu zhù huì xǐhuan tā
She is a funny girl, but you can't help liking her.

Exercise 11.2

Complete the following sentences to provide a full translation of the English:

1 这是一座漂亮的房子，_____。
zhè shì yī zuò piàoliang de fángzi | _____
This is a nice house, but it hasn't got a garden.

2 我累了，_____。 **wǒ lèi le | _____**
I was tired so I went to bed.

3 我进不了屋子，_____。 **wǒ jìn bu liǎo wūzi |** _____
  I can't get into the house because I can't find the key.
4 我们今晚上电影院去，_____。
  wǒmen jīn wǎn shàng diànyǐngyuàn qù | _____
  Let's go to the cinema tonight or we won't get to see the film.
5 这位医生虽然很有经验，_____。
  zhè/zhèi wèi yīshēng suīrán hěn yǒu jīngyàn | _____
  Although the doctor is experienced, I am still very worried.
6 那儿水太脏，_____。 **nàr shuǐ tài zāng |** _____
  The water there was so dirty that nobody wanted to swim.

Exercise 11.3

Translate the following into Chinese:

  1 As it's raining, you might as well stay at home.
  2 You won't get a good job unless you study hard.
  3 No matter how fast you run, you are bound to be late.
  4 As long as you are honest everyone will like you.
  5 If she isn't crying then she's making trouble.
  6 Are we eating at home or eating out tonight?
  7 Although he has been to Japan a few times, he can't speak any Japanese.
  8 Are you going to France or Italy for your holidays?
  9 They always talk about politics and so no one will go to see them.
 10 If the weather was good, I would either go fishing or go hill-walking.

UNIT TWELVE

Conjunctions and conjunctives linking clauses in compound sentences (2)

A Conjunctions and conjunctives (continued):

(1) if . . . (then) . . .

> conjunctions followed by conjunctives: 如果 **rúguǒ**/要是 **yàoshi** . . .
> 就 **jiù** . . . , 假使 **jiǎshǐ**/假如 **jiǎrú**/假若 **jiǎruò** . . . 就 **jiù** . . .

> 如果/要是再不下雨，水库里的水就会干了。
> **rúguǒ/yàoshi zài bù xià yǔ | shuǐkù li de shuǐ jiù huì gān le**
> If it doesn't rain any more the reservoir will dry up.

> 假使/假如/假若他五分钟内不来，我们就不等了。
> **jiǎshǐ/jiǎrú/jiǎruò tā wǔ fēn zhōng nèi bù lái | wǒmen jiù bù děng le**
> If he doesn't turn up in five minutes, we won't wait any longer.

Note: The phrase '. . . 的话' **de huà** is often used at the end of the first clause either by itself or together with a conjunction like 如果 **rúguǒ**:

> (如果) 明天下雪的话，我们就不去爬山了。
> **(rúguǒ) míngtiān xià xuě de huà | wǒmen jiù bù qù páshān le**
> If it snows tomorrow we won't go hill-walking/climbing.

Note: It is possible to form an 'if . . . then . . .' sentence without using a conjunction in the first clause:

> 明天下雪，我们就不去爬山了。 **míngtiān xià xuě | wǒmen jiù bù qù páshān le**
> If it snows tomorrow we won't go hill-walking/climbing.

(2) even though, although, even if

> paired conjunctions: 尽管 **jǐnguǎn** . . . 但是 **dànshì** . . .
> conjunctions followed by conjunctives: 尽管 **jǐnguǎn** . . . 还是 **háishi** . . . ,
> 即使 **jíshǐ** . . . 也 **yě** . . . , 哪怕 **nǎpà**/就算 **jiùsuàn** . . . 也 **yě** . . .

> 尽管他有很多钱，但是并不感到幸福。
> **jǐnguǎn tā yǒu hěn duō qián | dànshì bìng bù gǎndào xìngfú**
> Although he is very rich, he isn't happy.

尽管这道题很难，他还是做出来了。
jǐnguǎn zhè/zhèi dào tí hěn nán | tā *háishi* zuò chūlái le
Even though it was a difficult question, he was able to do it.

即使你很忙，也得抽空来一趟。
jíshǐ nǐ hěn máng | *yě* děi chōukòng lái yī tàng
Even if you are very busy, you'll have to find time to (come and) visit.

这双鞋哪怕/就算穿十年，也穿不破。
zhè/zhèi shuāng xié *nǎpà/jiùsuàn* chuān shí nián | *yě* chuān bu pò
Even if you wear this pair of shoes for ten years, they will not wear out/
you won't wear them out.

Note: Conjunctions like 哪怕 **nǎpà** and 就算 **jiùsuàn** refer to potential rather than actual events.

(3) . . . would rather . . . than . . .

paired conjunctions: 与其 **yǔqí** . . . 倒不如 **dào bùrú** . . . (*lit.* 'as regards'/
'compared with . . . ,' 'it does not compare with'/'is as good as . . .'),
宁可 **nìngkě** . . . 也不 **yě bù** . . .

与其出去看电影，倒不如在家看电视。
yǔqí chū qù kàn diànyǐng | *dào bùrú* zài jiā kàn diànshì
I would rather stay at home and watch television than go out and see
a film.
(*lit.* Rather than going out to see a film, it is not as good as watching
television at home.)

我宁可自己做，也不要别人帮。
wǒ *nìngkě* zìjǐ zuò | *yě bù* yào biéren bāng
I would rather do it myself than ask other people for help.

(4) . . . in order to . . . , so that . . .

conjunction: 以便 **yǐbiàn**

老师在黑板上把字写得很大，以便后排的同学也能看清楚。
**lǎoshī zài hēibǎn shang bǎ zì xiě de hěn dà | *yǐbiàn* hòu pái de tóngxué
yě néng kàn qīngchu**
The teacher wrote the characters very large on the blackboard so that
pupils on the back row could also see them clearly.

. . . (in order) to avoid

conjunctions: 以免 **yǐmiǎn**, 免得 **miǎnde**

These conjunctions are usually placed before the verb in the second clause:

请你放轻脚步，以免吵醒大家。
qǐng nǐ fàng qīng jiǎobù | *yǐmiǎn* **chǎo xǐng dàjiā**
Please walk quietly to avoid waking everybody up.

穿上你的外套，免得着凉。
chuān shàng nǐ de wàitào | *miǎnde* **zháoliáng**
Put on your coat to avoid catching cold/so that you won't catch cold.

(5) as soon as . . .

paired conjunctives: 一 **yī** . . . 就 **jiù** . . .

我一开口，他就打断我的话。 **wǒ** *yī* **kāikǒu** | **tā** *jiù* **dǎduàn wǒ de huà**
As soon as I opened my mouth, he interrupted me.

not until . . . , . . . and only then . . .

paired conjunctives: . . . 之后 **zhī hòu** . . . 才 **cái**

他这么说了之后，我才恍然大悟。
tā zhème shuō le zhī hòu | **wǒ** *cái* **huǎngrán dàwù**
It was only when/after he said so that it dawned on me/I realised.

(6) while . . . , also . . .

parallel conjunctives: 一边 **yībiān**/一面 **yīmiàn** . . . 一边 **yībiān**/一面 **yīmiàn** . . .

他一边/一面吃饭，一边/一面看书。
tā *yībiān/yīmiàn* **chīfàn** | *yībiān/yīmiàn* **kànshū**
He ate as he read./He read while he ate.

both . . . and . . . , . . . as well as . . .

parallel conjunctives: 又 **yòu** . . . 又 **yòu** . . .

他又会画画儿，又会写诗。 **tā** *yòu* **huì huà huàr** | *yòu* **huì xiě shī**
He can paint as well as write poems.

the more . . . the more . . .

parallel conjunctives: 越 **yuè** . . . 越 **yuè** . . .

电影越惊险，他越喜欢看。

diànyǐng *yuè* jīngxiǎn | tā *yuè* xǐhuan kàn

The more thrilling the film was, the more he enjoyed it.

雪越下越大。　**xuě *yuè* xià *yuè* dà**

The snow came down more and more heavily.

B　Clauses may also be linked in compound sentences by placing the same interrogative pronoun or adverb in each clause. In these sentences the interrogative pronouns or adverbs take on indefinite meanings ('anyone'/'whoever', 'anywhere'/ 'wherever', 'anything'/'whatever') and 就 **jiù** will often appear in the second clause.

谁有困难，我们就帮助谁。

shéi/shuí* yǒu kùnnan | wǒmen jiù bāngzhù *shéi/shuí

We will help anyone who is in difficulty./Whoever has difficulties, we will help them.

哪里有名胜古迹，哪里就有来观光的游客。

***nǎli* yǒu míngshèng gǔjī | *nǎli* jiù yǒu lái guānguāng de yóukè**

Anywhere/Wherever there is a place of scenic beauty or historical interest, there will be tourists coming to visit/to see it.

你想吃什么，就吃什么。　**nǐ xiǎng chī *shénme* | jiù chī *shénme***

You may eat anything/whatever you like. (*lit.* Whatever you want to eat, you may eat it.)

你怎么说，我就怎么做。　**nǐ *zénme* shuō | wǒ jiù *zénme* zuò**

I'll do it any way/whichever way you like. (*lit.* Whatever you say, I will do it that way.)

Exercise 12.1

Complete the following Chinese sentences with appropriate conjunctions or conjunctives to match the English:

1　他 _____ 绕道走，_____ 不踩在草地上。

　　tā _____ ràodào zǒu | _____ bù cǎi zài cǎodì shang

　　He would rather go round than tread on the grass.

2　_____ 她没有上过大学，_____ 她懂得很多。

　　_____ tā méiyǒu shàng guo dàxué | _____ tā dǒng de hěn duō

　　Even though she's never been to university she knows a lot.

3 _____ 困难再大，我们 _____ 能克服。

_____ **kùnnan zài dà | wǒmen** _____ **néng kèfú**

No matter if the difficulties get worse, we can still overcome them.

4 _____ 说是粗心大意，_____ 说是不负责任。

_____ **shuō shì cūxīn dàyì |** _____ **shuō shì bù fù zérèn**

It's not so much carelessness as irresponsibility.

5 我再说明一下，_____ 引起误会。

wǒ zài shuōmíng yīxià | _____ **yǐnqǐ wùhuì**

To avoid any misunderstanding, let me explain once again.

6 你 _____ 当初听我的话，现在 _____ 不会惹上这些麻烦了。

nǐ _____ **dāngchū tīng wǒ de huà | xiànzài** _____ **bù huì rě shàng zhè/ zhèi xiē máfan le**

If you had listened to me, you wouldn't have got into the trouble you are in now.

7 我提早来了，_____ 让你在会议前看一下我的讲稿。

wǒ tízǎo lái le | _____ **ràng nǐ zài huìyì qián kàn yīxià wǒ de jiǎnggǎo**

I came early so that you could read my speech before the meeting.

8 _____ 你有理，_____ 不应该发火啊!

_____ **nǐ yǒulǐ |** _____ **bù yīnggāi fāhuǒ a**

You shouldn't have lost your temper even if you were in the right.

9 等到草莓熟了，我 _____ 可以去采了。

děng dào cǎoméi shú le | wǒ _____ **kěyǐ qù cǎi le**

I'll pick the strawberries when they are ripe.

10 _____ 夜深了，他 _____ 在工作。

_____ **yè shēn le | tā** _____ **zài gōngzuò**

Although it was late, he was still working.

11 _____ 她打电话来，你 _____ 通知我。

_____ **tā dǎ diànhuà lái | nǐ** _____ **tōngzhī wǒ**

If she telephones, let me know.

12 我 _____ 踏进家门，外面 _____ 下起了倾盆大雨。

wǒ _____ **tà jìn jiāmén | wàimian** _____ **xià qǐ le qīngpén dà yǔ**

As soon as I stepped in the door, it began to pour down outside.

Exercise 12.2

Translate the sentences below into Chinese using the parallel constructions given in brackets:

1 They chatted over a cup of tea.
   (一边 **yībiān** . . . 一边 **yībiān** . . .)
2 She can drive as well as ride horses.
   (又 **yòu** . . . 又 **yòu** . . .)

3 The more angry she became, the more he laughed at her.
(越 **yuè** . . . 越 **yuè** . . .)
4 You can say whatever you like.
(什么 **shénme** . . . 什么 **shénme** . . .)
5 Wherever you go I'll go too.
(哪儿 **nǎr** . . . 哪儿 **nǎr** . . .)
6 So saying, he made for the door.
(一面 **yīmiàn** . . . 一面 **yīmiàn** . . .)
7 You may choose whoever is suitable.
(谁 **shéi/shuí** . . . 谁 **shéi/shuí** . . .)
8 The snowball got bigger and bigger as it rolled along.
(越 **yuè** . . . 越 **yuè** . . .)

Exercise 12.3

The following Chinese sentences are incorrect or inappropriate translations of
the English. Make the necessary corrections in each case:

1 邻居一开音乐，我才头疼。 **línjū yī kāi yīnyuè | wǒ cái tóu téng**
My head started to ache as soon as the neighbours started playing music.
2 她生气的话，我才去道歉。 **tā shēngqì de huà | wǒ cái qù dàoqiàn**
If she's annoyed then I'll go and apologise.
3 老师讲课的声音很大，为了大家能听清楚。
lǎoshī jiǎngkè de shēngyīn hěn dà | wèile dàjiā néng tīng qīngchu
The teacher spoke in a loud voice as she taught the lesson so that everyone
could hear clearly.
4 与其上馆子，倒自己煮。 **yǔqí shàng guǎnzi | dào zìjǐ zhǔ**
I'd rather cook myself than go to a restaurant.
5 会议开始了，他才没有赶到。 **huìyì kāishǐ le | tā cái méiyǒu gǎn dào**
He still hadn't arrived when the meeting started.
6 只有你努力，就一定能学好汉语。
zhǐyǒu nǐ nǔlì | jiù yīdìng néng xué hǎo hànyǔ
You'll be able to learn Chinese as long as you work hard.
7 穿上你的靴子，以便在雪地上滑倒。
chuān shàng nǐ de xuēzi | yǐbiàn zài xuědì shang huá dǎo
Put your boots on so you don't slip on the snow.
8 他一面弹琴，一面也唱歌。 **tā yīmiàn tán qín | yīmiàn yě chàng gē**
He can sing at the same time as playing the piano.
9 外面下着大雪，却他只穿着一件衬衫。
wàimian xià zhe dà xuě | què tā zhǐ chuān zhe yī jiàn chènshān
He had only a shirt on despite the heavy snow outside.
10 你喜欢喝什么，我就给你倒那个。
nǐ xǐhuan hē shénme | wǒ jiù gěi nǐ dào nà/nèi gè
I'll pour out for you whatever you'd like to drink.

Exercise 12.4

Translate the sentences below into Chinese:

1 Come and see me as soon as you get back.
2 Even if you get back late, come and see me.
3 I would rather get back today than wait to see you tomorrow.
4 I can't come and see you until I get back.
5 If you can't get back now, come and see me later.
6 I will come back immediately to avoid not seeing you.
7 I will see anyone who gets back today.
8 I will see you any time you can get back.

UNIT THIRTEEN
Conjunctions linking words or phrases (summary)

In this unit we will discuss in more detail conjunctions which link together words or phrases (see *Basic Chinese*, Unit 1), rather than sentences or clauses.

A Conjunctions meaning 'and'.

(1) 和 **hé** may be used to join nouns, pronouns, adjectives and verbs:

    (a) Nouns:

> 刀和叉 **dāo hé chā**
> knife and fork
> 饭碗和筷子 **fànwǎn hé kuàizi**
> bowl and chopsticks
> 爸爸和妈妈 **bàba hé māma**
> father and mother

    (b) Pronouns:

> 你和我 **nǐ hé wǒ**
> you and I
> 我和她 **wǒ hé tā**
> she and I/me and her

> Note that, unlike English, Chinese does not feel any polite obligation on the part of the speaker to put the other person first and him/herself second.

    (c) Adjectives (as attributives):

> 失落和忧伤的心情 **shīluò hé yōushāng de xīnqíng**
> a sad and lost feeling

> Note that when adjectives are used as predicatives, they are generally linked by the conjunction 而 **ér** 'also' (see section **E**):
>
> 那间屋子宽敞而明亮。 **nà/nèi jiān wùzi kuānchang ér míngliàng**
> That room is spacious and bright.

(d) Verbs:

讨论和研究这个问题 **tǎolùn hé yánjiū zhè/zhèi gè wèntí**
discuss and research into this problem

收集和珍藏古董 **shōují hé zhēncáng gǔdǒng**
collect and keep antiques

他认真地学习和工作。 **tā rènzhēn de xuéxí hé gōngzuò**
He studies and works conscientiously.

Note: verbal expressions may only be linked by 和 **hé** when they share the same object (e.g. 问题 **wèntí**, 古董 **gǔdǒng**, etc.) or adverbial (e.g. 认真地 **rènzhēn de**).

(2) 跟 **gēn**, 与 **yǔ** and 同 **tóng** may be used to replace 和 **hé** but only when they are used to link nouns and pronouns but not adjectives or verbs:

(a) 跟 **gēn** is more often used in the northern dialects:

刀跟叉 **dāo gēn chā**
knife and fork
我跟你 **wǒ gēn nǐ**
you and I/me

(b) 与 **yǔ** is more formal in tone:

碗与筷 **wǎn yǔ kuài**
bowls and chopsticks
你与她 **nǐ yǔ tā**
you and she/her

(c) 同 **tóng** is more often used in central and southern China:

袜子同鞋子 **wàzi tóng xiézi**
socks and shoes
你们同我们 **nǐmen tóng wǒmen**
you and we/us

Note: Although 和 **hé**, 跟 **gēn**, 与 **yǔ** and 同 **tóng** mean 'and' and are used to link words and phrases, these conjunctions are never used to link clauses.

One cannot say:

*你去游泳和我去打球。 **nǐ qù yóuyǒng hé wǒ qù dǎ qiú**
(*lit.* You go swimming and I'll play ball games.)

Please also note that 跟 **gēn** is also used as a coverb/preposition in comparison sentences (see *Basic Chinese*, Unit 12).

B   或 (者) **huò(zhě)** 'or' is used mostly to link nouns, pronouns or verbs. 或者 **huòzhě** is preferable when linking items of more than two syllables:

> 牛或羊 **niú huò yáng**
> oxen or sheep
> 这个或那个 **zhè/zhèi gè huò nà/nèi gè**
> this (one) or that (one)
> 今天或明天 **jīntiān huò míngtiān**
> today or tomorrow
> 椅子或者凳子 **yǐzi huòzhě dèngzi**
> chairs or stools
> 这个月或者下个月 **zhè/zhèi gè yuè huòzhě xià gè yuè**
> this month or next month
> 学习或者工作 **xuéxí huòzhě gōngzuò**
> work or study
> 擦窗户或者拖地板 **cā chuānghu huòzhě tuō dìbǎn**
> wipe the windows or mop the floor

Note: 或者 **huòzhě** may also be used to link clauses, whereas 或 **huò** may not:

明天你来找我，或者我去找你。 **míngtiān nǐ lái zhǎo wǒ | huòzhě wǒ qù zhǎo nǐ**
You come to my place tomorrow or I'll go to your place.

One does not say:

*明天你来找我，或我去找你。 **míngtiān nǐ lái zhǎo wǒ | huò wǒ qù zhǎo nǐ**
to translate 'You come to my place tomorrow or I'll go to your place'.

In alternative-questions 'or' is rendered as 还是 **háishi** (see *Basic Chinese*, Unit 19) and never as 或 (者) **huò(zhě)**:

> 你要这本还是 (要) 那本？ **nǐ yào zhè/zhèi běn háishi (yào) nà/nèi běn**
> Do you want this one (book/magazine, etc.) or that one (book/magazine, etc.)?

> 你喝茶还是喝咖啡？ **nǐ hē chá háishi hē kāfēi**
> Would you like tea or coffee?

> 他们这个月放假还是下个月放假？
> **tāmen zhè/zhèi gè yuè fàngjià háishi xià gè yuè fàngjià**
> Are they going on holiday this month or next month?

C   并 (且) **bìng(qiě)** 'and', 'moreover' lends a formal tone to the sentence and may be used only to link verbal expressions:

他学习并掌握了电脑的基本原理。
tā xuéxí bìng zhǎngwò le diànnǎo de jīběn yuánlǐ
He studied and mastered the basic principles of computing.

Note: 并且 **bìngqiě** but not 并 **bìng** may also be used to link clauses.

他扶起地上的老人，并且把他送进了医院。
tā fú qǐ dì shang de lǎorén | bìngqiě bǎ tā sòng jìn le yīyuàn
He helped the old man up from the floor and then took him to hospital.

D (以) 及 **(yǐ)jí** 'and' has a more formal tone than 和 **hé**, and is used to link a
list of individual items with a general term indicating a category:

衣服、帽子、鞋子 (以) 及其他商品 **yīfu | màozi | xiézi (yǐ)jí qítā shāngpǐn**
clothes, hats, shoes and other merchandise

游泳、拳击、举重 (以) 及各种各样的体育运动
yóuyǒng | quánjī | jǔzhòng (yǐ)jí gè zhǒng gè yàng de tǐyù yùndòng
swimming, boxing, weightlifting and all kinds of sports

E 而 **ér** is used to link two adjectives which are related in meaning and means
'and', or, if a contrast is implied, 'but':

生动而幽默的演讲 **shēngdòng ér yōumò de yǎnjiǎng**
a lively and humorous speech
深刻而难忘的印象 **shēnkè ér nánwàng de yìnxiàng**
a profound and unforgettable impression
这个故事真实而曲折。 **zhè/zhèi gè gùshi zhēnshí ér qūzhé**
The story is true but complex.

艳而不俗 **yàn ér bù sú**
colourful but not vulgar
甜而不腻 **tián ér bù nì**
sweet but not cloying

F The correlated conjunctions: 不但 **bùdàn**/不仅 **bùjǐn** . . . 而且 **érqiě** 'not
only . . . but also . . .', 要么 **yàome** . . . 要么 **yàome** . . . 'either . . . or . . .'/'if it
isn't . . . then it's . . .' and 无论 **wúlùn**/不管 **bùguǎn** . . . 还是 **háishi** 'no
matter . . . or . . .', 'whether . . . or not . . .', are used to join nouns, adjectives or
verbs (as well as clauses – see Unit 11):

他们不但白天而且黑夜还在工作。
tāmen bùdàn báitiān érqiě hēiyè hái zài gōngzuò
They worked day and night. (*lit.* They not only worked by day, but also
at night.)

他要么唱歌，要么跳舞，一刻不停。

tā yàome chàng gē | yàome tiàowǔ | yīkè bù tíng

If he's not singing then he's dancing; he just never stops.

无论刮风还是下雨，比赛照常进行。

wúlùn guā fēng háishi xià yǔ | bǐsài zhàocháng jìnxíng

The competition will go ahead whatever if it's windy or raining.

Note: Both conjunctions of a correlated pair should be followed by similar types of words or phrases. For example, if a verb immediately follows the first conjunction then a verb should also follow the second:

他不但骂我而且打我。 **tā bùdàn mà wǒ érqiě dǎ wǒ**
He not only abused me but hit me as well.
(Both 骂 **mà** and 打 **dǎ** are verbs.)

One cannot say:

*不但他骂我而且打我。 **bùdàn tā mà wǒ érqiě dǎ wǒ**
to translate 'He not only abused me but hit me as well'.

Exercise 13.1

Translate the following phrases into Chinese. In most cases more than one conjunction could be used.

1 pens and pencils
2 Saturday or Sunday
3 they and I
4 useless and boring
5 short but clear
6 you as well as me
7 whether by day or night
8 kittens, puppies, chickens and all kinds of small animals
9 roses, daffodils, daisies and all kinds of flowers
10 moon and stars
11 doctor or engineer
12 you or they
13 read and write
14 either by bus or by train

Exercise 13.2

Complete the Chinese sentences below, choosing the appropriate conjunction from the list provided to match the English translation. (Each conjunction may be used in more than one sentence.)

还是 **háishi**   不但 . . . 而且 . . . **bùdàn . . . érqiě . . .**
并且 **bìngqiě**   不管 . . . 还是 . . . **bùguǎn . . . háishi . . .**
而 **ér**   以及 **yǐjí**
或者 **huòzhě**   无论 . . . 还是 . . . **wúlùn . . . háishi . . .**

1 你长大以后想当医生 ———— 想当演员？
nǐ zhǎng dà yǐ hòu xiǎng dāng yīshēng ———— xiǎng dāng yǎnyuán
Do you want to be a doctor or an actor when you grow up?

2 这是一个酷热 ———— 干燥的夏天。
zhè shì yī gè kùrè ———— gānzào de xiàtiān
This is a very hot, dry summer.

3 昨晚的电影冗长 ———— 乏味。
zuó wǎn de diànyǐng rǒngcháng ———— fáwèi
That film yesterday was long and boring.

4 他 ———— 对朋友 ———— 对陌生人也很友好。
tā ———— duì péngyou ———— duì mòshēng rén yě hěn yǒuhǎo
He's not only good to his friends but also to strangers.

5 他们游览了长城、故宫、兵马俑 ———— 其他名胜古迹。
tāmen yóulǎn le chángchéng | gùgōng | bīngmǎyǒng ———— qítā míngshèng gǔjī
They visited the Great Wall, the Imperial Palace, the Terracotta Army and other places of interest.

6 你一定要给我写信 ———— 打电话。
nǐ yīdìng yào gěi wǒ xiě xìn ———— dǎ diànhuà
You must either ring me or write me a letter.

7 ———— 他家 ———— 我家都没有车库。
———— tā jiā ———— wǒ jiā dōu méi yǒu chēkù
Neither he nor I have a garage.

8 ———— 同意 ———— 不同意，你必须说出自己的意见。
———— tóngyì ———— bù tóngyì | nǐ bìxū shuō chū zìjǐ de yìjian
Whether you agree or disagree, you must give your own opinion.

9 他认识 ———— 了解小王。 **tā rènshi ———— liǎojiě xiǎo wáng**
He knows and understands Xiao Wang.

10 他吃了很多饭，———— 喝了很多酒。
tā chī le hěn duō fàn | ———— hē le hěn duō jiǔ
He ate a lot and also drank a lot.

Exercise 13.3

The Chinese sentences below all contain conjunctions used incorrectly. Rewrite the sentences, making corrections as necessary:

1 她喜欢购买而收藏首饰。 **tā xǐhuan gòumǎi ér shōucáng shǒushi**
She likes buying and hoarding jewellery.

2 这间教室明亮跟宽敞。 **zhě/zhèi jiān jiàoshì míngliàng gēn kuānchang**
This classroom is bright and spacious.

3 他擦桌子和我拖地板。 **tā cā zhuōzi hé wǒ tuō dìbǎn**
He wiped the table and I mopped the floor.

4 你想去巴黎或者纽约旅游？ **nǐ xiǎng qù bālí huòzhě niǔyuē lǚyóu**
Do you want to travel to Paris or New York?

5 请你给我打电话，或发传真？ **qǐng nǐ gěi wǒ dǎ diànhuà | huò fā chuánzhēn**
Will you ring me or send me a fax?

6 我买了电视机、录象机、音响与各种电器用品。
wǒ mǎi le diànshìjī | lùxiàngjī | yīnxiǎng yǔ gè zhǒng diànqì yòngpǐn
I bought a television set, a video recorder, a hi-fi and all sorts of electrical equipment.

7 这种蛋糕甜和不太腻。 **zhě/zhèi zhǒng dàngāo tián hé bù tài nì**
This kind of cake is sweet but not too sickly.

8 她进了房间和开了电灯。 **tā jìn le fángjiān hé kāi le diàndēng**
She came into the room and switched the light on.

9 他无论关心我，并且帮助我。 **tā wúlùn guānxīn wǒ | bìngqiě bāngzhù wǒ**
He not only showed concern for me but also helped me.

10 她要么吃很多，或者一点儿也不吃。
tā yàome chī hěn duō | huòzhě yīdiǎnr yě bù chī
She either eats a lot or eats nothing at all.

Exercise 13.4

Translate the following into Chinese:

1 On the desk there were five books and three magazines.
2 All the students were quietly reading or writing.
3 Are we playing football or tennis today?
4 Let's go today or tomorrow.
5 Shall we go today or tomorrow?
6 That shop sells sweaters, scarves, socks and all kinds of woollen garments.
7 The committee discussed and moreover resolved all the problems.
8 She is a strict but kind teacher.

UNIT FOURTEEN
Attributives (summary)

Attributives are words or expressions used to describe nouns. They are invariably placed before the noun they qualify and, in many cases, they require the use of the particle 的 **de** (see *Basic Chinese*, Unit 10 and Unit 11).

A An obvious example of an attributive is an adjective. The adjectival attributive will generally require 的 **de** if it is:

(1) A disyllabic adjective:

> 这是一朵美丽的花儿。 **zhè shì yī duǒ** *měilì de* **huār**
> This is a beautiful flower.

(2) A monosyllabic adjective modified by a degree adverb:

> 我收到了一封很长的信。 **wǒ shōudào le yī fēng** *hěn cháng de* **xìn**
> I received a very long letter.

(3) A monosyllabic adjective reduplicated:

> 一条弯弯的小路 **yī tiáo** *wānwān de* **xiǎo lù**
> a winding path
> 清清的水 *qīngqīng de* **shuǐ**
> clear water
> 蓝蓝的天 *lánlán de* **tiān**
> blue sky

Monosyllabic adjectives as attributives by themselves are usually placed before the noun without 的 **de**:

> 这是一片红叶。 **zhè shì yī piàn** *hóng* **yè**
> This is a red leaf.

那是一条蓝裙子。 **nà shì yī tiáo** *lán* **qúnzi**
That is a blue skirt.

山脚下有一个大湖。 **shānjiǎo xià yǒu yī gè** *dà* **hú**
There is a big lake at the foot of the hill.

Exceptions to the above rule are:

(1) 的 **de** may be omitted when a disyllabic adjective forms part of an established quadrisyllabic expression:

> 优良传统 **yōuliáng chuántǒng**
> fine traditions
> 根本原因 **gēnběn yuányīn**
> basic reason

(2) 的 **de** may also be omitted where there is more than one attribute and rhythmic patterns allow for one or more 的 **de** to be left out:

> 这是他的伟大 (的) 理想。 **zhè shì tā de wěidà (de) lǐxiǎng**
> This is his ambition. (*lit.* This is his lofty ideal.)

> 去中国访问是我哥哥 (的) 多年以来 (的) 最深切的愿望。
> **qù zhōngguó fǎngwèn shì wǒ gēge (de) duō nián yǐlái (de) zuì shēnqiè de yuànwàng**
> To go to China has been my elder brother's deep-felt hope for many years.

(3) 的 **de** may be added when a monosyllabic adjective is followed by other attributives:

> 这是一件新的皮大衣。 **zhè shì yī jiàn xīn de pí dàyī**
> This is a new leather coat.

B A noun or pronoun followed by 的 **de** may be used as an attributive to indicate 'possession':

李先生的自行车 **lǐ xiānsheng de zìxíngchē**
Mr Li's bicycle
中国的土地 **zhōngguó de tǔdì**
China's territory
伦敦的戏剧界 **lúndūn de xìjújiè**
London's dramatic world

那是我的照相机。 **nà shì wǒ de zhàoxiàngjī**
That is my camera.

Note: 的 **de** may be omitted in possessive attributives before human nouns where a close relationship is implied:

那是我母亲。 **nà shì wǒ mǔqīn**
That is my mother.
他是我表弟。 **tā shì wǒ biǎodì**
He is my cousin (usually, a cousin on one's mother's side).

The possessor may also be broadly understood to be the initiator of a certain action or attitude:

首相的讲话 **shǒuxiàng de jiǎnghuà**
the Prime Minister's speech
他们的行为 **tāmen de xíngwéi**
their behaviour
这是大家的建议。 **zhè shì dàjiā de jiànyì**
This is everyone's idea.

C   Nouns may function as attributives describing other nouns, and as such rarely incorporate 的 **de**:

我喜欢我们的中文老师。 **wǒ xǐhuan wǒmen de *zhōngwén* lǎoshī**
I like our Chinese teacher.
我买了一件皮外套。 **wǒ mǎi le yī jiàn *pí* wàitào**
I bought a leather jacket.
丝绸料子 ***sīchóu* liàozi**
silk material
英语电台 ***yīngyǔ* diàntái**
English broadcasting station

D   A verb or clause followed by 的 **de** may also be used as an attributive:

(1) A verb:

我买了一本刚出版的书。 **wǒ mǎi le yī běn *gāng chūbǎn de* shū**
I bought a book that had just been published./I bought a newly published book.

在花园里看书的那个人是不是你父亲？
***zài huāyuán li kànshū de* nà/nèi gè rén shì bù shì nǐ fùqīn**
Is the man (who is) reading in the garden your father?

(2) A clause:

> 我前天看的那个电影很有趣。
> **wǒ qiántiān kàn de nà/nèi gè diànyǐng hěn yǒuqù**
> The film I saw the day before yesterday was very interesting.

> 你刚才晾出去的衣服都干了。
> **nǐ gāngcái liàng chūqù de yīfu dōu gān le**
> The washing you hung out just now is dry.

E   The other common forms of attributive are:

(1) Demonstrative and/or number + measure word structures (see *Basic Chinese*, Unit 6):

> 那张纸 **nà/nèi zhāng zhǐ**
> that piece of paper (attributive: 那张 **nà/nèi zhāng**)
> 三个人 **sān gè rén**
> three people (attributive: 三个 **sān gè**)
> 这两本书 **zhè/zhèi liǎng běn shū**
> these two books (attributive: 这两本 **zhè/zhèi liǎng běn**)

(2) Postpositional phrases:

> 海上的轮船 *hǎi shang de* **lúnchuán**
> ships at sea
> 家里的人 *jiā li de* **rén**
> members of the family
> 山下的村庄 *shān xià de* **cūnzhuāng**
> the village at the foot of the hill

F   As a general rule, when different types of attributive qualify the same noun, they should be placed in the following order:

possessive attributive | demonstrative and/or numeral + measure word | verbal/clausal attributive | adjectival attributive | nominal attributive

For example:

> 我 (的) 同事 **wǒ (de) tóngshì**
> my colleague

我 (的)	同事
possessive attributive	noun

我 (的) 那两位同事 **wǒ (de) nà/nèi liǎng wèi tóngshì**
those two colleagues of mine

我 (的)	那两位	同事
possessive attributive	demonstrative/numeral/measure word	noun

我 (的) 那两位刚从美国来的同事
wǒ (de) nà/nèi liǎng wèi gāng cóng měiguó lái de tóngshì
those two colleagues of mine who have just come from America

我 (的)	那两位	刚从美国来的	同事
possessive attributive	demonstrative/ numeral/measure word	verbal attributive	noun

我 (的) 那两位刚从美国来的年轻的同事
wǒ (de) nà/nèi liǎng wèi gāng cóng měiguó lái de niánqīng de tóngshì
those two young colleagues of mine who have just come from America

我 (的)	那两位	刚从美国来的	年轻的	同事
possessive attributive	demonstrative/ numeral/ measure word	verbal attributive	adjectival attributive	noun

我 (的) 那两位刚从美国来的年轻的日本同事
wǒ (de) nà/nèi liǎng wèi gāng cóng měiguó lái de niánqīng de rìběn tóngshì
those two young Japanese colleagues of mine who have just come from America

我 (的)	那两位	刚从美国来的	年轻的	日本	同事
possessive attributive	demonstrative/ numeral/ measure word	verbal attributive	adjectival attributive	nominal attributive	noun

Other examples are:

这是两条我刚买的漂亮的丝绸连衣裙。
zhè shì liǎng tiáo *wǒ gāng mǎi de* piàoliang de sīchóu liányīqún
These are two beautiful silk dresses that I have just bought.

这是我的三个新招收的非常勤奋的博士研究生。
zhè shì wǒ de sān gè *xīn zhāoshōu de* fēicháng qínfèn de bóshì yánjiūshēng
These are three extremely hard-working PhD students of mine, who have recently enrolled.

Note: A verbal or clausal attributive may sometimes be placed before the demonstrative and/or numeral + measure word phrase:

刚出版的那本小说太动人了。
***gāng chūbǎn de* nà/nèi běn xiǎoshuō tài dòngrén le** (verbal)
That newly published novel is very moving.

我们今年春天种的那些葡萄好甜哪!
***wǒmen jīnnián chūntiān zhòng de* nà/nèi xiē pútáo hǎo tián na** (clausal)
The grapes we grew this spring are really sweet!

Note: When an adjectival attributive is modified by a degree adverb like 多么 duōme, it may also be placed before, as well as after, the demonstrative and/or numeral + measure word phrase:

这是多么危险的一条路啊! **zhè shì *duōme wēixiǎn de* yī tiáo lù a**
What a dangerous road this is!

or:

这是一条多么危险的路啊! **zhè shì yī tiáo *duōme wēixiǎn de* lù a**
What a dangerous road this is!

G   The noun after an attributive, if it is understood from the given (actual or verbal) context, may be omitted or understood, leaving the attributive itself to function as a noun. The attributive may originally be derived from any of the following categories:

(1)   A pronoun:

>   这是我的。 **zhè shì *wǒ de***
>   This one is mine.
>   他们的最好。 ***tāmen de* zuì hǎo**
>   Theirs is best.

(2)   A noun:

>   百货商店的比较便宜。 ***bǎihuò shāngdiàn de* bǐjiào piányi**
>   The ones in the department store are cheaper.

(3)   An adjective:

>   他喜欢吃辣的。 **tā xǐhuan chī *là de***
>   He likes (eating) peppery food.
>
>   我买了一件绿的,她买了一件黄的。
>   **wǒ mǎi le yī jiàn *lǜ de* | tā mǎi le yī jiàn *huáng de***
>   I bought a green one and she bought a brown one (jacket/shirt/blouse/coat, etc.).

(4)   A postpositional phrase:

>   家里的坏了。 ***jiā li de* huài le**
>   The one at home has gone wrong.

(5) A verb:

开车的是我的朋友。 *kāichē de* **shì wǒ de péngyou**
The driver (*lit.* the one driving the car) is my friend.

新做的比较合身。 *xīn zuò de* **bǐjiào héshēn**
The one which was newly made fits more nicely.

学汉语参加演讲比赛的讲得最好。
xué hànyǔ cānjiā yǎnjiǎng bǐsài de **jiǎng de zuì hǎo**
Those who studied Chinese and took part in the speech contest spoke best of all.

(6) A clause:

我要喝的是咖啡。 *wǒ yào hē de* **shì kāfēi**
What I would like is a cup of coffee.

大家都同意你说的。 **dàjiā dōu tóngyì** *nǐ shuō de*
Everybody agreed with what you said.

经济发展最快的要算中国。 *jīngjì fāzhǎn zuì kuài de* **yào suàn zhōngguó**
China may be counted as (the one) with the fastest economic development.

Exercise 14.1

Link together the Chinese attributives and nouns below, deciding whether to include 的 **de**, and then translate the resulting phrase into English:

EXAMPLES:
好 **hǎo**　　　学生 **xuésheng**　　好学生 **hǎo xuésheng** a good student
美丽 **měilì**　　城市 **chéngshì**　　美丽的城市 **měilì de chéngshì** a beautiful city

 1 新 **xīn**　　　　　　　朋友 **péngyou**
 2 古老 **gǔlǎo**　　　　　城市 **chéngshì**
 3 三块 **sān kuài**　　　　蛋糕 **dàngāo**
 4 很多 **hěn duō**　　　　人 **rén**
 5 那杯 **nà/nèi bēi**　　　茶 **chá**
 6 皮 **pí**　　　　　　　　裙子 **qúnzi**
 7 学习好 **xuéxí hǎo**　　孩子 **háizi**
 8 中文 **zhōngwén**　　　老师 **lǎoshī**
 9 这张 **zhè/zhèi zhāng**　地图 **dìtú**
10 热 **rè**　　　　　　　　牛奶 **niúnǎi**
11 跳舞 **tiàowǔ**　　　　　男孩 **nánhái**
12 我 **wǒ**　　　　　　　　爷爷 **yéye**

13 你 **nǐ**   房子 **fángzi**
14 公司里 **gōngsī li**   秘书 **mìshū**
15 木头 **mùtou**   桌子 **zhuōzi**
16 他们借 **tāmen jiè**   书 **shū**
17 干净 **gānjìng**   街道 **jiēdào**
18 有趣 **yǒuqù**   游戏 **yóuxì**
19 三岁 **sān suì**   儿子 **érzi**
20 英国 **yīngguó**   人 **rén**

Exercise 14.2

Construct a Chinese sentence which amalgamates in each case the information
provided in the three sentences, and translate the resulting sentence into English:

EXAMPLE:
这是一件衬衫。 **zhè shì yī jiàn chènshān**
This is a shirt.
这是新衬衫。 **zhè shì xīn chènshān**
This is a new shirt.
这是一件美丽的衬衫。 **zhè shì yī jiàn měilì de chènshān**
This is a beautiful shirt.

Answer: 这是一件美丽的新衬衫。 **zhè shì yī jiàn měilì de xīn chènshān**
This is a beautiful new shirt.

1 我想买一本书。 **wǒ xiǎng mǎi yī běn shū**
   我想买新书。 **wǒ xiǎng mǎi xīn shū**
   我想买英文书。 **wǒ xiǎng mǎi yīngwén shū**
2 那是一条裙子。 **nà shì yī tiáo qúnzi**
   那是旧裙子。 **nà shì jiù qúnzi**
   那是姐姐的裙子。 **nà shì jiějie de qúnzi**
3 那辆汽车是小李的。 **nà/nèi liàng qìchē shì xiǎo lǐ de**
   那辆汽车很便宜。 **nà/nèi liàng qìchē hěn piányi**
   那辆汽车是新买的。 **nà/nèi liàng qìchē shì xīn mǎi de**
4 她是一位老师。 **tā shì yī wèi lǎoshī**
   她是汉语老师。 **tā shì hànyǔ lǎoshī**
   她是出色的老师。 **tā shì chūsè de lǎoshī**
5 湖旁有一对年轻人。 **hú páng yǒu yī duì niánqīng rén**
   他们手拉着手。 **tāmen shǒu lā zhe shǒu**
   他们并肩走着。 **tāmen bìngjiān zǒu zhe**
6 有一只小鸟在树林里歌唱。 **yǒu yī zhī xiǎo niǎo zài shùlín li gēchàng**
   那是一只美丽的小鸟。 **nà shì yī zhī měilì de xiǎo niǎo**
   那是一片密密的树林。 **nà shì yī piàn mìmì de shùlín**

Exercise 14.3

Decide which of the three Chinese sentences in each of the cases below is the appropriate translation of the English:

1 I have a lot of Chinese friends.
    我认识很多中国朋友。 **wǒ rènshi hěn duō zhōngguó péngyou**
    我认识很多的中国朋友。 **wǒ rènshi hěn duō de zhōngguó péngyou**
    我认识中国的很多朋友。 **wǒ rènshi zhōngguó de hěn duō péngyou**

2 His lies were exposed.
    他说谎言被戳穿。 **tā shuō huǎngyán bèi chuōchuān**
    他的谎言被戳穿了。 **tā de huǎngyán bèi chuōchuān le**
    他谎言被戳穿了。 **tā huǎngyán bèi chuōchuān le**

3 Leeds is a famous city.
    利兹是有名的一个城市。 **lìzī shì yǒumíng de yī gè chéngshì**
    利兹是一个有名的城市。 **lìzī shì yī gè yǒumíng de chéngshì**
    利兹是一个有名城市。 **lìzī shì yī gè yǒumíng chéngshì**

4 The book of stories I have just bought is very interesting.
    我新买的那本故事书很有趣。 **wǒ xīn mǎi de nà/nèi běn gùshi shū hěn yǒuqù**
    我新买那本故事书很有趣。 **wǒ xīn mǎi nà/nèi běn gùshi shū hěn yǒuqù**
    我那本新买故事书很有趣。 **wǒ nà/nèi běn xīn mǎi gùshi shū hěn yǒuqù**

5 She is a good doctor.
    她是一个很好大夫。 **tā shì yī gè hěn hǎo dàifu**
    她是很好一个大夫。 **tā shì hěn hǎo yī gè dàifu**
    她是一个很好的大夫。 **tā shì yī gè hěn hǎo de dàifu**

6 This hot cup of coffee is mine.
    这杯是我的热的咖啡。 **zhè/zhèi bēi shì wǒ de rè de kāfēi**
    这杯我的咖啡是热的。 **zhè/zhèi bēi wǒ de kāfēi shì rè de**
    这杯热咖啡是我的。 **zhè/zhèi bēi rè kāfēi shì wǒ de**

Exercise 14.4

Translate the following into Chinese:

1 Complicated questions are usually very interesting.
2 The blue ones are the best.
3 Where is that book I bought yesterday?
4 The girl on the left is my younger sister; the one on the right is her friend.
5 That old Chinese professor who came last week to help you translate those Tang poems used to be my teacher.
6 I don't want to buy a magazine that is so expensive.
7 The train that leaves at 8.00 a.m. is an express.
8 The ones made in China are better than the ones made here.

UNIT FIFTEEN
Adverbials (summary)

A Adverbials are words and expressions used to modify verbs. They supply information relating to time, place, scope, manner, etc., and they precede the verb or, in some cases, the subject.

B Time and location expressions used as adverbials, unlike English, are placed before the verb (see *Basic Chinese*, Units 13 and 14):

学校明天开学。 **xuéxiào míngtiān kāixué** (time)
School starts tomorrow.

孩子们在院子里玩。 **háizimen zài yuànzi li wán** (location)
The children are playing in the courtyard.

Where a time expression and a location expression are both present, the time expression always comes first:

我们常常在厨房里吃饭。 **wǒmen chángcháng zài chúfáng li chīfàn**
We often eat in the kitchen.

Note: A time expression generally indicates a particular point of time. If it refers to a particular period of time, the words 整 **zhěng** or 整整 **zhěngzhěng** are often incorporated before the time expression in affirmative sentences, though they are not needed in negative sentences:

他整天/整晚都在学中文。 **tā zhěng tiān/zhěng wǎn dōu zài xué zhōngwén**
He was studying Chinese the whole day/evening.

她整整一个月都在休假。 **tā zhěngzhěng yī gè yuè dōu zài xiūjià**
She was on leave for that whole month.

But:

他一夜没睡着。 **tā yī yè méi shuì zháo**
He did not sleep a wink all that night.

她一个月没上班。 **tā yī gè yuè méi shàngbān**
She was away from work for that whole month.

For duration expressions, which as complements follow the verb, see *Basic Chinese*, Unit 14.

C   Adverbs like 都 **dōu** 'all', 'both', 也 **yě** 'also', 'too', 只 **zhǐ** 'only', 还 **hái** 'in addition to', 才 **cái** 'only then', 就 **jiù** 'then', 再 **zài** 'again' and 又 **yòu** 'once again' are placed immediately before the main or modal verb in the sentence:

他们都同意了。 **tāmen dōu tóngyì le**
They all agreed.

她也会游泳。 **tā yě huì yóuyǒng**
She can also swim.

我只有一个弟弟。 **wǒ zhǐ yǒu yī gè dìdi**
I have only got one younger brother.

我口袋里还有十镑钱。 **wǒ kǒudài li hái yǒu shí bàng qián**
I have still got ten pounds in my pocket.

他明天就走了。 **tā míngtiān jiù zǒu le**
He will be leaving tomorrow.

小李今天才写完论文。 **xiǎo lǐ jīntiān cái xiě wán lùnwén**
Xiao Li finished her dissertation (only) today./Xiao Li did not finish her dissertation till today.

咱们从头再来一遍。 **zánmen cóng tóu zài lái yī biàn**
Let's do it once more from the beginning.

她又睡过头了。 **tā yòu shuì guòtóu le**
She overslept again.

[handwritten margin note:] order of adverbs where more than one - see PCG p44
① - 也 + 都 + 很
② - 也 + 不
③ - 都,很 - never with 了 depends on meaning

One cannot say:

*又他来了。 **yòu tā lái le**
(*lit.* He turned up again.)

*他就明天走了。 **tā jiù míngtiān zǒu le**
(*lit.* He will be leaving tomorrow.)

D   The adverbs listed below introduce a tone of evaluation. The first set is used before the verb or modal verb and after the subject, while the second set may be placed either before the verb or modal verb or at the beginning of the sentence before the subject:

(1)

总算 **zǒngsuàn**	简直 **jiǎnzhí**
'after all'	'simply'
几乎 **jīhū**	偏偏 **piānpiān**
'almost'	'contrary to what was expected', 'unfortunately'
甚至 **shènzhì**	
'even', 'go so far as'	

火车总算来了。 **huǒchē zǒngsuàn lái le**
Here comes the train at last.

她简直不相信自己的耳朵。 **tā jiǎnzhí bù xiāngxìn zìjǐ de ěrduo**
She simply couldn't believe her ears.

他几乎忘了自己想说什么。 **tā jīhū wàng le zìjǐ xiǎng shuō shénme**
He almost forgot what he was going to say.

出门的时候，偏偏下起雪来了。
chūmén de shíhou | piānpiān xià qǐ xuě lái le
Just as [I] set out, it had to start snowing./Unfortunately it started to
snow just as I was setting out.

她甚至会说俄语。 **tā shènzhì huì shuō éyǔ**
She can even speak Russian.

(2)

当然 **dāngrán**	显然 **xiǎnrán**
'of course', 'naturally'	'obviously'
也许 **yěxǔ**	幸亏 **xìngkuī**
'probably', 'perhaps', 'maybe'	'fortunately'

我当然不同意。 **wǒ dāngrán bù tóngyì**
I naturally disagree./Of course I don't agree.

显然这很重要。 **xiǎnrán zhè hěn zhòngyào**
This is obviously very important.

明天也许会下雨。 **míngtiān yěxǔ huì xià yǔ**
It will probably rain tomorrow.

幸亏我没迟到。 **xìngkuī wǒ méi chídào**
Fortunately I wasn't late.

E   Adverbials of manner are derived from adjectives of two or more syllables. (Monosyllabic adjectives must be reduplicated or suffixed with reduplicated sound-connotative phonaesthemes or modified by a degree adverb.) These adverbials are placed before the verb in the sentence and are usually followed by the particle 地 **de** (see Unit 16):

她在认真地学舞蹈。 **tā zài rènzhēn de xué wǔdǎo**
She is working hard studying dance. (*lit.* She is diligently studying dance.)

朋友热情地招待了我。 **péngyou rèqíng de zhāodài le wǒ**
My friend gave me a warm reception. (*lit.* My friend warmly welcomed me.)

奶奶慢慢地上了火车。
nǎinai mànmàn de shàng le huǒchē (reduplicated monosyllable)
Grandma slowly got on the train.

爸爸急匆匆地跳上了公共汽车。
bàba jícōngcōng de tiào shàng le gōnggòng qìchē (monosyllabic and reduplicated phonaestheme)
Father hurriedly jumped onto the bus.

孩子很快地睡着了。
háizi hěn kuài de shuì zháo le (monosyllabic with modifier)
The child quickly fell asleep.

火车非常早地到达了伦敦。
huǒchē fēicháng zǎo de dàodá le lúndūn (monosyllabic with modifier)
The train arrived in London extremely early.

Note: A certain number of disyllabic adjectives also occur in reduplicated versions expressing more vivid descriptions.

他匆匆忙忙地向我走来。 **tā cōngcōngmángmáng de xiàng wǒ zǒu lái**
He came towards me in a great hurry.

他们高高兴兴地欢迎我们。 **tāmen gāogāoxìngxìng de huānyíng wǒmen**
They welcomed us with great joy.

F   Both monosyllabic and disyllabic adjectives may be used as adverbials of manner in imperatives. They are not suffixed with 地 **de**:

慢走! **màn zǒu**
Take care! (*lit.* Walk slowly.)

快过来! **kuài guò lái**
Come over here (quickly)!

认真学习! **rènzhēn xuéxí**
Study conscientiously!

Exercise 15.1

Rewrite the Chinese sentences below, adding the adverbials given, and 地 **de** where necessary, and then translate the resulting sentences into English:

EXAMPLE:
商店开门。 **shāngdiàn kāimén**
九点钟 **jiǔ diǎn zhōng**

Answer: 商店九点钟开门。 **shāngdiàn jiǔ diǎn zhōng kāimén**
The shop opened at nine o'clock.

1 我们见面了。 **wǒmen jiànmiàn le**
  在公园 **zài gōngyuán**
2 他看着我。 **tā kàn zhe wǒ**
  吃惊 **chījīng** in surprise
3 护士走进病房。 **hùshi zǒu jìn bìngfáng**
  急匆匆 **jícōngcōng**
4 弟弟工作。 **dìdi gōngzuò**
  在医院 **zài yīyuàn**
5 学生到图书馆去。 **xuésheng dào túshūguǎn qù**
  常常 **chángcháng**
6 妈妈会说英语了。 **māma huì shuō yīngyǔ le**
  慢慢 **mànmàn**
7 她走了。 **tā zǒu le**
  高高兴兴 **gāogāoxìngxìng**
8 病人没有吃饭。 **bìngrén méiyǒu chīfàn**
  整整一天 **zhěngzhěng yī tiān** all day

Exercise 15.2

Rewrite the following Chinese sentences, by adding an adverb chosen from the list to provide an accurate translation of the English:

甚至 **shènzhì**	总算 **zǒngsuàn**	也许 **yěxǔ**
简直 **jiǎnzhí**	幸亏 **xìngkuī**	几乎 **jīhū**
显然 **xiǎnrán**	偏偏 **piānpiān**	

1 He is obviously wrong.
  他错了。 **tā cuò le**
2 Unfortunately the electricity went off when I was watching television.
  我看电视的时候，停电了。 **wǒ kàn diànshì de shíhou | tíng diàn le**

3 The secretary was so angry that she could hardly (almost could not) speak.
秘书气得说不出话来。 **mìshū qì de shuō bu chū huà lái**

4 It was a good thing that I didn't catch that bus.
我没坐那辆车。 **wǒ méi zuò nà/nèi liàng chē**

5 I simply didn't want to meet her.
我不想见她。 **wǒ bù xiǎng jiàn tā**

6 This is probably true.
这件事是真的。 **zhè/zhèi jiàn shì shì zhēn de**

7 He told the truth at last.
他说出真相。 **tā shuō chū zhēnxiàng**

8 She can even fly an aeroplane.
她会驾驶飞机。 **tā huì jiàshǐ fēijī**

Exercise 15.3

There are errors in all the Chinese sentences below. Rewrite each one with the necessary corrections:

1 六点钟就爸爸回家。 **liù diǎn zhōng jiù bàba huí jiā**
Father will be home at six o'clock.

2 他们开会在礼堂。 **tāmen kāihuì zài lǐtáng**
They held a meeting at the hall.

3 我们在花园上午除草。 **wǒmen zài huāyuán shàngwǔ chú cǎo**
We were in the garden this morning mowing the lawn.

4 小李才今天写完论文。 **xiǎo lǐ cái jīntiān xiě wán lùnwén**
Xiao Li only finished her dissertation today.

5 明天会也许下雪。 **míngtiān huì yěxǔ xià xuě**
It will probably snow tomorrow.

6 我慢地喝了一杯茶。 **wǒ màn de hē le yī bēi chá**
I slowly drank a cup of tea.

7 她看电视一个人在家里。 **tā kàn diànshì yī gè rén zài jiā li**
She was watching television at home on her own.

8 那位医生工作了在这个医院三年。
nà/nèi wèi yīshēng gōngzuò le zài zhè/zhèi gè yīyuàn sān nián
The doctor has worked at this hospital for three years.

Exercise 15.4

Translate the following into Chinese:

1 The doctor didn't arrive till nine o'clock in the evening.

2 I will be doing some research in the library tomorrow.

3 I have not been to Beijing for five years.

4 He only bought two books.
5 Because I said I did not like it, she had to cry.
6 Those students can even speak Cantonese.
7 He explained the problem with great clarity.
8 I'm off now.
9 Please say it again.
10 Please speak a bit more slowly.

UNIT SIXTEEN
的 **de**, 得 **de**, 地 **de** (summary)

的, 得 and 地, which as syntactic markers are all pronounced **de** in Modern Standard Chinese, each have their own distinctive usages.

A 的 **de**

(1) For the use of 的 **de** as part of an attributive, see Unit 14.

(2) 的 **de** is also used to form part of the comment of a topic–comment structure generally in conjunction with 是 **shì**:

    (a) With nouns:

> 这本杂志是英文的。 **zhè/zhèi běn zázhì shì yīngwén de**
> This magazine is in English.

> 那把椅子是木头的。 **nà/nèi bǎ yǐzi shì mùtou de**
> That chair is made of wood.
> (*lit.* That chair is wooden.)

    (b) With non-gradable adjectives (i.e. adjectives which cannot be modified by a degree adverb like 很 **hěn** 'very', etc.):

> 我说的那个人是男的。 **wǒ shuō de nà/nèi gè rén shì nán de**
> The person I am talking about is male.

> 这是真的，不是假的。 **zhè shì zhēn de | bù shì jiǎ de**
> This is true, not false.

> 这张桌子是圆的。 **zhè/zhèi zhāng zhuōzi shì yuán de**
> This table is round.

Note: Gradable adjectives as predicatives/comments of course do not require 是 **shì** or 的 **de**:

> 这件衣服很漂亮。 **zhè/zhèi jiàn yīfu hěn piàoliang**
> This suit (of clothes) is (very) beautiful.

(c) With verbs:

> 我的头发是新烫的。 **wǒ de tóufa shì xīn tàng de**
> My hair was newly permed.
>
> 这双鞋是破的。 **zhè/zhèi shuāng xié shì pò de**
> This pair of shoes is rather worn.

(d) With clauses:

> 这个日记本是她送给我的。 **zhè/zhèi gè rìjìběn shì tā sòng gěi wǒ de**
> This diary was a gift from her.
>
> 那个菜是妈妈做的。 **nà/nèi gè cài shì māma zuò de**
> That dish was cooked by Mother.

(e) With reduplicated adjectives or verbs or set expressions, in these cases
     without 是 **shì**:

> 山路高高低低的。 **shānlù gāogāodīdī de**
> The mountain path is very uneven.
>
> 田野绿油油的。 **tiányě lǜyóuyóu de**
> The fields are emerald green.
>
> 桌子上乱七八糟的。 **zhuōzi shang luànqībāzāo de**
> The table is all messy.
>
> 同学们有说有笑的。 **tóngxuémen yǒu shuō yǒu xiào de**
> The students were talking and laughing.

(3) The 是 **shì** . . . 的 **de** structure is regularly used to emphasise the time, place,
     manner, purpose, etc. of an action that has taken place (see *Basic Chinese*,
     Unit 19):

> 他们是去的北京。 **tāmen shì qù de běijīng**
> They went to <u>Beijing</u>.
> 他们是昨天去的。 **tāmen shì zuótiān qù de**
> They went <u>yesterday</u>.
> 他们是坐飞机去的。 **tāmen shì zuò fēijī qù de**
> They went <u>by plane</u>.
> 他们是去买书的。 **tāmen shì qù mǎi shū de**
> They went <u>to buy (some) books</u>.

Note that 的 **de** is not present if the action is not in the past but is going to take place:

Per Lillian Chia, (correction of 'Wolverhampton W' text, Gr5 9718 etc) on 13. March 02, these V 得 complements of 'degree, extent, result — FOCUS on OUT COME

Unit 16   105

他们是去北京。 **tāmen shì qù běijīng**
They are going to <u>Beijing</u>.
他们是明天去。 **tāmen shì míngtiān qù**
They are going <u>tomorrow</u>.
他们是坐飞机去。 **tāmen shì zuò fēijī qù**
They are going <u>by plane</u>.
他们是去买书。 **tāmen shì qù mǎi shū**
They are going <u>to buy (some) books</u>.

(4) 的 **de** also occurs in the phrase 的话 **de huà** 'if':

你不同意的话，没有关系。 **nǐ bù tóngyì de huà | méiyǒu guānxì**
It doesn't matter if you don't agree.

天气不好的话，我们不去。 **tiānqì bù hǎo de huà | wǒmen bù qù**
We don't go if the weather is bad.

B 得 **de** is used immediately after verbs to introduce complements of manner or result: ✳

(1) With these complements it can follow either a verb or an adjective:

他学习得很认真。 **tā xuéxí de hěn rènzhēn** (manner)
He studies conscientiously.

他们谈得很投机。 **tāmen tán de hěn tóujī** (manner)
They had a congenial talk.

姑娘哭得眼睛都红了。 **gūniang kū de yǎnjing dōu hóng le** (result)
The girl's eyes were red with crying.
(*lit*. The girl cried so much that her eyes went red.)

她高兴得睡不着觉。 **tā gāoxìng de shuì bu zháo jiào** (result)
She was so happy that she couldn't sleep.

(2) As can be seen from (1) above, the complement may take various forms:

   (a) A degree adverb + an adjective:

     他们工作得非常努力。 **tāmen gōngzuò de fēicháng nǔlì**
     They work extremely hard.

   (b) A verbal expression:

     她高兴得跳起来了。 **tā gāoxìng de tiào qǐlái le**
     She jumped for joy. (*lit*. She was so happy that she jumped up.)

(c) A clause:

妹妹伤心得眼泪都流下来了。
mèimei shāngxīn de yǎnlèi dōu liú xiàlái le
Younger sister was so sad that she cried. (*lit.* Younger sister was sad so that tears rolled down.)

(d) A quadrisyllabic set expression:

他笑得前俯后仰的。 **tā xiào de qiánfǔ hòuyǎng de**
He laughed his head off./His body rocked with laughter. (*lit.* He laughed so much that his body went backwards and forwards.)

她跑得气喘吁吁的。 **tā pǎo de qìchuǎn xūxū de**
She was breathless with running. (*lit.* She ran so much that she was panting.)

他吃得津津有味的。 **tā chī de jīnjīn yǒu wèi de**
He ate with gusto.

(e) A reduplicated adjective, or an expression which incorporates a reduplicated adjective:

他把玻璃窗抹得干干净净的。
tā bǎ bōlichuāng mā de gāngānjìngjìng de
He wiped the windows spotlessly clean.

她热得脸红红的。 **tā rè de liǎn hónghóng de**
Her face was flushed with the heat. (*lit.* She was so hot that her face was all red.)

C 地 **de** marks adverbials of manner. These adverbials take the following forms (see Unit 15):

(1) A disyllabic adjective, or a monosyllabic adjective modified by a degree adverb:

她高兴地笑了。 **tā gāoxìng de xiào le**
She smiled happily.
他很快地走了过来。 **tā hěn kuài de zǒu le guòlái**
He came over very quickly.

(2) An onomatopoeic word:

他呼呼地睡着了。 **tā hūhū de shuì zháo le**
He fell sound asleep.
雨淅沥淅沥地下着。 **yǔ xīlì xīlì de xià zhe**
It was drizzling.

(3) A reduplicated phrase:

太阳慢慢地升起来了。 **tàiyáng mànmàn de shēng qǐlái le**
The sun came up slowly.

大家痛痛快快地玩了一天。 **dàjiā tòngtòngkuàikuài de wán le yī tiān**
Everybody thoroughly enjoyed themselves that day.

他一步一步地向前走去。 **tā yī bù yī bù de xiàng qián zǒu qù**
Step by step he plodded on. (*lit.* He step by step went forward.)

她一遍又一遍地朗诵着那首诗。
tā yī biàn yòu yī biàn de lǎngsòng zhe nà/nèi shǒu shī
She recited the poem again and again.

D   The difference between an adverbial of manner with 地 **de** and a complement of manner with 得 **de** is that the adverbial emphasises the actual manner in
which the action is carried out and the speaker recounts it, whereas the complement emphasises the manner in which the action is seen to be carried out and
the speaker comments on it. It therefore follows that the 地 **de** construction
produces a subject–predicate narration while the 得 **de** construction produces a
topic–comment sentence. Consider the following examples:

他在认认真真地学习。
tā zài rènrènzhēnzhēn de xuéxí (narrating what happened on one particular
occasion)
He is studying conscientiously. (i.e. he has conscientiously adopted this
attitude.)

他学习得认认真真的。 **tā xuéxí de rènrènzhēnzhēn de** (commenting)
He is studying conscientiously. (i.e. he is seen to be doing so.)

他好好地跟她说。 **tā hǎohǎo de gēn tā shuō** (narrating)
He spoke to her nicely. (i.e. was not abrupt, unkind, etc.)

他说得很好。 **tā shuō de hěn hǎo** (commenting)
He spoke well/put it well. (i.e. what he said was clear/convincing, etc.)

Exercise 16.1

Translate the following phrases into Chinese:

1 a busy road/street
2 a very old sofa
3 a winding path
4 the magazine I like reading
5 the shops at the station
6 the coat my mother bought yesterday
7 the village at the foot of the hill
8 the bike that I ride
9 a wooden table
10 a plastic container

Exercise 16.2

Bring together the Chinese attributives and nouns below, adding 的 **de** where necessary, and translate the resulting noun phrase into English. In some cases 的 **de** may be optional. Indicate where this is so.

1 很厚 **hěn hòu**	杂志 **zázhì**
2 短 **duǎn**	裙子 **qúnzi**
3 红色 **hóngsè**	玫瑰 **méiguì** 'rose'
4 我 **wǒ**	办公室 **bàngōngshì**
5 他 **tā**	侄女 **zhínǚ** 'niece'
6 当地 **dāngdì** 'local'	图书馆 **túshūguǎn**
7 海上 **hǎi shang**	轮船 **lúnchuán** 'ships'
8 旧 **jiù**	钟 **zhōng**
9 羊毛 **yángmáo** 'wool'	手套 **shǒutào**
10 聪明 **cōngming**	孩子 **háizi**
11 深深 **shēnshēn**	海洋 **hǎiyáng**
12 中文 **zhōngwén**	报纸 **bàozhǐ**

Exercise 16.3

Translate the following into Chinese:

1 This book is written in Chinese.
2 That is his map.
3 This is my new watch.
4 This is a story my mother told me.
5 Her school bag is new.
6 A boxing ring is square.

7 What he said was true.
8 This present was from my granddad.

Exercise 16.4

Complete the Chinese translations below using a 的 **de** phrase in each case:

1 我很喜欢 _____。 **wǒ hěn xǐhuan** _____
   I like the present you gave me.
2 _____ 是牛奶。 _____ **shì niúnǎi**
   What she liked to drink was milk.
3 房间里 _____。 **fángjiān li** _____
   The room is messy.
4 _____ 是我妹妹。 _____ **shì wǒ mèimei**
   The one wearing the red shirt is my younger sister.
5 _____ 不对。 _____ **bù duì**
   What you said is wrong.
6 _____ 我都要。 _____ **wǒ dōu yào**
   I'd like some red ones, yellow ones and blue ones.

Exercise 16.5

Complete the following Chinese sentences with 的 **de**, 得 **de** or 地 **de** as appropriate to make a correct translation of the English:

1 我慢慢 _____ 把门打开。 **wǒ mànmàn** _____ **bǎ mén dǎkāi**
   I opened the door slowly.
2 雨下 _____ 很大。 **yǔ xià** _____ **hěn dà**
   It's raining heavily.
3 他是一个经验丰富 _____ 律师。
   tā shì yī gè jīngyàn fēngfù _____ **lǜshī**
   He is a very experienced lawyer.
4 我彻底 _____ 理解你。 **wǒ chèdǐ** _____ **lǐjiě nǐ**
   I understand you perfectly.
5 她是商店 _____ 经理。 **tā shì shāngdiàn** _____ **jīnglǐ**
   She is the manager of the shop.
6 我昨晚睡 _____ 不好。 **wǒ zuó wǎn shuì** _____ **bù hǎo**
   I didn't sleep very well last night.
7 他开车开 _____ 很小心。 **tā kāichē kāi** _____ **hěn xiǎoxīn**
   He is a careful driver.
8 医生高兴 _____ 笑了。 **yīshēng gāoxìng** _____ **xiào le**
   The doctor smiled happily.
9 他一遍又一遍 _____ 问我。 **tā yī biàn yòu yī biàn** _____ **wèn wǒ**
   He asked me over and over again.

10 孩子兴奋 ——— 跳起来。 **háizi xīngfèn** ——— **tiào qǐlái**
The child jumped up in excitement.
11 老师把书放 ——— 整整齐齐的。
lǎoshī bǎ shū fàng ——— **zhěngzhěngqíqí de**
The teacher arranged the books neatly.
12 雪片纷纷扬扬 ——— 飞舞着。 **xuěpiàn fēnfēnyángyáng** ——— **fēiwǔ zhe**
It was snowing heavily. (*lit.* Snowflakes came down flying, dancing.)

Exercise 16.6

There is an error in each of the following Chinese sentences. Make the necessary correction in each case:

1 我的朋友是一个坚强得人。 **wǒ de péngyou shì yī gè jiānqiáng de rén**
My friend is a very strong person.
2 每个学生都写地很好。 **měi gè xuésheng dōu xiě de hěn hǎo**
Every student wrote very well.
3 亚洲的经济发展的很快。 **yàzhōu de jīngjì fāzhǎn de hěn kuài**
The Asian economy is developing very quickly.
4 那位高大地运动员是我弟弟。 **nà/nèi wèi gāodà de yùndòngyuán shì wǒ dìdi**
That tall athlete is my younger brother.
5 他开车开地很危险。 **tā kāichē kāi de hěn wēixiǎn**
He is a dangerous driver.
6 回答问题前你应该仔细得想想。
huídá wèntí qián nǐ yīnggāi zǐxì de xiǎngxiǎng
You should think carefully before you answer the question.

Exercise 16.7

Translate the following into Chinese:

1 He runs very fast.
2 I lay down quietly.
3 I slept very well last night.
4 The manager is working very hard.
5 The manager is obviously working very hard.
6 The teacher teaches well.
7 The little girl was beautifully dressed.
8 The person, who spoke most clearly, was the new teacher, who had not spoken before.
9 Who is that man sitting quietly at the back?
10 The people who could not buy tickets were so angry that they all shouted loudly.

UNIT SEVENTEEN
'Every', 'each' – 每 **měi**, 各 **gè** and indefinite pronouns

A 每 **měi** 'every', like a demonstrative, is normally followed by a measure. It is also regularly linked with the adverb 都 **dōu**:

这儿的每个孩子都很活泼。 **zhèr de měi gè háizi dōu hěn huópo**
All the children here are very lively.

你的每本书都很有趣。 **nǐ de měi běn shū dōu hěn yǒuqù**
All your books are interesting./Every one of your books is interesting.

他每天都到河边去钓鱼。 **tā měi tiān dōu dào hé biān qù diào yú**
He goes to the river every day to do some fishing.

Like a demonstrative, it is also often followed by a numeral + measure phrase. In these cases it is not necessarily linked with 都 **dōu**, and there is generally another numeral + measure phrase in the predicate:

我们每两个月去一次。 **wǒmen měi liǎng gè yuè qù yī cì**
We go/went there every two months.

每三小时吃两粒。 **měi sān xiǎoshí chī liǎng lì**
Take two pills every three hours.

B 各 **gè** 'each' has a slightly more formal tone. Unlike 每 **měi** 'every', 各 **gè** 'each' only occurs with particular types of nouns, such as communities, countries, institutions, categories, etc. which may also be taken as collective measures:

各国 **gè guó**
every country
各国人民 **gè guó rénmín**
people of every country

各部门 **gè bùmén**
every department
各部门领导 **gè bùmén lǐngdǎo**
leadership of every department

各单位 **gè dānwèi**
every unit
各单位负责人 **gè dānwèi fùzé rén**
responsible people from every unit

各民族 **gè mínzú**
every nationality
各族人民 **gè zú rénmín**
people of all nationalities

各方面 **gè fāngmiàn**
every aspect
各方面意见 **gè fāngmiàn yìjian**
all points of view (*lit.* opinions from every angle)

各 **gè** is also used frequently with 位 **wèi** to address a group of people or with 人 **rén** to mean 'everyone', 'each person':

各位先生，各位女士 . . . **gè wèi xiānsheng | gè wèi nǚshì**
ladies and gentlemen . . .

各人有各人的主张。 **gè rén yǒu gè rén de zhǔzhāng**
Everyone holds a different view/advocates a different approach. (*lit.* Each person has each person's view/idea.)

Unlike 每 **měi**, which emphasises totality, 各 **gè** emphasises individuality and may be used as a pronoun in some reduplicated structures:

各顾各 **gè gù gè**
each for oneself
各有各的特点 **gè yǒu gè de tèdiǎn**
Each has its own characteristics.

各有各的想法 **gè yǒu gè de xiǎngfǎ**
Each has his/her own axe to grind.
各就各位，预备，跑! **gè jiù gè wèi | yùbèi | pǎo**
On your marks; get set; go!

C   The notion of totality may also be expressed by interrogative pronouns (e.g. 谁 **shéi/shuí**, 什么 **shénme**, 哪儿 **nǎr**, etc.) which are used as indefinite pronouns

meaning 'everyone', 'everything', 'everywhere', etc., generally in association
with the adverb 都 **dōu** (see Unit 12 Section **B**):

谁都愿意去。 **shéi/shuí dōu yuànyì qù**
Everybody is willing to go.
我什么都要。 **wǒ shénme dōu yào**
I want everything./I'll take anything.
谁都可以来。 **shéi/shuí dōu kěyǐ lái**
Everybody/anyone can come.
哪儿都行。 **nǎr dōu xíng**
Anywhere will do.
怎样都可以。 **zényàng dōu kěyǐ**
Any way will do.
她谁都认识。 **tā shéi/shuí dōu rènshi**
She knows everybody.

Note: A sentence like 她谁都认识。 **tā shéi/shuí dōu rènshi**, depending on the pause or context,
may also mean 'everybody knows her' since either 她 **tā** or 谁 **shéi/shuí** may be taken as the subject
or object of 认识 **rènshi**.

In negative statements, 都 **dōu** may be replaced by 也 **yě**, a usage particularly
common with speakers from north China:

谁也不相信他的话。 **shéi/shuí yě bù xiāngxìn tā de huà**
Nobody believes what he says.

(天黑了，) 我什么也看不见。 **(tiān hēi le l) wǒ shénme yě kàn bu jiàn**
It is/was dark and I can't/couldn't see anything at all.

(我很累，) 哪儿也不愿意去。 **(wǒ hěn lèi l) nǎr yě bù yuànyì qù**
I am so tired that I don't want to go anywhere.

什么 **shénme** may also be used attributively in this structure:

她什么东西也没 (有) 带。 **tā shénme dōngxi yě méi(yǒu) dài**
She didn't take anything with her.

谁也不知道发生了什么事情。
shéi/shuí yě bù zhīdao fāshēng le shénme shìqing
Nobody knows what has happened.

怎么 **zénme** is always used adverbially:

她怎么也不肯说。 **tā zénme yě bù kěn shuō**
She refused to say anything no matter what the situation.

我已经知道怎么办了。 **wǒ yǐjing zhīdao zénme bàn le**
I already know how to do it.

D   Apart from the indefinite use of interrogative pronouns, the notion of totality may also be expressed by the use of the adjective 任何 **rènhé** 'any' and pronouns like 大家 **dàjiā** 'everybody', 一切 **yīqiè** 'everything', 到处 **dàochù** 'everywhere', etc.:

任何人都愿意帮助他。 **rènhé rén dōu yuànyì bāngzhù tā**
Everybody was willing to help him.

我不吃任何肉类的食品。 **wǒ bù chī rènhé ròulèi de shípǐn**
I don't touch any food made from meat.

大家都来了。 **dàjiā dōu lái le**
Everyone has come.

一切都准备好了。 **yīqiè dōu zhǔnbèi hǎo le**
Everything is ready.

到处都是花儿。 **dàochù dōu shì huār**
There are flowers everywhere.

E   Reduplicating a measure word also conveys the meaning 'every', 'each', 'all'. The reduplication always precedes the verb and is often followed by the adverb 都 **dōu**:

个个都很高兴。 **gègè dōu hěn gāoxìng**
Everyone is happy.

张张桌子都很脏。 **zhāngzhāng zhuōzi dōu hěn zāng**
All the tables are dirty.

条条大路通罗马。 **tiáotiáo dà lù tōng luómǎ**
All roads lead to Rome.

Note that the last example, as a form of proverb, naturally falls into a seven-syllable rhythm, which explains why 都 **dōu** is absent here.

Note: Some nouns may sometimes be used/regarded as measure words and follow the same reduplication rule to mean 'every', 'each', 'all':

人人都会说英文。 **rénrén dōu huì shuō yīngwén**
Everybody can speak English.

家家户户都有冰箱。 **jiājiāhùhù dōu yǒu bīngxiāng**
Every household has a fridge.

Exercise 17.1

Fill in the blanks in the Chinese sentences below with either 每 **měi** or 各 **gè** to match the English translations:

1 老师要求我们 _____ 分钟写三十个汉字。
lǎoshī yāoqiú wǒmen _____ fēn zhōng xiě sān shí gè hànzì
The teacher asked us to write thirty characters every minute.

2 这个班的学生 _____ 人有 _____ 人的特点。
zhè/zhèi gè bān de xuésheng _____ rén yǒu _____ rén de tèdiǎn
The students in this class each have their own characteristics.

3 小猫 _____ 天吃三顿，_____ 顿都吃鱼。
xiǎo māo _____ tiān chī sān dùn | _____ dùn dōu chī yú
The kitten eats fish three times a day.
(*lit.* The kitten eats three times a day. Each time it eats fish.)

4 花园里有 _____ 种花草。**huāyuán li yǒu _____ zhǒng huācǎo**
There are many different kinds of plants in the garden.

5 _____ 人都需要朋友。_____ **rén dōu xūyào péngyou**
Everyone needs friends.

6 他说的 _____ 句话都有道理。**tā shuō de _____ jù huà dōu yǒu dàoli**
Everything he says is reasonable.

7 学校 _____ 星期休息两天。**xuéxiào _____ xīngqī xiūxi liǎng tiān**
School is closed for two days every week.

8 出席会议的 _____ 位代表都发了言。
chūxí huìyì de _____ wèi dàibiǎo dōu fā le yán
All the representatives attending the meeting gave a speech.

9 女儿 _____ 个月都去看望爸爸。
nǚ'ér _____ gè yuè dōu qù kànwàng bàba
The daughter goes to see her father every month.

10 世界 _____ 民族人民团结起来。**shìjiè _____ mínzú rénmín tuánjié qǐlái**
People of the world, unite!

Exercise 17.2

Complete the following Chinese sentences using indefinite pronouns/adverbs (converted from interrogatives) to provide a translation of the English:

1 _____ 都羡慕他。_____ **dōu xiànmù tā**
Everyone envies her.

2 他 _____ _____ 都知道。**tā _____ dōu zhīdao**
He knows everything.

3 _____ 都猜到了。_____ **dōu cāi dào le**
Everyone guessed right.

4　你说什么？我没说 ＿＿＿ ＿＿＿ 。 **nǐ shuō shénme | wǒ méi shuō** ＿＿＿
　　What did you say? I didn't say anything.

5　我 ＿＿＿ ＿＿＿ 都找过了，还是没(有)找到。
　　wǒ ＿＿＿ **dōu zhǎo guo le | háishi méi(yǒu) zhǎo dào**
　　I have searched everywhere but I still can't find it.

6　在这个小镇上，我 ＿＿＿ 都认识。
　　zài zhè/zhèi ge xiǎo zhèn shang | wǒ ＿＿＿ **dōu rènshi**
　　I know everyone in this town.

7　＿＿＿ 都来帮助老人搬家。 ＿＿＿ **dōu lái bāngzhù lǎorén bānjiā**
　　Everyone came to help the old people move house.

8　＿＿＿ ＿＿＿ 都准备好了，可以出发了。
　　＿＿＿ **dōu zhǔnbèi hǎo le | kěyǐ chūfā le**
　　Everything is ready so we can leave now.

9　小张 ＿＿＿ ＿＿＿ 也不肯跟我去。 **xiǎo zhāng** ＿＿＿ **yě bù kěn gēn wǒ qù**
　　Xiao Zhang was unwilling to go with me no matter what.

10　他们没提 ＿＿＿ ＿＿＿ 问题。 **tāmen méi tí** ＿＿＿ **wèntí**
　　They didn't raise any questions.

Exercise 17.3

Some of the Chinese sentences below contain errors. Identify the sentences with mistakes and correct them:

1　哥哥各年夏天都去游泳。 **gēge gè nián xiàtiān dōu qù yóuyǒng**
　　My elder brother goes swimming every summer.

2　每个孩子吃一块蛋糕。 **měi gè háizi chī yī kuài dàngāo**
　　Each child may have a piece of cake.

3　每电影都很惊险。 **měi diànyǐng dōu hěn jīngxiǎn**
　　All the films are exciting.

4　这些字各个写五遍。 **zhè/zhèi xiē zì gè gè xiě wǔ biàn**
　　Write each of these characters five times.

5　各人都需要自由。 **gè rén dōu xūyào zìyóu**
　　Everyone needs freedom.

6　奶奶吃什么没味道。 **nǎinai chī shénme méi wèidao**
　　Grandmother can't taste anything, whatever she eats.

7　他说的一切我都理解。 **tā shuō de yīqiè wǒ dōu lǐjiě**
　　I understood all that he said.

8　每个地方也有草坪。 **měi gè dìfang yě yǒu cǎopíng**
　　There are lawns everywhere.

Exercise 17.4

Replace the expressions in bold italic type in the Chinese sentences below with one of the following: 什么 **shénme**, 谁 **shéi/shuí** or 哪儿 **nǎr**:

1 学校里每个人都认识王校长。
xuéxiào li *měi gè rén* **dōu rènshi wáng xiàozhǎng**
Everybody in the school knows head teacher Wang.

2 他今天不舒服，一点东西也不想吃。
tā jīntiān bù shūfu | yīdiǎn dōngxi yě bù xiǎng chī
He's feeling ill today and can't eat a thing (can't eat anything at all).

3 大家都说安妮好。 *dàjiā* **dōu shuō ānní hǎo**
Everyone says Anne is a good person.

4 每个地方都找过了，钥匙还是没(有)找到。
měi gè dìfang **dōu zhǎo guo le | yàoshi háishi méi(yǒu) zhǎo dào**
We looked everywhere, but we couldn't find the key.

5 一切都在好起来。 *yīqiè* **dōu zài hǎo qǐlái**
Everything is getting better.

6 人人都信任她。 *rénrén* **dōu xìnrèn tā**
Everyone trusts her.

7 她任何地方都/也不想去。 **tā** *rènhé dìfang* **dōu/yě bù xiǎng qù**
She doesn't want to go anywhere.

8 他不喝任何有汽的饮料。 **tā bù hē** *rènhé* **yǒu qì de yǐnliào**
She doesn't touch any fizzy drinks.

Exercise 17.5

Translate the following into Chinese:

1 There are restaurants everywhere in Beijing.
2 My son rings me every other day.
3 You don't have to do anything.
4 Everyone in the office finishes work every day at 5.30.
5 I don't recognise anyone in this photograph.
6 Every time he opened his mouth, we all laughed.
7 Any time will do.
8 There aren't any small shops anywhere here any more.

UNIT EIGHTEEN
Comparisons with 比 **bǐ** and 没有 **méiyǒu** (summary)

A X 比 **bǐ** Y + adjective is the basic construction expressing a comparison:

玫瑰花比茉莉花香。 **méiguìhuā bǐ mòlìhuā xiāng**
Roses smell sweeter than jasmine.

菠菜比白菜好吃。 **bōcài bǐ báicài hǎochī**
Spinach is tastier than cabbage.

A complement of degree may be placed after the adjective:

菠菜比白菜好吃一点儿。 **bōcài bǐ báicài hǎochī yīdiǎnr**
Spinach is a bit tastier than cabbage.

这个故事比那个故事有趣得多。
zhè/zhèi gè gùshi bǐ nà/nèi gè gùshi yǒuqù de duō
This story is much more interesting than that one.

我比她大三岁。 **wǒ bǐ tā dà sān suì**
I am three years older than her.

The degree adverbs 更 **gèng** or 还 **hái** may be placed before the adjective for emphasis, with the optional use of the particle 呢 **ne** at the end of the sentence:

玫瑰花比茉莉花还香 (呢)。 **méiguìhuā bǐ mòlìhuā hái xiāng (ne)**
Roses smell even sweeter than jasmine.

这个故事比那个故事更有趣 (呢)。
zhè/zhèi gè gùshi bǐ nà/nèi gè gùshi gèng yǒuqù (ne)
This story is even more interesting than that one.

Similarity, on the other hand, is expressed by the construction X 跟 **gēn** Y 一样 **yīyàng** 'the same (*lit*. one kind)' + adjective:

玫瑰花跟茉莉花一样香。 **méiguìhuā gēn mòlìhuā yīyàng xiāng**
Roses smell as sweet as jasmine.

菠菜跟白菜一样好吃。 **bōcài gēn báicài yīyàng hǎochī**
Spinach is as tasty as cabbage.

B   If the comparison is not directly between X and Y, but between the quality
or result of their actions, then a complement of manner or result must naturally
be introduced in the form of 得 **de** + adjective (see *Basic Chinese*, Unit 12).
Under these circumstances the 比 **bǐ** Y phrase may be placed either before the
adjective or before the verb:

这个运动员跳得比那个运动员高。
zhè/zhèi gè yùndòngyuán tiào de bǐ nà/nèi gè yùndòngyún gāo
这个运动员比那个运动员跳得高。
zhè/zhèi gè yùndòngyuán bǐ nà/nèi gè yùndòngyuán tiào de gāo
This athlete jumps higher than that athlete.

你唱得比她好听。 **nǐ chàng de bǐ tā hǎotīng**
你比她唱得好听。 **nǐ bǐ tā chàng de hǎotīng**
You sing better than she does.

哥哥常常睡得比我早。 **gēge chángcháng shuì de bǐ wǒ zǎo**
哥哥常常比我睡得早。 **gēge chángcháng bǐ wǒ shuì de zǎo**
My elder brother often goes to bed earlier than I do.

Note: Where the verb has an object and has to be repeated after the object, the same rule applies
with the 比 **bǐ** Y phrase going before the adjective or the repeated verb:

你唱歌唱得比她好听。 **nǐ chàng gē chàng de bǐ tā hǎotīng**
你唱歌比她唱得好听。 **nǐ chàng gē bǐ tā chàng de hǎotīng**
You sing better than she does.

小张做算术题做得比小李更快。 **xiǎo zhāng zuò suànshùtí zuò de bǐ xiǎo lǐ gèng kuài**
小张做算术题比小李做得更快。 **xiǎo zhāng zuò suànshùtí bǐ xiǎo lǐ zuò de gèng kuài**
Xiao Zhang does sums even more quickly than Xiao Li.

你说英文说得比我流利。 **nǐ shuō yīngwén shuō de bǐ wǒ liúlì**
你说英文比我说得流利。 **nǐ shuō yīngwén bǐ wǒ shuō de liúlì**
You speak English more fluently than I do.

One cannot say:

*你比她唱歌唱得好听。 **nǐ bǐ tā chàng gē chàng de hǎotīng**

The 跟 **gēn** Y phrase in similarity expressions is located in the same alternative
positions as 比 **bǐ** Y in verb–complement and verb–object–verb–complement
sentences:

她长得跟她母亲一样漂亮。 **tā zhǎng de gēn tā mǔqīn yīyàng piàoliang**
她跟她母亲长得一样漂亮。 **tā gēn tā mǔqīn zhǎng de yīyàng piàoliang**
She looks as pretty as her mother.

我跑得跟他一样快。 **wǒ pǎo de gēn tā yīyàng kuài**
我跟他跑得一样快。 **wǒ gēn tā pǎo de yīyàng kuài**
I run/ran as fast as he does/did.

你那天吃饭吃得跟他一样多。 **nǐ nà/nèi tiān chīfàn chī de gēn tā yīyàng duō**
你那天吃饭跟她吃得一样多。 **nǐ nà/nèi tiān chīfàn gēn tā chī de yīyàng duō**
You ate as much as she did that day.

你写汉字写得跟他一样好。 **nǐ xiě hànzì xiě de gēn tā yīyàng hǎo**
你写汉字跟他写得一样好。 **nǐ xiě hànzì gēn tā xiě de yīyàng hǎo**
You write Chinese characters as well as he does.

C   If the modal verbs 能 **néng** or 会 **huì** are used in a comparison or similarity construction, X 比 **bǐ** Y or X 跟 **gēn** Y 一样 **yīyàng** precedes the modal verb:

他比我能说话。 **tā bǐ wǒ néng shuōhuà**
He is more eloquent than I am.

你跟我一样会游泳。 **nǐ gēn wǒ yīyàng huì yóuyǒng**
You know how to swim as well as I do.

D   It is also possible for a comparison or similarity construction to focus on an adverbial of time, location, etc.:

你今天穿得比昨天漂亮。 **nǐ jīntiān chuān de bǐ zuótiān piàoliang**
你今天比昨天穿得漂亮。 **nǐ jīntiān bǐ zuótiān chūan de piàoliang**
You are better dressed today than yesterday.

你今年说汉语说得比去年好。 **nǐ jīnnián shuō hànyǔ shuō de bǐ qùnián hǎo**
你今年说汉语比去年说得好。 **nǐ jīnnián shuō hànyǔ bǐ qùnián shuō de hǎo**
You speak Chinese better this year than last year.

这个孩子在家里跟在学校里一样乖。
zhè/zhèi gè háizi zài jiā li gēn zài xuéxiào li yīyàng guāi
This child behaves as well at home as at school.

The comparison can also relate to different objects:

他看电影看得比戏剧多。 **tā kàn diànyǐng kàn de bǐ xìjú duō**
他看电影比戏剧看得多。 **tā kàn diànyǐng bǐ xìjú kàn de duō**
He sees more films than plays.

你说中文说得跟法文一样好。
nǐ shuō zhōngwén shuō de gēn fǎwén yīyàng hǎo
你说中文跟法文说得一样好。
nǐ shuō zhōngwén gēn fǎwén shuō de yīyàng hǎo
You speak Chinese as well as French.

E   In topic | subject-predicate sentences, once the topic is presented, comparisons can be made with different parts of the comment in a similar way:

汉字你写得比我漂亮。 **hànzì nǐ xiě de bǐ wǒ piàoliang**
You can write Chinese characters much better than I can. (*lit.* As far as Chinese characters are concerned, you can write them much better than I can.)

足球你今年踢得比去年好。 **zúqiú nǐ jīnnián tī de bǐ qùnián hǎo**
You play better football this year than last year.

这儿的天气你比我习惯。 **zhèr de tiānqì nǐ bǐ wǒ xíguàn**
You are more used to the climate here than I am.

那个地方你比我熟悉。 **nà/nèi gè dìfang nǐ bǐ wǒ shúxī**
You know that place better than I do.

这儿的情况我现在比过去了解。
zhèr de qíngkuàng wǒ xiànzài bǐ guòqù liǎojiě
I understand more about the situation here now than I did before.

F   If the comparison or similarity expression relates to the attributives of a noun, it is not necessary to repeat the noun:

他的衣服比我 (的) 多。 **tā de yīfu bǐ wǒ (de) duō**
He has more clothes than I do.

这儿的天气比那儿 (的) 好。 **zhèr de tiānqì bǐ nàr (de) hǎo**
The climate here is better than the climate there.

今天买的香蕉比上星期的大。
jīntiān mǎi de xiāngjiāo bǐ shàng xīngqī de dà
The bananas I bought today are bigger than the ones I bought last week.

这辆车跟那辆一样新。 **zhè/zhèi liàng chē gēn nà/nèi liàng yīyàng xīn**
This car is as new as that one.

It is not necessary to repeat the noun, though it is not wrong to do so:

他的衣服比我的衣服多。 **tā de yīfu bǐ wǒ de yīfu duō**
He has more clothes than I have.

这儿的天气比那儿的天气好。 **zhèr de tiānqì bǐ nàr de tiānqì hǎo**
The climate here is better than the climate there.

G The negative of comparison may be formed by placing 不 **bù** before 比 **bǐ**:

这辆车不比那辆新。 **zhè/zhèi liàng chē bù bǐ nà/nèi liàng xīn**
This car is no(t) newer than that one.

这个电视节目不比那个有意思。
zhè/zhèi gè diànshì jiémù bù bǐ nà/nèi gè yǒu yìsi
This television programme is no(t) more interesting than that one.

Note: 不见得 **bù jiàn dé** is often used before 比 **bǐ** to reduce the impact of the negative:

他学得不见得比我好。 **tā xué de bù jiàn dé bǐ wǒ hǎo**
He doesn't necessarily learn better than I do.

他们射球射得不见得比我们准。 **tāmen shè qiú shè de bù jiàn dé bǐ wǒmen zhǔn**
他们射球不见得射得比我们准。 **tāmen shè qiú bù jiàn dé shè de bǐ wǒmen zhǔn**
They did not necessarily score better goals than we did.

这个不见得比那个有用。 **zhè/zhèi gè bù jiàn dé bǐ nà/nèi gè yǒuyòng**
This is not necessarily more useful than that.

这条裙子不见得比那条漂亮。 **zhè/zhèi tiáo qúnzi bù jiàn dé bǐ nà/nèi tiáo piàoliang**
This skirt is not necessarily prettier than that one.

H A more common way to express a negative comparison is to use the structure X 没有 **méiyǒu** Y (那么 **nàme**) + adjective:

我没有你 (那么) 聪明。 **wǒ méiyǒu nǐ (nàme) cōngming**
I'm not as intelligent as you.

这首歌没有那首 (那么) 好听。
zhè/zhèi shǒu gē méiyǒu nà/nèi shǒu (nàme) hǎotīng
This song is not as nice as that one.

你说汉语没有她 (说得) (那么) 流利。
nǐ shuō hànyǔ méiyǒu tā (shuō de) (nàme) liúlì
You don't speak Chinese as fluently as she does.

你吃得没有我多。 **nǐ chī de méiyǒu wǒ duō**
You don't/didn't eat as much as I do/did.

Note also that this structure can occur in the positive to ask a comparison question (see Unit 19):

他有你 (那么) 高吗? **tā yǒu nǐ (nàme) gāo ma**
Is he as tall as you?

他们下棋有没有你 (下得) (那么) 好? **tāmen xià qí yǒu méiyǒu nǐ (xià de) (nàme) hǎo**
Do they play chess as well as you do?

I It must be pointed out that, as we saw with modal verbs (Section **C** above), verbal expressions in addition to adjectives may be used to indicate the degree or extent of comparison or similarity:

她比你喜欢吃鱼。 **tā bǐ nǐ xǐhuan chī yú**
She likes (eating) fish more than you do.

这儿的天气你没有我习惯。 **zhèr de tiānqì nǐ méiyǒu wǒ xíguàn**
You are not as used to the weather here as I am.

那些中学生跟这些大学生一样也会说中文。
nà/nèi xiē zhōngxuésheng gēn zhè/zhèi xiē dàxuésheng yīyàng yě huì shuō zhōngwén
Those secondary school students, like these university students, can also speak Chinese.

Exercise 18.1

Complete the Chinese translations below by filling in the gaps with 比 **bǐ**, 不比 **bù bǐ**, 跟 **gēn** or 没有 **méiyǒu**:

1 This piece of luggage is heavier than that piece.
这件行李 ＿＿＿＿ 那件重。 **zhè/zhèi jiàn xínglǐ ＿＿＿＿ nà/nèi jiàn zhòng**
2 It's quicker to phone than to write a letter.
打电话 ＿＿＿＿ 写信快。 **dǎ diànhuà ＿＿＿＿ xiě xìn kuài**
3 This hotel isn't as expensive as that one.
这个旅馆 ＿＿＿ ＿＿＿ 那个 (旅馆) 那么贵。
zhè/zhèi gè lǚguǎn ＿＿＿＿ nà/nèi gè (lǚguǎn) nàme guì
4 My car is the same colour as Xiao Li's.
我汽车的颜色 ＿＿＿＿ 小李的一样。
wǒ qìchē de yánsè ＿＿＿＿ xiǎo lǐ de yīyàng
5 My room is as large as Xiao Hong's.
我的房间 ＿＿＿＿ 小红的一样大。
wǒ de fángjiān ＿＿＿＿ xiǎo hóng de yīyàng dà

6　You haven't been here as long as I have.

你在这儿的时间 _____ _____ 我长。

nǐ zài zhèr de shíjiān _____ **wǒ cháng**

7　I didn't get up as early as you did.

我起床起得 _____ _____ 你早。　**wǒ qǐchuáng qǐ de** _____ **nǐ zǎo**

8　I feel better today than I did yesterday.

我今天觉得 _____ 昨天好。　**wǒ jīntiān juéde** _____ **zuótiān hǎo**

9　I don't play tennis as often as you do.

我打网球 _____ _____ 你打得次数多。

wǒ dǎ wǎngqiú _____ **nǐ dǎ de cìshù duō**

10　Your chair is more comfortable than mine.

你的椅子 _____ 我的舒服。　**nǐ de yǐzi** _____ **wǒ de shūfu**

11　He can run just as fast as she can.

他跑得 _____ 她一样快。　**tā pǎo de** _____ **tā yīyàng kuài**

12　This rope is not the same length as that one.

这根绳子 _____ _____ 那根绳子一样长。

zhè/zhèi gēn shéngzi _____ _____ **nà/nèi gēn shéngzi yīyàng cháng**

Exercise 18.2

Combine the two pieces of information below to make a Chinese sentence of
comparison or similarity. In each case, start with the first piece of information.
Sometimes more than one structure of comparison is possible:

EXAMPLE:

小张今年十八岁。　**xiǎo zhāng jīnnián shí bā suì**

Xiao Zhang is eighteen.

小李今年二十一岁。　**xiǎo lǐ jīnnián èr shí yī suì**

Xiao Li is twenty-one.

Answer: 小张比小李小三岁。　**xiǎo zhāng bǐ xiǎo lǐ xiǎo sān suì**

Xiao Zhang is three years younger than Xiao Li.

1　我身高一米七十。　**wǒ shēn gāo yī mǐ qī shí**

I'm 1.7 metres tall.

他身高一米八十。　**tā shēn gāo yī mǐ bā shí**

He is 1.8 metres tall.

2　这个故事很复杂。　**zhè/zhèi gè gùshi hěn fùzá**

This story is very complicated.

那个故事不很复杂。　**nà/nèi gè gùshi bù hěn fùzá**

That story isn't very complicated.

3　他去年只认识几个汉字。　**tā qùnián zhǐ rènshi jǐ gè hànzì**

He only knew a few Chinese characters last year.

他现在认识不少汉字。 **tā xiànzài rènshi bù shǎo hànzì**
He knows a lot of Chinese characters now.

4 这个运动员跑第一名。 **zhè/zhèi gè yùndòngyuán pǎo dì yī míng**
This athlete came first.

那个运动员跑第二名。 **nà/nèi gè yùndòngyúan pǎo dì èr míng**
That athlete came second.

5 小李跳舞跳得很好。 **xiǎo lǐ tiàowǔ tiào de hěn hǎo**
Xiao Li is a very good dancer.

我跳舞跳得一般。 **wǒ tiàowǔ tiào de yībān**
I'm an average dancer.

6 加拿大很大。 **jiānádà hěn dà**
Canada is a very large country.

英国不很大。 **yīngguó bù hěn dà**
Britain is not very big.

7 小王教书教得不太认真。 **xiǎo wáng jiāoshū jiāo de bù tài rènzhēn**
Xiao Wang isn't a very conscientious teacher.

陈老师教书教得很认真。 **chén lǎoshī jiāoshū jiāo de hěn rènzhēn**
Miss Chen is a very conscientious teacher.

8 这扇门油漆得很白。 **zhè/zhèi shàn mén yóuqī de hěn bái**
This door is painted white.

那扇门油漆得也很白。 **nà/nèi shàn mén yóuqī de yě hěn bái**
That door is also painted white.

Exercise 18.3

There are errors in each of the following Chinese sentences. Rewrite them in the correct form:

1 这条街道比那条很宽。 **zhè/zhèi tiáo jiēdào bǐ nà/nèi tiáo hěn kuān**
This street is even wider than that street.

2 我比我侄子写诗得好。 **wǒ bǐ wǒ zhízi xiě shī de hǎo**
I am better at writing poems than my nephew.

3 小李对工作没比你对工作负责。
xiǎo lǐ duì gōngzuò méi bǐ nǐ duì gōngzuò fùzé
Xiao Li isn't as responsible with (his) work as you are.

4 他不比以前那样喜欢串门了。
tā bù bǐ yǐqián nà/nèi yàng xǐhuan chuànmén le
He doesn't like visiting people as much as he used to.

5 爸爸跟妈妈经常帮助人一样。 **bàba gēn māma jīngcháng bāngzhù rén yīyàng**
My father helps people as regularly as my mother does.

6 伦敦比利兹拥挤多。 **lúndūn bǐ lìzī yōngjǐ duō**
London is far more crowded than Leeds.

Exercise 18.4

Translate the following into Chinese:

1 I don't know as many people as you do.
2 She can play the piano better than he can.
3 Her essay was longer than yours.
4 My computer breaks down more easily than yours does. (出毛病 **chū máobìng** 'to break down')
5 This spring isn't as warm as last spring.
6 He doesn't play tennis as well as you do.
7 This one is as big as that one.
8 There are as many people here today as there were yesterday.
9 The population of India is still not as big as that of China.
10 The one that is more attractive than this one is not as expensive as this one.

UNIT NINETEEN
Various uses of 有 **yǒu** (summary)

A 有 **yǒu** meaning 'to have' (see *Basic Chinese*, Unit 11) may be preceded by an animate or inanimate subject to indicate possession:

我哥哥有一辆自行车。 **wǒ gēge yǒu yī liàng zìxíngchē**
My elder brother has a bicycle.

他有两个儿子。 **tā yǒu liǎng gè érzi**
He has got two sons.

小李有一台电脑。 **xiǎo lǐ yǒu yī tái diànnǎo**
Xiao Li has a computer.

大象有一条长鼻子。 **dàxiàng yǒu yī tiáo cháng bízi**
The elephant has a long trunk.

玫瑰有刺。 **méiguì yǒu cì**
Roses have thorns.

中文系有两百个学生。 **zhōngwénxì yǒu liǎng bǎi gè xuésheng**
The department of Chinese has two hundred students.

这个公园有四个入口处。 **zhè/zhèi gè gōngyuán yǒu sì gè rùkǒuchù**
This park has four entrances.

一周有七天。 **yī zhōu yǒu qī tiān**
A week has seven days.

B 有 **yǒu** also indicates existence 'there is/are . . .' (see *Basic Chinese*, Unit 11) and regularly follows a location phrase:

(1) Coverbal location phrase (see *Basic Chinese*, Unit 24):

沿路有很多大树。 **yán lù yǒu hěn duō dà shù**
There are many tall trees along the road.

靠墙有一张大床。 **kào qiáng yǒu yī zhāng dà chuáng**
There is a large bed against the wall.

朝东有两扇窗户。 **cháo dōng yǒu liǎng shàn chuānghu**
There are two windows facing east.

(2) Postpositional location phrase (see *Basic Chinese*, Unit 13):

门前有块草坪。 **mén qián yǒu kuài cǎopíng**
There is a lawn in front of the house (*lit.* in front of the door).

树下有只松鼠。 **shù xià yǒu zhī sōngshǔ**
There is a squirrel under the tree.

岩石上有很多贻贝。 **yánshí shang yǒu hěn duō yíbèi**
There are a lot of mussels on the rocks.

花园里有不少玫瑰。 **huāyuán li yǒu bù shǎo méiguì**
There are quite a few roses in the garden.

Note: 是 **shì** is also used to indicate existence. However, with 是 **shì** the location is emphasised, whereas with 有 **yǒu** the the emphasis is on the object that exists:

房子前有两棵大树。 **fángzi qián yǒu liǎng kē dà shù**
There are two tall trees in front of the house.

房子前是两棵大树。 **fángzi qián shì liǎng kē dà shù**
In front of the house (there) are two tall trees.

Note: 是 **shì** often indicates that the object(s) is/are the sole occupant(s) of a location, especially when accompanied by 全 **quán** 'all', 'entirely' and 都 **dōu** 'all':

窗台上全是花。 **chuāngtái shang quán shì huā**
The windowsill is full of flowers.

地上都是水。 **dì shang dōu shì shuǐ**
There's water all over the place.

C 有 **yǒu** also indicates existence when used with a preceding time phrase:

昨天有太阳。 **zuótiān yǒu tàiyáng**
There was some sunshine yesterday.

今晚有个音乐会。 **jīn wǎn yǒu gè yīnyuèhuì**
There will be a concert tonight.

唐代有不少诗人。 **tángdài yǒu bù shǎo shīrén**
There were quite a few poets in the Tang Dynasty.

D   The subject of a narrative sentence tends to be of definite reference. However, when 有 **yǒu** is placed before the subject, it makes the subject indefinite:

汽车停在门前。 **qìchē tíng zài mén qián**
The car is parked in front of the house (*lit.* in front of the door). (definite reference)
有 (一) 辆汽车停在门前。 **yǒu (yī) liàng qìchē tíng zài mén qián**
There is a car parked in front of the house (*lit.* in front of the door). (indefinite reference)

鸟在树上唱歌。 **niǎo zài shù shang chàng gē**
The bird is singing in the tree. (definite reference)
有 (一) 只鸟在树上唱歌。 **yǒu (yī) zhī niǎo zài shù shang chàng gē**
There is a bird singing in the tree. (indefinite reference)

Note: 鸟 **niǎo** 'bird' in the third example may, of course, be regarded as of indefinite reference if the sentence is used in a descriptive rather than narrative mode.

E   有 **yǒu** is sometimes used with a verbal object to indicate that a change or development has taken place. Only under such circumstances can 有 **yǒu** be attached with an aspect marker:

她的中文有 (了) 很大的进步。 **tā de zhōngwén yǒu (le) hěn dà de jìnbù**
She has made great progress with her Chinese.

亚洲的经济有了明显的发展。 **yàzhōu de jīngjì yǒu le míngxiǎn de fāzhǎn**
The economy of Asia has clearly developed.

他家的收入有了增加。 **tā jiā de shōurù yǒu le zēngjiā**
His family income has increased.

她家的生活水平有了提高。 **tā jiā de shēnghuó shuǐpíng yǒu le tígāo**
The living standard of her family has improved.

这儿的气候有了变化。 **zhèr de qìhòu yǒu le biànhuà**
There have been changes in the weather conditions here.

F   有 **yǒu** and its negative 没 (有) **méi(yǒu)** occur with abstract noun objects to form adjectival phrases:

有趣 **yǒuqù**	有道理 **yǒu dàoli**
interesting	reasonable
有可能 **yǒu kěnéng**	有空 **yǒukòng**
possible	free, having free time

有力气 **yǒu lìqi**
strong enough

有钱 **yǒuqián**
rich, wealthy

有礼貌 **yǒu lǐmào**
polite

有学问 **yǒu xuéwèn**
learned

有经验 **yǒu jīngyàn**
experienced

有办法 **yǒu bànfǎ**
resourceful

有勇气 **yǒu yǒngqì**
courageous

有志气 **yǒu zhìqi**
ambitious

有意思 **yǒu yìsi**
interesting

没有道理 **méi(yǒu) dàoli**
unreasonable, illogical

没有可能 **méi(yǒu) kěnéng**
impossible

没有文化 **méi(yǒu) wénhuà**
uneducated

没有办法 **méi(yǒu) bànfǎ**
having no way of doing something

没有志气 **méi(yǒu) zhìqi**
unmotivated

没有钱 **méi(yǒu) qián**
poor, penniless

没有意思 **méi(yǒu) yìsi**
boring

Being adjectival phrases, they may be modified by degree adverbs:

那个工程师很有经验。 **nà/nèi gè gōngchéngshī *hěn* yǒu jīngyàn**
The engineer has had a lot of experience.

这个故事十分有趣。 **zhè/zhèi gè gùshi *shífēn* yǒuqù**
This story is extremely interesting.

G   有的 **yǒu de** 'some' either precedes a noun as an attributive or refers back to a stated (or understood) group:

有的工人星期六不上班。 **yǒu de gōngrén xīngqī liù bù shàngbān**
Some workers do not go to work on Saturdays.

沙滩上有很多人，有的在晒太阳，有的在聊天，有的在捡贝壳。
shātān shang yǒu hěn duō rén | yǒu de zài shài tàiyáng | yǒu de zài liáotiān | yǒu de zài jiǎn bèiké
There were many people on the beach, some sunbathing, some chatting and some collecting shells.

花园里有很多花，有的是红的，有的是黄的，有的是紫的，有的是粉红的。
huāyuán li yǒu hěn duō huā | yǒu de shì hóng de | yǒu de shì huáng de | yǒu de shì zǐ de | yǒu de shì fěnhóng de
There are many flowers in the garden, some red, some yellow, some purple and others pink.

Note: This use of 有 **yǒu** may also be seen in the following idiomatic expressions:

有些 **yǒuxiē**	有些人 **yǒuxiē rén**
some	some people
有点儿 **yǒudiǎnr**	有点儿紧张 **yǒudiǎnr jǐnzhāng**
a little	a little nervous
有时 **yǒushí**	有时快，有时慢 **yǒushí kuài	yǒushí màn**
sometimes	sometimes quick, sometimes slow

H   有 **yǒu** is used with numbers and measures to express estimation:

这条鱼有两斤重吗？ **zhè/zhèi tiáo yú yǒu liǎng jīn zhòng ma**
Does this fish weigh about two catties?

这根绳子大约有两米长。 **zhè/zhèi gēn shéngzi dàyuē yǒu liǎng mǐ cháng**
This rope is about two metres long.

大厅里有三百人吗？ **dà tīng li yǒu sān bǎi rén ma**
Are there about three hundred people in the hall?

从这儿到车站没有半英里路。 **cóng zhèr dào chēzhàn méi yǒu bàn yīnglǐ lù**
It's less than half a mile from here to the station.

I   The negative form of 有 **yǒu**, 没 (有) **méi(yǒu)**, negates a past action (see *Basic Chinese*, Unit 17):

他昨天没有打壁球。 **tā zuótiān méiyǒu dǎ bìqiú**
He didn't play squash yesterday.

去年她没回家乡。 **qùnián tā méi huí jiāxiāng**
She didn't go back to her home town last year.

Exercise 19.1

Complete the Chinese translations below with a phrase beginning with 有 **yǒu**:

1 Mr. Wang is an experienced teacher.
王先生是一个 _____。 **wáng xiānsheng shì yī gè _____**
2 There are a lot of doctors in this hospital.
这个医院 _____。 **zhè/zhèi gè yīyuàn _____**

3 It's going to rain this afternoon.
   今天下午 _____。 **jīntiān xiàwǔ** _____
4 I have three brothers altogether.
   我一共 _____。 **wǒ yīgòng** _____
5 There are a few shops along this road.
   沿路 _____。 **yán lù** _____
6 Living standards have improved a lot.
   生活水平 _____。 **shēnghuó shuǐpíng** _____

Exercise 19.2

Rephrase the following Chinese sentences using 有 **yǒu** or 没 (有) **méi (yǒu)** as part of the new sentence in each case:

1 一年分春，夏，秋，冬四季。 **yī nián fēn chūn | xià | qiū | dōng sìjì**
   A year has four seasons: spring, summer, autumn and winter.
2 天气闷热得很，一点风也不刮。
   tiānqì mènrè de hěn | yīdiǎn fēng yě bù guā
   The weather is very humid and there is no wind at all.
3 我家一共四口人。 **wǒ jiā yīgòng sì kǒu rén**
   There are four people altogether in our family.
4 昨晚在礼堂举办了一个舞会。 **zuó wǎn zài lǐtáng jǔbàn le yī gè wǔhuì**
   There was a party in the hall last night.
5 那棵小树长得跟一个大人那么高了。
   nà/nèi kē xiǎo shù zhǎng de gēn yī gè dàrén nàme gāo le
   That small tree has grown as tall as an adult.
6 现在大概十二点了吧？ **xiànzài dàgài shí èr diǎn le ba**
   It's about twelve o'clock now, isn't it?
7 这个人对什么都不感兴趣。 **zhè/zhèi gè rén duì shénme dōu bù gǎn xìngqù**
   S/he has no interest in anything.
8 门前是块草坪。 **mén qián shì kuài cǎopíng**
   There is a lawn in front of the house.

Exercise 19.3

Rewrite the Chinese sentences below using 有的 **yǒu de**:

1 动物园里动物很多，天上飞的，地下跑的，水里游的都有。
   dòngwùyuán li dòngwù hěn duō | tiān shang fēi de | dì xià pǎo de | shuǐ li yóu de dōu yǒu
   There are a lot of animals in the zoo: ones that fly, ones that run and ones that swim.

2 河边有不少人，钓鱼的，看书的，散步的，晒太阳的都有。

hé biān yǒu bù shǎo rén | diào yú de | kànshū de | sànbù de | shài tàiyáng de dōu yǒu

There are a lot of people down by the river. There are people fishing, reading books, going for walks and sunbathing.

3 妹妹有很多皮鞋，红的，黑的，白的都有。

mèimei yǒu hěn duō píxié | hóng de | hēi de | bái de dōu yǒu

My younger sister has a lot of shoes: red ones, black ones and white ones.

Exercise 19.4

Translate the adjectives below into Chinese adjectival phrases with 有 **yǒu**:

interesting	hopeless
possible	rich
impolite	powerful
experienced	resourceful
daring	brainy

Exercise 19.5

Translate the following into Chinese:

1 A year has twelve months.
2 There is a big bridge in the centre of town.
3 Some of the books in our library are in English and some in Chinese.
4 On Wednesday afternoon there is a football match.
5 The students learning Chinese have all made great progress.
6 Today's lecture was very interesting.
7 Is there a telephone here?
8 The question you ask is unreasonable and I have no way of replying.

UNIT TWENTY
Idiomatic uses of 是 **shì** (summary)

A 是 **shì** 'to be' links the topic of a sentence with a nominal comment, which defines what the topic is (or is not):

他是一个邮递员。 **tā shì yī gè yóudìyuán**
He is a postman.

那位医生是我妹妹。 **nà/nèi wèi yīshēng shì wǒ mèimei**
That doctor is my younger sister.

这是一台电脑。 **zhè shì yī tái diànnǎo**
This is a computer.

鲸鱼是哺乳动物。 **jīngyú shì bǔrǔ dòngwù**
Whales are mammals.

她不是工程师。 **tā bù shì gōngchéngshī**
She is not an engineer.

这不是玫瑰花。 **zhè bù shì méiguìhuā**
This is not a rose.

鲸鱼不是鱼。 **jīngyú bù shì yú**
Whales are not fish.

Note: Being a commentative verb, 是 **shì** *cannot* be used with the aspect markers 着 **zhe**, 了 **le**, 过 **guo** or 在 **zài**, which are mainly used in subject–predicate sentences for narrative purposes.

One cannot say:

*她是了一个运动员。 **tā shì le yī gè yùndòngyuán**
(*lit.* She is an athlete.)
*他是过一个医生。 **tā shì guo yī gè yīshēng**
(*lit.* He has been a doctor.)
*我是着一个工程师。 **wǒ shì zhe yī gè gōngchéngshī**
(*lit.* I am (at present) an engineer.)
*他们 (正) 在是学生。 **tāmen (zhèng)zài shì xuésheng**
(*lit.* They are students.)

Note: Nouns indicating time, age, height, weight, etc. may be used as nominal comments without 是 **shì**:

今天星期五。 **jīntiān xīngqī wǔ**
Today is Friday.

他今年十九岁。 **tā jīnnián shí jiǔ suì**
He is nineteen this year.
她一米五。 **tā yī mǐ wǔ**
She is one metre and a half tall.
婴儿四公斤。 **yīng'ér sì gōngjīn**
The baby weighs four kilos.

是 **shì** must, however, be included in the negative form of these sentences:

今天不是星期三。 **jīntiān bù shì xīngqī sān**
It's not Wednesday today.
他今年不是二十一岁。 **tā jīnnián bù shì èr shí yī suì**
He isn't twenty-one this year.

B   是 **shì** is not generally used with adjectival comments:

这个孩子很可爱。 **zhè/zhèi gè háizi hěn kě'ài**
This child is (very) sweet.
这件事非常重要。 **zhè/zhèi jiàn shì fēicháng zhòngyào**
This matter is incredibly important.
那个运动员十分高大。 **nà/nèi gè yùndòngyuán shífēn gāodà**
That athlete is extremely tall.

However, it does occur with adjectives under particular circumstances:

(1) For emphasis:

他是聪明。 **tā shì cōngming**
He *is* intelligent.
这个杯子是很脏。 **zhè/zhèi gè bēizi shì hěn zāng**
This glass/cup *is* dirty.

(2) When implying some degree of reservation:

这个孩子是很可爱，可是 ... **zhè/zhèi gè háizi shì hěn kě'ài | kěshì** ...
The child is quite lovely, but ...

这件事儿是重要，不过 ... **zhè/zhèi jiàn shìr shì zhòngyào | bùguò** ...
This is an important matter, but ...

The reservation can be made more marked if the adjective occurs before and after 是 **shì**:

这件事重要是重要，可是 ...
zhè/zhèi jiàn shì zhòngyào shì zhòngyào shì zhòngyào | kěshì ...
The matter is indeed important, but ...

(3) When the adjective is non-gradable (e.g. 男 **nán** 'male', 女 **nǚ** 'female', 真 **zhēn** 'true', 假 **jiǎ** 'false', 圆 **yuán** 'round', 方 **fāng** 'square', 红 **hóng** 'red', 绿 **lǜ** 'green' etc.) (see Unit 16); in this case the adjective is followed by 的 **de**:

我们的语法老师是男的。 **wǒmen de yǔfǎ lǎoshī shì nán de**
Our grammar teacher is a man. (*lit.* male)

他的头发是假的。 **tā de tóufa shì jiǎ de**
He wears a wig. (*lit.* His hair is false.)

那些玫瑰都是粉红的。 **nà/nèi xiē méiguì dōu shì fěnhóng de**
All those roses are pink.

这样做是不对的。 **zhè/zhèi yàng zuò shì bù duì de**
It is/was wrong to do so./To do it like this is/was wrong.

C 是 **shì**, like 有 **yǒu**, may also feature in a sentence beginning with a location phrase. The difference is that 是 **shì** emphasises the location, whereas 有 **yǒu** emphasises merely the object that exists (see Unit 19):

果盆里是各种水果。 **guǒpén li shì gè zhǒng shuǐguǒ**
In the fruit bowl are various kinds of fruit.

鱼缸里都是热带鱼。 **yúgāng li dōu shì rèdài yú**
The tank is full of tropical fish.

山顶上是座庙。 **shāndǐng shang shì zuò miào**
On the top of the hill is a temple.

But:

山顶上有 (一) 座庙。 **shāngdǐng shang yǒu (yī) zuò miào**
There is a temple on the top of the hill.

D 是 **shì** may also be used as an intensifier in subject–predicate sentences. Its function is to highlight a particular element of the narration for the purpose of contrast or emphasis, and it turns the whole sentence into a topic–comment construction.

If the sentence refers to something that has already happened (i.e. a past fact), 是 **shì** is used in conjunction with 的 **de**:

他昨天到这儿来。 **tā zuótiān dào zhèr lái**
He came here yesterday.
他是昨天到这儿来的。 **tā *shì* zuótiān dào zhèr lái *de***
He came here *yesterday.*

If the sentence refers to something that is about to happen (i.e. a future possibility), 是 **shì** is used on its own:

他明天走。 **tā míngtiān zǒu**
He leaves tomorrow.
他是明天走。 **tā** *shì* **míngtiān zǒu**
He leaves *tomorrow*.

Different elements of a sentence may be highlighted:

(1) If the subject is to be highlighted, 是 **shì** is placed immediately before the subject (with 的 **de** coming at the end of the sentence if the action of the verb in the sentence refers to the past).

  (a) With 的 **de**:

    我把洗衣机弄坏了。 **wǒ bǎ xǐyījī nòng huài le** (subject–predicate)
    I broke the washing machine.

    是我把洗衣机弄坏 (了) 的。
    shì **wǒ bǎ xǐyījī nòng huài** (**le**) *de* (topic–comment)
    I was the one who broke the washing machine.

    张先生叫李明站起来。
    zhāng xiānsheng jiào lǐ míng zhàn qǐlái (subject–predicate)
    Mr Zhang asked Li Ming to stand up.

    是张先生叫李明站起来的。
    shì **zhāng xiānsheng jiào lǐ míng zhàn qǐlái** *de* (topic–comment)
    It was Mr Zhang who asked Li Ming to stand up.

  (b) Without 的 **de**:

    谁去？ **shéi/shuí qù**
    Who's going?
    是谁去？ *shì* **shéi/shuí qù**
    Who's going then?

    Note: The subject–predicate construction may be embedded in a bigger topic | subject–predicate sentence:

    (a) With 的 **de**:

      这本小说是她写的。
      zhè/zhèi běn xiǎoshuō *shì* **tā xiě** *de*
      She wrote this novel.

那套西装是他买的。
nà/nèi tào xīzhuāng *shì* **tā mǎi** *de*
He bought that suit.

衣服都是妈妈折叠好的。 **yīfu dōu** *shì* **māma zhédié hǎo** *de*
It was Mother who folded all those clothes.

(b) Without 的 **de**:

这件事儿是你去办，还是我去办？
zhè/zhèi jiàn shìr *shì* **nǐ qù bàn | háishi wǒ qù bàn**
Are you going to deal with this matter or am I?

(2) If the adverbial is to be highlighted, 是 **shì** is placed immediately before the
adverbial (and if the action of the verb in the sentence refers to the past,
with 的 **de** coming either at the end of the sentence following the verb or
between the verb and its object if there is one):

(a) With 的 **de**:

他是一九五九年出生的。
tā *shì* **yī jiǔ wǔ jiǔ nián chūshēng** *de* (time expression)
He was born in 1959.

代表团是前个月到的。
dàibiǎotuán *shì* **qián gè yuè dào** *de* (time expression)
The delegation arrived the month before last.

她是上星期去的伦敦。
tā *shì* **shàng xīngqī qù** *de* **lúndūn** (time expression)
She went to London last week.

孩子们是三点半放的学。
háizimen *shì* **sān diǎn bàn fàng** *de* **xué** (time expression)
It was half past three when the children were let out of school.

她是在上海进的大学。
tā *shì* **zài shànghǎi jìn** *de* **dàxué** (location expression)
She went to the university in Shanghai.

他们是在体育馆打的羽毛球。
tāmen *shì* **zài tǐyùguǎn dǎ** *de* **yǔmáoqiú** (location expression)
They played badminton at the gym.

我们是坐船去的荷兰。

wǒmen *shì* **zuò chuán qù** *de* **hélán** (coverbal phrase 坐船 **zuò chuán** 'by boat')

We went to Holland *by boat.*

她是用毛笔写的标语。

tā *shì* **yòng máobǐ xiě** *de* **biāoyǔ** (coverbal phrase 用毛笔 **yòng máobǐ** 'with a brush')

She wrote the slogan *with a brush.*

我是为你买的这本字典。

wǒ *shì* **wèi nǐ mǎi** *de* **zhè/zhèi běn zìdiǎn** (coverbal phrase 为你 **wé nǐ** 'for you')

I bought this dictionary *for you.*

(b) Without 的 **de**:

我是为你着想。 **wǒ** *shì* **wèi nǐ zhuóxiǎng**

It's for your good./I'm thinking about you/your interests.

(3) If the object is to be highlighted, 是 **shì** is placed before the verb (and if the action of the verb in the sentence refers to the past, 的 **de** comes between the verb and the object):

(a) With 的 **de**:

哥哥是读的博士学位。 **gēge** *shì* **dú** *de* **bóshì xuéwèi**

Elder brother studied for a *PhD.*

导游是说的西班牙语。 **dǎoyóu** *shì* **shuō** *de* **xībānyáyǔ**

The tourist guide was speaking *Spanish.*

我昨天是喝的葡萄酒。 **wǒ zuótiān** *shì* **hē** *de* **pútáojiǔ**

I drank *wine* yesterday.

(b) Without 的 **de**:

我是想去找他。 **wǒ** *shì* **xiǎng qù zhǎo tā**

I really want to go and see him.

Note: Similarly in topic | subject–predicate sentences:

胡萝卜她是刨的丝。 **húluóbo tā** *shì* **páo** *de* **sī**
She shredded the carrots. (*lit.* Carrots she made into shreds.)

E   是 **shì** as an intensifier may, of course, take the negative 不是 **bù shì** and alternative 是不是 **shì bù shì** 'whether . . . or not' forms:

他们是后天到，不是明天到。 **tāmen** *shì* **hòutiān dào** | *bù shì* **míngtiān dào**
They will arrive the day after tomorrow, not tomorrow.

你们是不是走路来的？ **nǐmen** *shì bù shì* **zǒulù lái** *de*
Did you come on foot?

有心脏病的人是不是不能跑步？
yǒu xīnzàngbìng de rén *shì bù shì* **bù néng pǎobù**
Is it true that people who suffer from heart disease cannot go jogging?

F   From the above examples we can see that when the verb in the sentence refers to the past or to the future, it does not carry an aspect marker. If an aspect marker is present, 是 **shì** by itself is sufficient for the intensifying purpose and 的 **de** does not have to occur at the end of the sentence:

是妈妈在看管行李。 *shì* **māma** *zài* **kānguǎn xíngli**
Mother is/was looking after the luggage.

爸爸是戴着一副黑眼镜。 **bàba** *shì* **dài** *zhe* **yī fù hēi yǎnjìng**
Father is/was really wearing a pair of sunglasses.

舅舅是在海里见过鲨鱼。 **jiùjiu** *shì* **zài hǎi li jiàn** *guo* **shāyú**
Uncle has indeed seen sharks in the sea.

是消防员救出了烧伤的弟弟。
shì **xiāofángyuán jiù chū** *le* **shāo shāng de dìdi**
It was the fireman who rescued my younger brother who had been injured/burnt in the fire.

G   是 **shì** may also be used as an assertion indicator. It is placed immediately before a verb or verb phrase, which indicates a habitual action, usually with 的 **de** coming at the end of the sentence:

我是住在巴黎 (的)。 **wǒ** *shì* **zhù zài bālí** (*de*)
I live in Paris.

她是吃素的。 **tā** *shì* **chīsù** *de*
She is a vegetarian. (*lit*. She eats vegetarian food.)

The verb may be preceded by coverbal phrases, modal verbs or negators:

西方人是用刀叉吃饭的。 **xīfāng rén** *shì yòng dāochā* **chīfàn** *de*
Western people eat with *a knife and fork*.

她是会说俄语的。 **tā *shì huì* shuō éyǔ *de***
She *can* speak Russian.

我是不吃肉的。 **wǒ *shì bù* chī ròu *de***
I (really) don't eat meat.

Exercise 20.1

Translate the following sentences into Chinese, deciding whether or not to use 是 **shì**:

1 My younger brother is a postman.
2 That athlete is incredibly tall.
3 It's raining.
4 This is not a computer.
5 Roses are red.
6 They are not engineers.
7 There is a fruit bowl on the table.
8 The fish in the tank are not tropical fish.
9 He is a doctor.
10 This meeting is very important.
11 The lake is very deep.
12 Time's up.
13 It's late.
14 There is a dog over there.

Exercise 20.2

Decide in which of the Chinese sentences below 是 **shì** may be omitted:

1 现在是九点钟。 **xiànzài shì jiǔ diǎn zhōng**
  It is nine o'clock.
2 那些玫瑰是假的。 **nà/nèi xiē méiguì shì jiǎ de**
  Those roses are not real/are artificial.
3 我是明天动身。 **wǒ shì míngtiān dòngshēn**
  I'll set off tomorrow.
4 今天不是星期三。 **jīntiān bù shì xīngqī sān**
  It isn't Wednesday today.
5 奶奶是七十六岁。 **nǎinai shì qī shí liù suì**
  Grandma is seventy-six years old.
6 书桌上是一台电脑。 **shūzhuō shang shì yī tái diànnǎo**
  On the desk is a computer.

7 我借的是英文字典。 **wǒ jiè de shì yīngwén zìdiǎn**
The dictionary I borrowed is an English dictionary.
8 这台电脑是我买的。 **zhè/zhèi tái diànnǎo shì wǒ mǎi de**
I bought this computer.

Exercise 20.3

Rewrite the following Chinese sentences adding emphasis as indicated in the brackets, and using 是 **shì** (. . . 的 **de**) as an intensifier:

1 他前年来英国。 **tā qiánnián lái yīngguó**
He came to Britain the year before last. (Emphasise 'the year before last'.)
2 体操比赛在体育馆举行。 **tǐcāo bǐsài zài tǐyùguǎn jǔxíng**
The gymnastic competition was held at the gymnasium. (Emphasise 'at the gymnasium'.)
3 学生骑自行车去学校。 **xuésheng qí zìxíngchē qù xuéxiào**
The student went to the school by bike. (Emphasise 'by bike'.)
4 护士给病人喂药。 **hùshi gěi bìngrén wèi yào**
The nurse was giving the medicine to the patient. (Emphasise 'the nurse'.)
5 他告诉我这个秘密。 **tā gàosu wǒ zhè/zhèi gè mìmì**
He told me this secret. (Emphasise 'he'.)
6 这双鞋比那双鞋漂亮。 **zhè/zhèi shuāng xié bǐ nà/nèi shuāng xié piàoliang**
This pair of shoes is more attractive than that pair. (Emphasise the truth of the statement.)
7 她愿意做我的朋友。 **tā yuànyì zuò wǒ de péngyou**
She is willing to be my friend. (Emphasise 'is willing'.)
8 我不喜欢游泳。 **wǒ bù xǐhuan yóuyǒng**
I don't like swimming. (Emphasise 'don't like'.)
9 他卖旧书。 **tā mài jiù shū**
He sells old books. (Emphasise 'old books'.)
10 中国人用筷子吃饭。 **zhōngguó rén yòng kuàizi chīfàn**
Chinese people eat with chopsticks. (Emphasise 'with chopsticks'.)
11 她三年前学打字。 **tā sān nián qián xué dǎzì**
She learnt to type three years ago. (Emphasise 'three years ago'.)
12 闹钟把我闹醒了。 **nàozhōng bǎ wǒ nào xǐng le**
The alarm clock woke me up. (Emphasise 'the alarm clock'.)

Exercise 20.4

Reformulate the following Chinese sentences as questions of enquiry using the 是不是 **shì bù shì** format to emphasise the verbal element in each case:

1 你妹妹喜欢看科学幻想小说。
   nǐ mèimei xǐhuan kàn kēxué huànxiǎng xiǎoshuō
   Your younger sister likes reading science fiction.
2 他能用筷子搛菜。 **tā néng yòng kuàizi jiān cài**
   He can pick up food using chopsticks.
3 这件事很重要。 **zhè/zhèi jiàn shì hěn zhòngyào**
   This is terribly important.
4 吃完饭，他帮你洗碗。 **chī wán fàn | tā bāng nǐ xǐ wǎn**
   He helped you to do the washing up after the meal.
5 爸爸前天把篱笆修好了。 **bàba qiántiān bǎ líba xiū hǎo le**
   Father mended the fence the day before yesterday.
6 妈妈昨晚用烤炉烤鸡。 **māma zuó wǎn yòng kǎolú kǎo jī**
   Yesterday evening, mother roasted chicken in the oven.

Exercise 20.5

Translate the following into Chinese:

1 This place was a cinema before, but now it's a club.
2 We did not come by train.
3 That sweater is attractive, but I can't afford it.
4 The car he has bought is a red one.
5 Tomorrow is Friday.
6 My wife is 30 this year.
7 Did you buy that watch in Hong Kong?
8 They are coming to visit us on Saturday, not Friday.
9 I went to university in 1990 but he didn't go till 1992.
10 Are you going to pay for tonight's dinner or am I?

UNIT TWENTY-ONE
The aspect marker 了 le (summary)

A The aspect marker 了 le is placed immediately after the verb to indicate that an action has been completed. This may be expressed in English translation by the perfect or past tense:

我寄了两封信。 **wǒ jì le liǎng fēng xìn**
I sent/I've sent two letters.

我昨天寄了两封信。 **wǒ zuótiān jì le liǎng fēng xìn**
I sent two letters yesterday.

The object of a verb with 了 le is generally modified by a numeral + measure phrase, etc.:

我寄了一封信。 **wǒ jì le yī fēng xìn**
I have sent a letter.

我们开了两个小时的会。 **wǒmen kāi le liǎng gè xiǎoshí de huì**
We spent two hours in a meeting.

他穿了我的大衣。 **tā chuān le wǒ de dàyī**
He put on my overcoat.

If there is an unmodified object after a verb followed by 了 le, the sentence sounds incomplete in Chinese:

*我寄了信。 **wǒ jì le xìn**
(*lit.* I have sent letters.)
*我们开了会。 **wǒmen kāi le huì**
(*lit.* We had a meeting.)

Completion of the sentence can be achieved by adding the sentence particle 了 le or another verbal expression with 了 le:

我写了信了。 **wǒ xiě le xìn le**
I have written the letter.

我写了信就回家了。 **wǒ xiě le xìn jiù huí jiā le**
I went home after I had written the letter. (*lit.* I wrote the letter and (then) went home.)

他锁了门出去了。 **tā suǒ le mén chū qù le**
He locked the door and went out.

她关了灯就睡觉了。 **tā guān le dēng jiù shuìjiào le**
She switched off the light and went straight to bed.

B   Aspect marker 了 **le** can also be used after adjectives, essentially turning them into verbs. This transformation is made clear when the verbs are followed by numeral + measure phrases:

他重了两公斤。 **tā zhòng le liǎng gōngjīn**
He put on two kilograms (in weight).
(*lit.* He has become heavier (to the extent of) two kilograms.)

妹妹今年高了两公分。 **mèimei jīnnián gāo le liǎng gōngfēn**
Younger sister has grown two centimetres taller this year.

If the numeral + measure phrase is not present, and the 了 **le** after the adjective comes at the end of the sentence, the 了 **le** can be viewed as a fusion of the aspect marker and sentence particle 了 **le** (see Unit 8):

树叶绿了。 **shùyè lǜ le**
The leaves on the trees have turned green.

衣服干了。 **yīfu gān le**
The clothes have dried.

天气暖和了。 **tiānqì nuǎnhuo le**
It has got warmer.

经理瘦了。 **jīnglǐ shòu le**
The manager has got thinner.

C   Aspect marker 了 **le** occurs frequently with verbs incorporating result complements:

小偷撬开了我家的门。 **xiǎotōu qiào kāi le wǒ jiā de mén**
A burglar broke into our home. (*lit.* The burglar prised open our home's door.)

弟弟弄脏了大家的衣服。 **dìdi nòng zāng le dàjiā de yīfu**
Younger brother dirtied everybody's clothes.

自行车修好了。 **zìxíngchē xiū hǎo le**
The bicycle has been repaired.

鸡蛋煮熟了。 **jīdàn zhǔ shú/shóu le**
The boiled egg is ready. (*lit.* The egg has been boiled-done.)

Note: In this situation it therefore often coincides with the sentence particle 了 **le** at the end of the sentence, as can be seen from the last two examples.

D   If the verb in a sentence is followed by a complement of direction, the aspect marker 了 **le** may occur either between the verb and the complement or after the complement (see Unit 2):

妹妹哭了起来/哭起来了。 **mèimei kū le qǐlái/kū qǐlái le**
Younger sister started to cry/weep.

消防队员把孩子救了出来/救出来了。
xiāofángduìyuán bǎ háizi jiù le chūlái/jiù chūlái le
The fireman rescued the child (from the house).

E   If the verb in a sentence is followed by a complement of frequency or duration, the aspect marker 了 **le** must occur between the verb and the complement:

那个调皮的孩子被老师批评了几次。
nà/nèi gè tiáopí de háizi bèi lǎoshī pīpíng le jǐ cì
That naughty child was reprimanded several times by the teacher.

那个犯人被关了三年。 **nà/nèi gè fànrén bèi guān le sān nián**
That criminal was imprisoned for three years.

F   了 **le** is used to indicate that something happened briefly in the past, when it is inserted between reduplicated monosyllabic verbs, or between the verb and 一下 **yīxià**, 一会儿 **yīhuìr**, etc.:

她看了看我。 **tā kàn le kàn wǒ**
She glanced at me.

我翻了翻今天的报纸。 **wǒ fān le fān jīntiān de bàozhǐ**
I flicked through today's papers.

我听了一下音乐。 **wǒ tīng le yīxià yīnyuè**
I listened to some music for a while.

我打了一会儿太极拳。 **wǒ dǎ le yīhuìr tàijíquán**
I did some Tai Ji exercises.

G Aspect marker 了 **le** does not occur in the following circumstances:

(1) In statements of habitual action:

她常常喝啤酒。 **tā chángcháng hē píjiǔ**
She often drinks beer.

我每天看报。 **wǒ měi tiān kàn bào**
I read the paper every day.

One cannot say:

*她常常喝了啤酒。 **tā chángcháng hē le píjiǔ**
to translate 'She often drinks beer'.
*我每天看了报。 **wǒ měi tiān kàn le bào**
to translate 'I read the paper every day'.

(2) With coverbs:

我坐公共汽车上学。 **wǒ zuò gōnggòng qìchē shàngxué**
I went to school by bus.

他用毛笔画画儿。 **tā yòng máobǐ huà huàr**
He painted with a Chinese brush.

One cannot say:

*我坐了公共汽车上学。 **wǒ zuò le gōnggòng qìchē shàngxué**
to translate 'I went to school by bus'.
*他用了毛笔画画儿。 **tā yòng le máobǐ huà huàr**
to translate 'He painted with a Chinese brush'.

(3) With the first verb in a serial construction (see Unit 5), particularly when the
first verb is 来 **lái** or 去 **qù**:

她星期天来看我。 **tā xīngqī tiān lái kàn wǒ**
She came to see me on Sunday.

他去海边度假。 **tā qù hǎi biān dùjià**
He has gone to the seaside/coast for a holiday.

One does not usually say:

> *她星期天来了看我。 **tā xīngqī tiān lái le kàn wǒ**
> to translate 'She came to see me on Sunday'.
> *他去了海边度假。 **tā qù le hǎi biān dùjià**
> to translate 'He has gone to the seaside/coast for a holiday'.

(4) With the negator 没 (有) **méi(yǒu)** (see *Basic Chinese*, Unit 17):

One cannot say:

> *我没 (有) 看了京剧。 **wǒ méi(yǒu) kàn le jīngjù**
> (*lit.* I haven't seen any Beijing operas (before).)
> *我没去了上海。 **wǒ méi qù le shànghǎi**
> (*lit.* I didn't go to Shanghai.)

Note: However, the negator 没 (有) **méi(yǒu)** is used with the aspect marker 过 **guo**:

我没看过京剧。 **wǒ méi kàn guo jīngjù**
I have never seen Beijing opera before.
我没去过上海。 **wǒ méi qù guo shànghǎi**
I have never been to Shanghai.

(5) With verbs indicating attitude:

> 我喜欢踢足球。 **wǒ xǐhuan tī zúqiú**
> I like playing football.
>
> 我怕吃海鲜。 **wǒ pà chī hǎixiān**
> I don't like eating seafood.

One cannot say:

> *我喜欢了踢足球。 **wǒ xǐhuan le tī zúqiú**
> to translate 'I like playing football'.
> *我怕了吃海鲜。 **wǒ pà le chī hǎixiān**
> to translate 'I don't like eating seafood'.

(6) With verbs expressing decision, intention, hope, etc.:

> 暑假我打算去旅行。 **shǔjià wǒ dǎsuàn qù lǚxíng**
> I have decided to go travelling during the summer vacation.
>
> 她准备/希望明年换汽车。 **tā zhǔnbèi/xīwàng míngnián huàn qìchē**
> She is planning/hoping to change her car next year.

One cannot say:

*暑假我打算了去旅行。 **shǔjià wǒ dǎsuàn le qù lǚxíng**
to translate 'I have decided to go travelling during the summer vacation'.
*她准备了/希望了明年换汽车。
tā zhǔnbèi le/xīwàng le míngnián huàn qìchē
to translate 'She is planning/hoping to change her car next year'.

Exercise 21.1

Decide which of the Chinese sentences below are incorrect and make corrections where necessary:

1 My shoes are wearing out.
   我的鞋子快破了。 **wǒ de xiézi kuài pò le**
2 I picked some mushrooms.
   我采了蘑菇。 **wǒ cǎi le mógu**
3 He has gone to see the dentist.
   他去了看牙医。 **tā qù le kàn yáyī**
4 His niece often wrote to him.
   他侄女常常给他写了信。 **tā zhínǚ chángcháng gěi tā xiě le xìn**
5 She came to the party.
   她来了参加舞会。 **tā lái le cānjiā wǔhuì**
6 I have never tried lobsters.
   我从没吃了龙虾。 **wǒ cóng méi chī le lóngxiā**
7 He used a broom to sweep up.
   他用了扫帚扫地。 **tā yòng le sàozhou sǎo dì**
8 I went travelling on my bike.
   我骑了自行车旅行。 **wǒ qí le zìxíngchē lǚxíng**
9 The grass is dry now.
   草干了。 **cǎo gān le**
10 I have never studied Japanese before.
   我没学过日语。 **wǒ méi xué guo rìyǔ**
11 I used to like reading novels.
   我过去爱了看小说。 **wǒ guòqù ài le kàn xiǎoshuō**
12 He decided to buy a computer.
   他准备了买电脑。 **tā zhǔnbèi le mǎi diànnǎo**
13 The accountant counted some money.
   会计数数了钱。 **kuàijì shǔ shǔ le qián**
14 The teacher glanced at her watch.
   老师看一下了手表。 **lǎoshī kàn yīxià le shǒubiǎo**
15 The gardener did some watering.
   花匠浇了浇花。 **huājiàng jiāo le jiāo huā**

Exercise 21.2

Complete the Chinese translations below, most of which require the use of 了 **le** as both aspect marker and sentence particle:

1 Younger brother has got his clothes all wet.
  弟弟的衣服全 ———— 。 **dìdi de yīfu quán** ————

2 The leaves have turned brown.
  树叶 ———— 。 **shùyè** ————

3 The rainfall here was ten centimetres less this year.
  今年这儿的降雨量 (比去年) ———— 十公分。
  jīnnián zhèr de jiàngyǔliàng (bǐ qùnián) ———— **shí gōngfēn**

4 The meal is ready.
  饭 ———— 。 **fàn** ————

5 The lock has been prised open.
  锁被 ———— 。 **suǒ bèi** ————

6 The door has been locked.
  门 ———— 。 **mén** ————

7 The light has been switched on.
  灯 ———— 。 **dēng** ————

8 The flower pot was broken by younger sister.
  花盆让妹妹给 ———— 。 **huāpén ràng mèimei gěi** ————

9 She has recovered from her illness.
  她的病 ———— 。 **tā de bìng** ————

10 Grandpa is getting very old.
   爷爷 ———— 。 **yéye** ————

11 Uncle (on father's side) has fallen ill.
   叔叔 ———— 。 **shūshu** ————

12 There is a full moon again.
   月亮又 ———— 。 **yuèliang yòu** ————

13 The watch is broken.
   手表 ———— 。 **shǒubiǎo** ————

14 The flowers have withered.
   花儿 ———— 。 **huār** ————

15 The letter was posted.
   信 ———— 。 **xìn** ————

16 The floor has been swept.
   地 ———— 。 **dì** ————

17 Everybody has arrived.
   人人 ———— 。 **rénrén** ————

18 The meeting has ended.
   会 ———— 。 **huì** ————

19 The car has been repaired.
   汽车 ———— 。 **qìchē** ————

20 Somebody has dirtied the carpet.

地毯给人 ———。 **dìtǎn gěi rén** ———

Exercise 21.3

Translate the following sentences into Chinese, paying attention to the need for an aspect marker or a sentence particle 了 **le** or both:

1 I have written two letters.
2 My friend bought today's paper.
3 The patient had some medicine this morning.
4 The window was broken.
5 He has grown three centimetres.
6 The television has been repaired.
7 The students have graduated.
8 We visited the museum.
9 I studied Chinese for three years.
10 I have been studying Chinese for three years.
11 We're leaving this afternoon.
12 I don't drink beer any more.

Exercise 21.4

Translate the following passage into English:

天黑了。太阳已经下了了山。小鸟回到了自己的窝里。 **tiān hēi le | tàiyáng yǐjing xià le shān | xiǎo niǎo huí dào le zìjǐ de wō li** 月亮升起来了。湖面上吹来了一阵风。四周的树沙沙地响了一下。 **yuèliang shēng qǐlái le | húmiàn shang chuī lái le yī zhèn fēng | sìzhōu de shù shāshā de xiǎng le yīxià** 这时候，爸爸回来了。 **zhè/zhèi shíhou | bàba huí lái le** 他进了门，在门毯上擦了擦鞋，脱了帽子，挂好了大衣，回过头来吻了吻我，就到厨房里去了。 **tā jìn le mén | zài méntǎn shang cā le cā xié | tuō le màozi | guà hǎo le dàyī | huí guò tóu lái wěn le wěn wǒ | jiù dào chúfáng li qù le** 妈妈已经为他准备好了饭菜。爸爸坐下来，喝了一口茶，朝妈妈笑了笑，就拿起了刀叉，大口大口地吃起来了。 **māma yǐjing wèi tā zhǔnbèi hǎo le fàncài | bàba zuò xiàlái | hē le yī kǒu chá | cháo māma xiào le xiào | jiù ná qǐ le dāochā | dà kǒu dà kǒu de chī qǐlái le** 不到一会儿，爸爸吃完了饭，回到大厅里。他把我叫到他的身边，问：'你做完了功课没有？你想看电视吗？' 我点了点头，他就走过去，把电视机开了。这时候妈妈已经洗了碗，抹干净（了）桌子，走出（了）厨房，坐下来跟我们一起看电视了。 **bù dào yīhuìr | bàba chī wán le fàn | huí dǎo dàtīng li | tā bǎ wǒ jiào dào tā de shēnbiān | wèn | nǐ zuò wán le gōngkè méiyǒu | nǐ xiǎng kàn diànshì ma | wǒ diǎn le diǎn tóu | tā jiù zǒu guòqù | bǎ diànshìjī kāi le | zhè/zhèi shíhou māma yǐjing xǐ le wǎn | mā gānjìng (le) zhuōzi | zǒu chū (le) chúfáng | zuò xiàlái gēn wǒmen yīqǐ kàn diànshì le**

UNIT TWENTY-TWO

The aspect markers 着 zhe, (正) 在 (zhèng)zài and 过 guo (summary)

A 着 zhe is an aspect marker placed directly after the verb to indicate a range of meanings related to a continuing state or action:

(1) A continuing state resulting from an action:

> 她戴着一副金丝眼镜。 **tā dài zhe yī fù jīnsī yǎnjìng**
> She is/was wearing a pair of gold-rimmed spectacles. (The action of putting on the glasses resulted in her wearing them.)
> 他穿着一双运动鞋。 **tā chuān zhe yī shuāng yùndòngxié**
> He is/was wearing a pair of sports shoes.
> 她围着一条红围巾。 **tā wéi zhe yī tiáo hóng wéijīn**
> She is/was wearing a red scarf.
> 她披着一件风衣。 **tā pī zhe yī jiàn fēngyī**
> She has/had an overcoat round her shoulders.
> 他举着一面旗。 **tā jǔ zhe yī miàn qí**
> He is/was holding up a flag.
> 她背着一个背包。 **tā bēi zhe yī gè bèibāo**
> She is/was carrying a rucksack.

(2) Preceded by a 在 **zài** location phrase to express a continuing state or action in a particular place. In these cases, if the verb in the sentence has an object, 着 **zhe** may be dropped:

> 她在沙发上坐着。 **tā zài shāfā shang zuò zhe**
> She is/was sitting on the sofa.

> 鱼在玻璃缸里游着。 **yú zài bōligāng li yóu zhe**
> The fish are/were swimming in the glass tank.

> 邮递员在门口等着。 **yóudìyuán zài ménkǒu děng zhe**
> The postman is/was waiting at the door.

游客们在海滩上晒 (着) 太阳。
yóukèmen zài hǎitān shang shài (zhe) tàiyáng
Thc tourists are/were sunbathing on the beach.

羊群在草地上吃草。 **yángqún zài cǎodì shang chī cǎo**
The flock of sheep is/was feeding on the grass.

(3) After a location phrase to indicate not only the fact that something exists, but also, to some extent, the manner of its existence:

广场上竖立着一座铜像。 **guǎngchǎng shang shùlì zhe yī zuò tóngxiàng**
A bronze statue stands/stood in the square.

屋里亮着灯。 **wū li liàng zhe dēng**
There is/was a light shining in the room. (*lit.* In the room was shining a lamp.)

桌子上放着一台收音机。 **zhuōzi shang fàng zhe yī tái shōuyīnjī**
There is/was a radio on the desk. (*lit.* On the table is/was placed a radio.)

屋檐下挂着不少灯笼。 **wūyán xià guà zhe bù shǎo dēnglóng**
There are/were a lot of lanterns hanging from the eaves.

Note: Negative sentences are rarely found with verbs suffixed with 着 **zhe** unless the speaker/ writer wishes to emphasise the fact that what should have been the case is obviously not the case at the time referred to:

这回屋檐下没挂着灯笼。 **zhè/zhèi huí wūyán xià méi guà zhe dēnglóng**
This time there were no lanterns hanging from the eaves.

她并没有戴着金丝眼镜。 **tā bìng méiyǒu dài zhe jīnsī yǎnjìng**
She is/was certainly not wearing a pair of gold-rimmed spectacles.

他没在图书馆看书。 **tā méi zài túshūguǎn kànshū**
He is/was not reading in the library.

(4) One action occurring at the same time as another:

他呼喊着走进屋子。 **tā hūhǎn zhe zǒu jìn wūzi**
He came into the room, shouting.

她提着皮包下了飞机。 **tā tí zhe píbāo xià le fēijī**
She got off the plane carrying a briefcase.

他哼着曲子走了。 **tā hēng zhe qǔzi zǒu le**
He left humming a tune.

和尚敲着木鱼念经。 **héshang qiāo zhe mùyú niànjīng**
The monk recited the scriptures while tapping a wooden fish (a percussion instrument used by Buddhist monks when reciting scriptures).

他冒着大雨跑了出去。 **tā mào zhe dà yǔ pǎo le chūqù**
He went/ran out, braving the heavy rain.

(5) With certain coverbs and prepositions:

邻居隔着树篱跟我打招呼。 **línjū gé zhe shùlí gēn wǒ dǎ zhāohu**
My neighbour greeted me across the hedge.

汽车沿着大路疾驶。 **qìchē yán zhe dà lù jíshǐ**
The car was speeding down/along the motorway.

护士朝着病人笑了笑。 **hùshi cháo zhe bìngrén xiào le xiào**
The nurse smiled at the patient. (*lit.* facing the patient)

(6) A continuing action leading to an involuntary result (i.e. verb + 着 **zhe** repeated and followed by another verb or verb phrase indicating the consequence):

她说着说着哭起来了。 **tā shuō zhe shuō zhe kū qǐlái le**
As she was talking she began to cry.

她哭着哭着睡着了。 **tā kū zhe kū zhe shuì zháo le**
She cried and cried until she fell asleep.

她睡着睡着做起梦来。 **tā shuì zhe shuì zhe zuò qǐ mèng lái**
As she slept she began to dream.

孩子跑着跑着摔了一交。 **háizi pǎo zhe pǎo zhe shuāi le yī jiāo**
As the child was running she tripped and fell.

(7) With a monosyllabic adjective and followed by 呢 **ne** to emphasise a particular state of affairs:

市中心的广场大着呢！ **shìzhōngxīn de guǎngchǎng dà zhe ne**
The square in the city centre is very big indeed!

这道题难着呢！ **zhè/zhèi dào tí nán zhe ne**
This question is really very difficult!

他心里急着呢！ **tā xīn li jí zhe ne**
He (*lit.* in his heart) is extremely anxious.

B   To indicate continuation, persistence or consistent repetition of an action over a period of time, the aspect marker to use is (正) 在 (**zhèng**)**zài**, which is placed immediately before the verb with an optional 着 **zhe** following the verb:

小溪在淙淙地流 (着)。 **xiǎo xī zài cóngcóng de liú (zhe)**
The stream was flowing gently.

钟在滴答滴答地响 (着)。 **zhōng zài dīdā dīdā de xiǎng (zhe)**
The clock is ticking away.

蟋蟀在不停地叫 (着)。 **xīshuài zài bù tíng de jiào (zhe)**
The cricket is chirping away.

同学们正在做 (着) 实验。 **tóngxuémen zhèngzài zuò (zhe) shíyàn**
The students are/were doing experiments.

孩子们正在做功课。 **háizimen zhèngzài zuò gōngkè**
The children are/were doing their lessons (at this very moment).

大家正在热烈地议论 (着) 这件事。
tàjiā zhèngzài rèliè de yìlùn (zhe) zhè/zhèi jiàn shì
Everybody is/was engaged in a heated discussion about this matter.

As a general rule, 正在 **zhèngzài** is more emphatic than 在 **zài**. Sometimes the sentence particle 呢 **ne** may be incorporated at the end of the statement to emphasise further the progress of an action or activity:

她在弹钢琴呢。 **tā zài tán gāngqín ne**
She is/was playing the piano.

他们正在谈论 (着) 这件事呢。
tāmen zhèngzài tánlùn (zhe) zhè/zhèi jiàn shì ne
They are/were discussing this matter at the moment.

C   过 **guo** occurs after a verb or adjective to express a past experience or state:

(1) Past experience (with a verb):

我参观过那个古堡。 **wǒ cānguān guo nà/nèi gè gǔbǎo**
I have visited that castle before.

我见过她。 **wǒ jiàn guo tā**
I've met her (before).

他当过飞行员。 **tā dāng guo fēixíngyuán**
He was once a pilot.

这个问题他们讨论过三次。 **zhè/zhèi gè wèntí tāmen tǎolùn guo sān cì**
They have discussed this problem three times.

(2) A past situation (with an adjective) which may in fact have changed:

这个孩子以前胖过，现在瘦了。
zhè/zhèi gè háizi yǐqián pàng guo | xiànzài shòu le
This child used to be fat, but he is (quite) slim/thin now.

他从来没有这么认真过。 **tā cónglái méiyǒu zhème rènzhēn guo**
He has never been so conscientious.

(3) A verb or adjective followed by 过 **guo** is always negated with 没 (有) **méi** (**yǒu**), not 不 **bù**:

我没吃过龙虾。 **wǒ méi chī guo lóngxiā**
I have never tried lobsters.

我没(有)穿过牛仔裤。 **wǒ méi(yǒu) chuān guo niúzǎikù**
I have never worn jeans.

他的病没好过。 **tā de bìng méi hǎo guo**
He has never recovered from his illness.

One cannot say:

*我不去过非洲。 **wǒ bù qù guo fēizhōu**
(*lit.* I have never been to Africa.)

D   The differences between the aspect markers 过 **guo** and 了 **le** are:

(1) 了 **le** emphasises completion, thus referring to an action on a particular occasion while 过 **guo** emphasises experience, thus referring to actions against a more general historical background:

我吃了两碗米饭。 **wǒ chī le liǎng wǎn mǐfàn**
I ate two bowls of rice.

我吃过米饭。 **wǒ chī guo mǐfàn**
I have eaten rice before. (i.e. I know what it tastes like.)

(2) 了 **le** is dropped when negated by 没 (有) **méi(yǒu)** but 过 **guo** is not:

我没 (有) 吃龙虾。 **wǒ méi(yǒu) chī lóngxiā**
I didn't eat/touch the lobster.

我没 (有) 吃过龙虾。 **wǒ méi(yǒu) chī guo lóngxiā**
I have never eaten lobsters before.

Exercise 22.1

Complete the Chinese sentences below using 着 **zhe**, (正) 在 **(zhèng)zài**, 过 **guo** or 了 **le** as appropriate:

1 以前我去 _____ 他家，今天他来 _____ 我家。
   yǐqián wǒ qù _____ **tā jiā | jīntiān tā lái** _____ **wǒ jiā**
   I have been to his house before, and today he came to my place.
2 昨天她穿 _____ 一件长风衣，今天穿 _____ 一件短风衣。
   zuótiān tā chuān _____ **yī jiàn cháng fēngyī | jīntiān chuān** _____
   yī jiàn duǎn fēngyī
   She was wearing a long coat yesterday but she's wearing a short one today.
3 病人 _____ _____ 吃药。 **bìngrén** _____ **chī yào**
   At present, the patient is taking medicine/having medication.
4 广场上竖立 _____ 一座石像。
   guǎngchǎng shang shùlì _____ **yī zuò shíxiàng**
   A stone statue stands in the square.
5 过道里亮 _____ 灯。 **guòdào li liàng** _____ **dēng**
   The lights are on in the corridor.
6 护士端 _____ 药进 _____ 病房。
   hùshi duān _____ **yào jìn** _____ **bìngfáng**
   The nurse came into the sickroom with some medicines.
7 同学隔 _____ 马路跟我打招呼。
   tóngxué gé _____ **mǎlù gēn wǒ dǎ zhāohu**
   My classmate greeted me from across the road.
8 我丈夫没去 _____ 非洲。 **wǒ zhàngfu méi qù** _____ **fēizhōu**
   My husband has never been to Africa.
9 爷爷病 _____，现在好 _____。 **yéye bìng** _____ **| xiànzài hǎo** _____
   My grandfather was ill but he's better now.
10 她 _____ _____ 弹 _____ 吉他唱歌。 **tā** _____ **tán** _____ **jítā chàng gē**
    She is singing and playing the guitar.
11 我们去看他的时候，他 _____ _____ 看电视。
    wǒmen qù kàn tā de shíhou | tā _____ **kàn diànshì**
    When we went to see him, he was just watching television.
12 他们 _____ _____ 做什么？他们 _____ _____ 下棋 (_____)。
    tāmen _____ **zuò shénme | tāmen** _____ **xiàqí (**_____**)**
    What are they doing? They're playing chess.

Exercise 22.2

The following Chinese sentences all contain errors. Make the necessary correction in each case:

1 汽车沿了大路疾驶。 **qìchē yán le dà lù jíshǐ**
   The car was speeding down the motorway.
2 学生们打着篮球。 **xuéshengmen dǎ zhe lánqiú**
   The students were playing basketball.
3 奶奶戴了一顶帽子。 **nǎinai dài le yī dǐng màozi**
   Grandma was wearing a hat.
4 她说了说了笑了起来。 **tā shuō le shuō le xiào le qǐlái**
   As she spoke she began to laugh.
5 我去了那个古堡。 **wǒ qù le nà/nèi gè gǔbǎo**
   I have visited that castle before.
6 经理从来没有跟我们生了气。 **jīnglǐ cónglái méi(yǒu) gēn wǒmen shēng le qì**
   The manager has never got angry with us.
7 这回爸爸没穿了牛仔裤。 **zhè/zhèi huí bàba méi chuān le niúzǎikù**
   This time my father was not wearing jeans.
8 我没有学了化学。 **wǒ méi(yǒu) xué le huàxué**
   I have never studied chemistry.
9 她买过很多激光唱片。 **tā mǎi guo hěn duō jīguāng chàngpiàn**
   She has bought a lot of compact discs.
10 我缝着衣服。 **wǒ féng zhe yīfu**
   I am sewing.

Exercise 22.3

Rewrite the Chinese sentences below using adjective + 着 **zhe** + 呢 **ne**:

1 这个运动员非常高。 **zhè/zhèi gè yùndòngyuán fēicháng gāo**
   That athlete is extremely tall.
2 我心里很着急。 **wǒ xīn li hěn zhāojí**
   I am very anxious.
3 我们的老师很严。 **wǒmen de lǎoshī hěn yán**
   Our teacher is very strict.
4 他有很多很多朋友。 **tā yǒu hěn duō hěn duō péngyou**
   He has lots of friends.
5 那道题目很难。 **nà/nèi dào tímù hěn nán**
   That question is very difficult.
6 这件事可真怪。 **zhè/zhèi jiàn shì kě zhēn guài**
   This is a really strange business./This is really strange.

Exercise 22.4

Translate the following into Chinese:

1 Have you ever seen Peking opera?
2 They were sitting there waiting for the lawyer to arrive.
3 There is someone outside smoking a cigar.
4 She walked in smiling.
5 There were several political posters hanging on the wall.
6 He ran and ran until his legs ached.
7 I have never been so happy.
8 I was once a newspaper reporter. (新闻记者 **xīnwén jìzhě** 'newspaper reporter')
9 When I went to see him, he was watching television.
10 What is that man doing?

UNIT TWENTY-THREE
The idiomatic uses of 来着 **lái zhe**, 呗 **bei**, 嘛 **ma**, 罢了 **bà le**, 么 **me** and 吧 **ba**

A 来着 **lái zhe** is used in spoken Chinese at the end of a sentence to convey two separate meanings:

(1) To indicate that the action of the verb has only just taken place:

> 她刚才去学开车来着。 **tā gāngcái qù xué kāichē lái zhe**
> She has just been for her driving lesson.

> 上午有人找你来着。 **shàngwǔ yǒu rén zhǎo nǐ lái zhe**
> Someone came to look for you just this morning.

> 他给谁打电话来着？ **tā gěi shéi/shuí dǎ diànhuà lái zhe**
> Who did he ring just now?

(2) To form questions which indicate that the speaker once had knowledge of the answer, but is unable to recall the information exactly at the moment of speaking:

> 你刚才说什么来着？ **nǐ gāngcái shuō shénme lái zhe**
> What did you say just now? (I can't quite remember.)

> 你的电话号码是多少来着？ **nǐ de diànhuà hàomǎ shì duōshǎo lái zhe**
> What's your telephone number again?

B Both 嘛 **ma** and 呗 **bei** occur at the end of a statement implying that what is being said is obvious. 嘛 **ma** expresses a sense of contradiction, whereas 呗 **bei** conveys a tone of self-assertion:

> 这很简单嘛！ **zhè hěn jiǎndān ma**
> (But) this is very simple. (How could you think otherwise?)
> 这很简单呗！ **zhè hěn jiǎndān bei**
> This is very simple. (You don't need me to tell you that!)

我没生她的气，她是我朋友嘛！
wǒ méi shēng tā de qì | tā shì wǒ péngyou ma
Of course I wasn't angry with her, she is my friend. (Despite what you/others might think.)

我没生她的气，她是我朋友呗！
wǒ méi shēng tā de qì | tā shì wǒ péngyou bei
I wasn't angry with her. She is my friend. (Don't you realise?)

你为什么买这么贵的鞋？ **nǐ wèi shénme mǎi zhème guì de xié**
Why did you buy such expensive shoes?

我喜欢嘛！ **wǒ xǐhuan ma**
I like them. (Why shouldn't I?)

我喜欢呗！ **wǒ xǐhuan bei**
Because I like them. (That's all./That's that.)

C 罢了 **bà le** is generally used at the end of a sentence which contains 不过 **bùguò**, 只是 **zhǐshì** 'only' or 无非 **wúfēi** 'only', 'just', 'simply' to dismiss something as unimportant:

我只是开玩笑罢了。 **wǒ zhǐshì kāi wánxiào bà le**
I was only joking.

她不过想躺一下罢了。 **tā bùguò xiǎng tǎng yīxià bà le**
She just wanted to lie down for a while.

他无非着了点儿凉罢了。 **tā wúfēi zháo le diǎnr liáng bà le**
He has just caught a cold, that's all.

D 么 **me** introduces a pause when the speaker needs time to think and wants to call attention to a particular point:

这件事么，我记不起来了。 **zhè/zhèi jiàn shì me | wǒ jì bu qǐlái le**
Oh that? . . . I can't really remember much about it.

我的意见么，很简单。 **wǒ de yìjian me | hěn jiǎndān**
My suggestion . . . is very simple.

你累了么，就早点休息吧。 **nǐ lèi le me | jiù zǎo diǎn xiūxi ba**
You're tired? . . . Well go to bed early then.

E 吧 **ba**, in addition to being a sentence particle indicating a suggestion (see *Basic Chinese*, Unit 20), also has some colloquial usages:

(1) To express indecision, when available courses of action all seem impossible or problematic:

去吧，没空；不去吧，不好意思。
qù ba | méi kòng | bù qù ba | bù hǎo yìsi
I don't really have time to go, but I'd be embarrassed if I didn't.

到餐馆去吃吧，太贵；自己做饭吃吧，太累。
dào cānguǎn qù chī ba | tài guì | zìjǐ zuòfàn chī ba | tài lèi
It's too expensive to eat out, but I'm too tired to cook.

(2) To convey a tone of resignation in the pattern 'verb/adjective + 就 **jiù** + the same verb/adjective + 吧 **ba**, + clause':

丢就丢了吧，再买一个。 **diū jiù diū le ba | zài mǎi yī gè**
If it's lost, it's lost; I'll just have to buy another one.

喝就喝吧，可别喝醉了。 **hē jiù hē ba | kě bié hē zuì le**
If you want to drink, drink, but don't get drunk.

瘦就瘦吧，反正没病。 **shōu jiù shōu ba | fǎnzhèng méi bìng**
If I'm thin, I'm thin, so long as I'm not ill.

Exercise 23.1

Complete the following Chinese sentences with 来着 **lái zhe**, 罢了 **bà le**, 呗 **bei** or 嘛 **ma** as appropriate:

1 他刚才去打电话 _____ _____。 **tā gāngcái qù dǎ diànhuà** _____
   He has just been to make a phone call.
2 他只是打了一个电话 _____ _____。 **tā zhǐshì dǎ le yī gè diànhuà** _____
   He was only making a phone call.
3 她家的新地址是什么 _____ _____？
   tā jiā de xīn dìzhǐ shì shénme _____
   What's her new address again?
4 那件事我忘了 _____。 **nà/nèi jiàn shì wǒ wàng le** _____
   I have forgotten that matter and that's that.
5 我愿意去农场工作 _____。 **wǒ yuànyì qù nóngchǎng gōngzuò** _____
   I'm willing to go and work on the farm, and that's all there is to it.
6 她不工作，无非是她爸爸有钱 _____ _____。
   tā bù gōngzuò | wúfēi shì tā bàba yǒuqián _____
   She needn't work, because her father is rich, that's all.
7 这条路去海边最近 _____。 **zhè/zhèi tiáo lù qù hǎi biān zuì jìn** _____
   Of course this is the quickest way to the seaside, you know that.

8 我信不过他 ———— 。 **wǒ xìn bu guò tā** ————
  I don't trust him, that's all.
9 会计说什么 ———— ————? **kuàijì shuō shénme** ————
  What was it the accountant just said?
10 这个孩子只是有点咳嗽 ———— ————。
  zhè/zhèi gè háizi zhǐshì yǒu diǎn késou ————
  This child has just got a bit of a cough, that's all.

Exercise 23.2

Rewrite the Chinese sentences below using 么 **me** or 吧 **ba** to match the English:

1 这个问题很复杂。 **zhè/zhèi gè wèntí hěn fùzá**
  This question is . . . very complicated.
2 你饿了就先吃。 **nǐ è le jiù xiān chī**
  If you are hungry, then eat.
3 去看电影，没钱；待在家里，无聊。
  qù kàn diànyǐng | méi qián | dāi zài jiā li | wúliáo
  As for going to the cinema, I haven't got any money but staying at home is
  so boring.
4 坐飞机危险；坐轮船太慢。 **zuò fēijī wēixiǎn | zuò lúnchuán tài màn**
  As for going by air, it's dangerous but going by ship takes too long.
5 他当领导不行。 **tā dāng lǐngdǎo bù xíng**
  For him to be a leader . . . won't do.
6 让我去我就去。 **ràng wǒ qù wǒ jiù qù**
  If you ask me to go . . . , I'll go.

Exercise 23.3

There are errors in all the Chinese sentences below. Make the necessary corrections in each case:

1 你要走就走么，我也没(有)办法。 **nǐ yào zǒu jiù zǒu me | wǒ yě méi(yǒu) bànfǎ**
  If you are going, go; there's nothing I can do about it.
2 碎就碎了嘛，再买一个新的呗。 **suì jiù suì le ma | zài mǎi yī gè xīn de bei**
  If it's broken, it's broken; just go and buy another one.
3 他当然会做，他是数学家吧。 **tā dāngrán huì zuò | tā shì shùxuéjiā ba**
  Of course he can do it. He's a mathematician.
4 这次考得不好，以后努力么。 **zhè/zhèi cì kǎo de bù hǎo | yǐhòu nǔlì me**
  I didn't get a good mark this time so I'll have to put in a bit more effort.
5 那很容易么。 **nà hěn róngyì me**
  But that's no problem, is it?
6 这个人吧，我记不起来了。 **zhè/zhèi gè rén ba | wǒ jì bu qǐlái le**
  That person? . . . I'm sorry, I can't really remember her/him.

Exercise 23.4

Translate the following into Chinese:

1 Now what were you saying?
2 I was just going to ask a question; that's all.
3 To say I won would be arrogant; to say I didn't would be untrue.
4 If you aren't willing to talk to me . . . , I won't come again.
5 If it's expensive, it's expensive; anyway you can't afford it.
6 He is the manager of this company! (i.e. not an ordinary member of staff)
7 I just wanted to make you happy.
8 He can speak Chinese very well! (i.e. I'm angry that you seem to disagree.)

UNIT TWENTY-FOUR
The idiomatic uses of 呢 **ne**

A 呢 **ne** can be used in a number of different question structures:

(1) It is often placed at the end of a question-word question to introduce a tone of slight impatience or reflection (e.g. 'I wonder . . .'):

> 你想喝点什么呢？ **nǐ xiǎng hē diǎn shénme ne**
> What would you like to drink then? (slight impatience)
> Let me see, what you would like to drink? (reflection)

> 他上哪儿去了呢？ **tā shàng nǎr qù le ne**
> I wonder where he has gone? (reflection)
> Where's he off to then?/Where is he then? (slight impatience)

(2) It occurs in alternative (还是 **háishi**) questions. It is usually placed at the end of each clause, but may sometimes be omitted after the last clause:

> 你想喝茶呢，还是想喝咖啡呢？
> **nǐ xiǎng hē chá ne | háishi xiǎng hē kāfēi ne**
> Would you like tea or coffee?

> 她喜欢去游泳呢，还是去爬山呢，还是在家里睡觉呢？
> **tā xǐhuan qù yóuyǒng ne | háishi qù pá shān ne | háishi zài jiā li shuìjiào ne**
> Does she want to go swimming or hillwalking, or stay at home and sleep?

> 你想骑车去呢，还是想开车去？
> **nǐ xiǎng qí chē qù ne | háishi xiǎng kāichē qù**
> Do you want to go there by bicycle or by car?

(3) It may also be placed at the end of affirmative-negative questions:

> 你今晚去不去朋友家呢？ **nǐ jīn wǎn qù bù qù péngyou jiā ne**
> Are you going to your friend's house tonight?

我可不可以在这儿抽烟呢？ **wǒ kě bù kěyǐ zài zhèr chōuyān ne**
May I smoke here?

这个句子对不对呢？ **zhè/zhèi gè jùzi dùi bù dùi ne**
Is this sentence correct?

(4) It is sometimes used with a noun or pronoun to form an abbreviated question with the meaning 'how/what about . . . ?'. This formulation is possible only when the context has already been made clear:

我喝咖啡，你呢？ **wǒ hē kāfēi | nǐ ne**
I would like some coffee. How about you?

大人去跳舞，孩子们呢？ **dàrén qù tiàowǔ | háizimen ne**
The adults are going dancing. What about the children?

他是教师，他的朋友呢？ **tā shì jiàoshī | tā de péngyou ne**
He is a teacher. What does his friend do?

今天不行，明天呢？ **jīntiān bù xíng | míngtiān ne**
Today won't do, what about tomorrow?

Note: When the context has not been specified, noun/pronoun + 呢 **ne** will always mean 'Where is/are . . . ?':

妈妈，我的鞋子呢？ **māma | wǒ de xiézi ne**
Mum, where are my shoes?

照相机呢？ **zhàoxiàngjī ne**
Where is the camera?

你的朋友呢？ **nǐ de péngyou ne**
Where is your friend?

(5) It may be placed at the end of questions containing 怎么 **zénme**/怎么这么 **zénme zhème** + adjectival/verbal predicate to create an exclamation to the effect of 'How/Why on earth . . . ?'/'How come . . . ?':

饭怎么煮焦了呢？ **fàn zénme zhǔ jiāo le ne**
How come the rice is burnt?

外面怎么下起雨来了呢？ **wàimian zénme xià qǐ yǔ lái le ne**
Oh no, it's raining! (*lit.* How come it's started to rain outside?)

这孩子怎么这么瘦呢？ **zhè háizi zénme zhème shòu ne**
Why on earth is this child so thin?

(6) It may be placed at the end of negative questions containing 为什么 **wèi shénme** to produce the rhetorical effect of 'Why don't you . . . ?', etc., which is equivalent to a suggestion:

你为什么不去呢？ **nǐ wèi shénme bù qù ne**
Why don't you go?
咱们为什么不马上开始呢？ **zánmen wèi shénme bù mǎshàng kāishǐ ne**
Why don't we start right now?

B 呢 **ne** also occurs frequently in spoken Chinese with statements under the following circumstances, in each case expressing a particular tone:

(1) To affirm a continuous state or action (with a somewhat challenging tone):

我在写信呢！ **wǒ zài xiě xìn ne**
(Can't you see) I'm writing a letter!

爸爸在喂猫呢！ **bàba zài wèi māo ne**
Dad is feeding the cat. (What did you think he was doing?)

屋子里有人在睡觉呢！ **wūzi li yǒu rén zài shuìjiào ne**
There's someone sleeping in the room! (Can't you stop making that kind of noise?)

衣服在外面晾着呢！ **yīfu zài wàimian liàng zhe ne**
The clothes are being hung outside to dry! (That's where they are. What else would you expect?, etc.)

(2) To indicate a surmise (with adverbials like 可能 **kěnéng** 'possible', 说不定 **shuō bu dìng** 'not too sure if . . .'):

客人可能已经走了呢。 **kèren kěnéng yǐjing zǒu le ne**
The visitor(s) might have already left.

他的病说不定已经好了呢。 **tā de bìng shuō bu dìng yǐjing hǎo le ne**
He might be well again./He might have got over his illness.
(*lit.* His illness not-for-sure has already recovered.)

(3) To imply sudden realisation/enlightenment (often with disbelief), regularly with 还 **hái** 'still':

她冬天还穿着短裙子呢！ **tā dōngtiān hái chuān zhe duǎn qúnzi ne**
She wears a short skirt even in winter! (I can't believe it!)

他提升了。怪不得这么高兴呢！
tā tíshēng le | guàibude zhème gāoxìng ne
He has been promoted. No wonder he's so happy.

(4) To convey sarcasm (reversing the meaning of the basic statement), often
with adverbials like 才 **cái** 'only then':

我才相信你呢！ **wǒ cái xiāngxìn nǐ ne**
I am the one who will believe you. (i.e. Don't you expect me to believe
you.)

你才理他呢！ **nǐ cái lǐ tā ne**
You're the only one who will listen to him! (i.e. If I were you, I would
certainly ignore him.)

Exercise 24.1

Rewrite the Chinese sentences below using the most simple noun/pronoun + 呢
ne structure:

1 你的玩具熊在哪儿？ **nǐ de wánjùxióng zài nǎr**
   Where is your teddy-bear?
2 笔在这儿。哪儿有纸？ **bǐ zài zhèr | nǎr yǒu zhǐ**
   The pen's here. Where's the paper?
3 我晚上十点钟睡觉，你晚上几点睡？
   wǒ wǎnshang shí diǎn zhōng shuìjiào | nǐ wǎnshang jǐ diǎn shuì
   I go to bed at ten o'clock. What time do you go to bed?
4 我的眼镜放在哪儿了呢？ **wǒ de yǎnjìng fàng zài nǎr le ne**
   Where are my glasses?
5 你在做实验。他们在做什么？ **nǐ zài zuò shíyàn | tāmen zài zuò shénme**
   You were doing experiments. What were they doing?
6 你侄儿到哪儿去了？ **nǐ zhír dào nǎr qù le**
   Where has your nephew gone?

Exercise 24.2

Translate the following Chinese sentences into English:

1 你姐姐会做饭，你自己呢？ **nǐ jiějie huì zuòfàn | nǐ zìjǐ ne**
2 你打算进城去呢，还是回家去？
   nǐ dǎsuàn jìnchéng qù ne | háishi huí jiā qù
3 我可 (以) 不可以坐在这儿呢？ **wǒ kě(yǐ) bù kěyǐ zuò zài zhèr ne**
4 哥哥，我的笔记本呢？ **gēge | wǒ de bǐjìběn ne**

5 新来的主任在开会呢。 **xīn lái·de zhǔrèn zài kāihuì ne**
6 火车站离这儿远得很呢。 **huǒchēzhàn lí zhèr yuǎn de hěn ne**
7 我的钱包怎么不见了呢？ **wǒ de qiánbāo zénme bù jiàn le ne**
8 你为什么不自己动手呢？ **nǐ wèi shénme bù zìjǐ dòngshǒu ne**
9 我才管他呢。 **wǒ cái guǎn tā ne**
10 怪不得他们请我吃饭呢。 **guàibude tāmen qǐng wǒ chīfàn ne**
11 这件事妈妈还不知道呢。 **zhè/zhèi jiàn shì māma hái bù zhīdao ne**
12 什么都已经准备好了呢。 **shénme dōu yǐjing zhǔnbèi hǎo le ne**

Exercise 24.3

Construct alternative-questions with 呢 **ne**, using words and phrases below:

1 今晚 **jīn wǎn** 你 **nǐ** 去电影院 **qù diànyǐngyuàn** 去朋友家 **qù péngyou jiā**
2 她 **tà** 是 **shì** 医生 **yīshēng** 护士 **hùshi**
3 你 **nǐ** 看小说 **kàn xiǎoshuō** 听音乐 **tīng yīnyuè**
4 他 **tā** 骑车去 **qí chē qù** 开车去 **kāichē qù**
5 孩子们 **háizimen** 在花园里 **zài huāyuán li** 在街上 **zài jiē shang** 玩儿 **wánr**
6 你 **nǐ** 想 **xiǎng** 养猫 **yǎng māo** 养狗 **yǎng gǒu**

Exercise 24.4

Translate the following into Chinese using 呢 **ne**:

1 Where would you like to go for dinner then?
2 Look! The kitten is drinking the milk.
3 Granddad is reading the newspaper as well.
4 Fancy that, an eighty-year-old man going swimming in the sea!
5 How come your clothes are wet?
6 What would you like to buy then?
7 Can't you see, the child is drawing a picture.
8 What on earth is she writing?
9 Does this train go to London or doesn't it?
10 Do you really want to read this novel?

UNIT TWENTY-FIVE
Onomatopoeia and interjection

A Onomatopoeic words by definition imitate natural sounds, and Chinese, like other languages, has its own conventions regarding their formulation:

喔喔喔 **wōwōwō**
cock-a-doodle-doo!
哗哗哗 **huāhuāhuā**
the gurgling (of a stream)
隆隆 **lónglóng**
the rumble of thunder
嘭嘭 **pēngpēng**
knock! knock! (on a door)
扑通 **pūtōng**
plop! (into water)
滴滴答答 **dīdīdādā**
drip! drip! (of water)
滴答滴答 **dīdā dīdā**
tick! tock! (of a clock)
汪汪 **wāngwāng**
woof! woof! (of a dog)
喵 **miāo**
miaow! (of a cat)

B Generally speaking, onomatopoeic expressions are used as adverbials or attributives:

(1) Adverbials:

风呼呼地刮着。 **fēng hūhū de guā zhe**
The wind is/was howling.

小鸟在枝头叽叽喳喳地叫着。 **xiǎo niǎo zài zhītóu jījīzhāzhā de jiào zhe**
The little birds are/were chirping in the trees. (*lit.* on the boughs)

蜜蜂在花丛中嗡嗡地飞着。
mìfēng zài huācóng zhōng wēngwēng de fēi zhe
The bees are/were humming among the flowers.

(2) Attributives:

我听见一阵砰砰的枪声。 **wǒ tīngjiàn yī zhèn pēngpēng de qiāng shēng**
I heard a burst of gunfire.

窗外传来淅沥淅沥的雨声。 **chuāng wài chuán lái xīlì xīlì de yǔ shēng**
The patter of the rain came from outside (the window).

突然响起了劈里啪啦的鞭炮声。
tūrán xiǎng qǐ le pīlipālā de biānpào shēng
Suddenly, there came the crackle of firecrackers.

哐啷的一声把孩子吵醒了。 **kuānglāng de yī shēng bǎ háizi chǎo xǐng le**
A clanking noise woke the baby up.

Note: The word modified by an onomatopoeic attributive generally has to incorporate the component 声 shēng meaning 'sound', 'voice' or 'noise'.

C Interjections are used to express different emotions. They may stand alone or with an accompanying sentence:

(1) 唉 **ài** regret:

唉，他真不幸！ **ài | tā zhēn bùxìng**
Oh, he's really unlucky!

唉，他又病了！ **ài | tā yòu bìng le**
Oh dear, he is ill again!

(2) 哎呀 **āiyā** pleasant or unpleasant surprises:

哎呀，你儿子大学毕业了！ **āiyā | nǐ érzi dàxué bìyè le**
Gosh! Your son has graduated from university already!

哎呀，你怎么搞的！ **āiyā | nǐ zénme gǎo de**
Oh dear, what a mess you have made of it!

(3) 哼 **hng** anger or displeasure:

哼，你还怪我！ **hng | nǐ hái guài wǒ**
How can you blame me?

哼，她懂什么？ **hng | tā dǒng shénme**
Humph, what does she know?

(4) 呸 **pēi** contempt:

呸，滚你的蛋！ **pēi | gǔn nǐ de dàn**
Bah, get lost!

呸，你算什么东西？ **pēi | nǐ suàn shénme dōngxi**
Bah, who do you think you are?

(5) 哦 **ò** or 噢 **ō** sudden enlightenment or realisation:

哦，我明白了。 **ò | wǒ míngbai le**
Oh, I see./Oh, I understand.

噢，时间到了。 **ō | shíjiān dào le**
Oh, time's up./It's time.

(6) 嗬 **hē** admiration:

嗬，真棒! **hē | zhēn bàng**
Hey, that's great!

嗬，天晴了。 **hē | tiān qíng le**
Hey, the rain has stopped.

(7) 嗯 **ǹg** acknowledging hearing or agreeing to something that has been said:

嗯，我知道了。 **ǹg | wǒ zhīdao le**
Hmm, I know.

嗯，我就来。 **ǹg | wǒ jiù lái**
Hmm, I'll be with you in a minute.

(8) 嘿 **hēi** delight:

嘿，多漂亮啊！ **hēi | duō piàoliang a**
Gosh, how beautiful it is!

嘿，我中奖了！ **hēi | wǒ zhòngjiǎng le**
Wow! I've won the prize!

D 啊 **a** is the most versatile interjection of all. With different tones, it may express different emotions:

(1) 啊 **ā** (first tone) surprise:

啊，是你呀！ **ā | shì nǐ ya**
Oh, it's you!

啊，太阳出来啦！ **ā | tàiyáng chū lái la**
Oh look, the sun has come out!

(2) 啊 **á** (second tone) asking for further confirmation:

啊，你说什么？ **á | nǐ shuō shénme**
What was it you said?

啊，你不同意吗？ **á | nǐ bù tóngyì ma**
Did you say you didn't agree?

(3) 啊 **ǎ** (third tone) doubt and astonishment:

啊，这是怎么回事呢？ **ǎ | zhè shì zénme huí shì ne**
Oh, what is all this (about)?

啊，他上哪儿去了呢？ **ǎ | tā shàng nǎr qù le ne**
Where could he have gone?

(4) 啊 **à** (fourth tone) agreement or admiration:

啊，我去吧！ **à | wǒ qù ba**
All right, I'll go!

啊，多精彩的比赛呀！ **à | duō jīngcǎi de bǐsài ya**
Ah, what an amazing game!

Exercise 25.1

Complete the Chinese sentences below, filling in the blanks in each case with one of the onomatopoeic phrases listed, and adding 的 **de** or 地 **de** or neither as appropriate:

劈里啪啦 **pīlipālā**   哐啷 **kuānglāng**   嘭嘭 **pēngpēng**   哗哗(哗) **huāhuā(huā)**
淅沥淅沥 **xīlì xīlì**   喔喔喔 **wōwōwō**   扑通 **pūtōng**   隆隆 **lónglóng**

1 公鸡 ＿＿＿ 叫着。 **gōngjī ＿＿＿ de jiào zhe**
The cock crowed.

2 _____ 一声，青蛙跳进了池塘。 _____ **yī shēng | qīngwā tiào jìn le chítáng**
The frog jumped into the pond with a splash.

3 户外传来 _____ 鞭炮声。 **hùwài chuán lái** _____ **biānpào shēng**
The crackle of firecrackers could be heard outside.

4 大江 _____ 流向大海。 **dà jiāng** _____ **liú xiàng dà hǎi**
The river babbled on towards the sea.

5 陌生人 _____ 敲着门。 **mòshēng rén** _____ **qiāo zhe mén**
The stranger banged on the door.

6 雨 _____ 下了一夜。 **yǔ** _____ **xià le yī yè**
The rain came pattering down throughout the night.

7 我听见 _____ 雷声。 **wǒ tīngjiàn** _____ **léi shēng**
I heard the rumble of thunder.

8 _____ 一声，脸盆掉在地上。 _____ **yī shēng | liǎnpén diào zài dì shang**
The basin fell to the floor with a crash.

Exercise 25.2

Complete the following Chinese sentences, expressing the emotion indicated in
parentheses by choosing an interjection from the list provided:

唉 **ài** 哎呀 **āiyā** 哼 **hng** 呸 **pēi** 哦 **ò** 嗬 **hē** 嗯 **ńg** 嘿 **hēi**

1 _____，他怎么会不及格呢？ _____ **| tā zénme huì bù jígé ne**
Why didn't he pass the examination? (disappointment)

2 _____，我考上大学了！ _____ **| wǒ kǎo shàng dàxué le**
I've passed the university qualifying exams! (delight)

3 _____，我们一起去吧！ _____ **| wǒmen yīqǐ qù ba**
Okay, let's go together! (agreement)

4 _____，演出简直好极了！ _____ **| yǎnchū jiǎnzhí hǎo jí le**
The performance was really excellent! (admiration)

5 _____，原来是这么回事？ _____ **| yuánlái shì zhème huí shì**
Oh, it's like that is it? (realisation)

6 _____，你这个流氓！ _____ **| nǐ zhè/zhèi gè liúmáng**
You're such a rogue! (contempt)

7 _____，我从来没有相信过她！
_____ **| wǒ cónglái méi(yǒu) xiāngxìn guo tā**
I have never trusted her! (displeasure)

8 _____，这个孩子这么高了！ _____ **| zhè/zhèi gè háizi zhème gāo le**
Goodness me! Look how tall this child has grown! (surprise)

9 _____，奶奶又咳嗽了！ _____ **| nǎinai yòu késou le**
Oh no, Grandma is coughing again! (regret)

10 _____，谁让你说这样的话！
_____ **| shéi/shuí ràng nǐ shuō zhè/zhèi yàng de huà**
Who taught you to say such things? (anger)

Exercise 25.3

Decide which tone 啊 **a** should be in the Chinese sentences below:

1 啊，中国有这么多自行车呀！**a | zhōngguó yǒu zhème duō zìxíngchē ya**
  There are so many bicycles in China!
2 啊，你真的不知道？**a | nǐ zhēn de bù zhīdao**
  You really don't know?
3 啊，你明天到底去不去呀？**a | nǐ míngtiān dàodǐ qù bù qù ya**
  Well, are you going tomorrow or not?
4 啊，这幢大楼只用了两个月就建成啦？
  a | zhè/zhèi zhuàng dàlóu zhǐ yòng le liǎng gè yuè jiù jiàn chéng la
  What! This enormous building only took two months to build?
5 啊，我就来。**a | wǒ jiù lái**
  All right, I'm coming.
6 啊，庄稼长得真好哇！**a | zhuāngjia zhǎng de zhēn hǎo wa**
  What a wonderful crop!
7 啊，那只兔子会咬人？**a | nà/nèi zhī tùzi huì yǎo rén**
  What! That rabbit bites people!?
8 啊，汽车来了！**a | qìchē lái le**
  Oh look, the bus is coming!

Exercise 25.4

Translate the following into Chinese:

1 She fell into the lake with a splash.
2 I could hear the old clock ticking in the hall.
3 Oh, now I understand what she means.
4 Hey, that blue sweater is really attractive.
5 Oh dear, it's started raining.
6 Oh, look! Dad has come home.

KEY TO EXERCISES

Unit 1

Exercise 1.1 1 小孩儿把玻璃窗打破了。 **xiǎoháir bǎ bōlichuāng dǎ pò le**
2 小红把头发梳了一下。 **xiǎo hóng bǎ tóufa shū le yīxià** 3 请把这些药吃了。
qǐng bǎ zhè/zhèi xiē yào chī le 4 她把那笔钱从银行里取了出来。 **tā bǎ nà/nèi
bǐ qián cóng yínháng li qǔ le chūlái** 5 老师把这个问题解释得很清楚。 **lǎoshī
bǎ zhè/zhèi gè wèntí jiěshì de hěn qīngchu** 6 我把你的衣服放在衣柜里了。
wǒ bǎ nǐ de yīfu fàng zài yīguì li le

Exercise 1.2 1 老师把讲义发给学生。 **laǒshī bǎ jiǎngyì fā gěi xuésheng**
The teacher distributed the hand-outs to the students. 2 他把衣服洗了。 **tā bǎ
yīfu xǐ le** He washed the clothes. 3 护士把药片递给病人。 **hùshi bǎ yàopiàn
dì gěi bìngrén** The nurse passed/handed the pills to the patient. 4 我把钥匙留
在家里了。 **wǒ bǎ yàoshi liú zài jiā li le** I left my key(s) at home. 5 警察把
小偷抓住了。 **jǐngchá bǎ xiǎotōu zhuā zhù le** The policeman caught the thief.
6 司机把汽车修好了。 **sījī bǎ qìchē xiū hǎo le** The driver repaired the car.

Exercise 1.3 1 小孩把杯子打破了。 **xiǎohái bǎ bēizi dǎ pò le** 2 老师把
书放在桌子上。 **lǎoshī bǎ shū fàng zài zhuōzi shang** 3 我必须把信写完。
wǒ bìxū bǎ xìn xiě wán 4 她把石头扔到海里去了。 **tā bǎ shítou rēng dào hǎi
li qù le** 5 厨师把鸡烤熟了。 **chúshī bǎ jī kǎo shú/shóu le** 6 请把火车票拿
好。 **qǐng bǎ huǒchēpiào ná hǎo** 7 小李吃了一个苹果。 **xiǎo lǐ chī le yī gè
píngguǒ** Xiao Li has eaten *an* apple. cf. 小李把苹果吃了。 **xiǎo lǐ bǎ píngguǒ
chī le** Xiao Li has eaten *the* apple. 8 她把生词记住了。 **tā bǎ shēngcí jì zhù le**
9 护士没把门关上。 **hùshi méi bǎ mén guān shàng** 10 请不要把这件事告诉他。
qǐng bù yào bǎ zhè/zhèi jiàn shì gàosu tā

Exercise 1.4 1 在 **zài** 里 **li** 2 两次 **liǎng cì**/两遍 **liǎng biàn** 3 完 **wán**
4 回来 **huílái** 5 在 **zài** 上 **shang** 6 作自己的女儿 **zuò zìjǐ de nǚ'ér** 7 一下
yīxià/(一)数 **(yī) shǔ** 8 半(个)小时/半个钟头 **bàn (gè) xiǎoshí/bàn gé zhōngtóu**

Exercise 1.5 1 不要/别忘了把你的钥匙带上。 **bù yào/bié wàng le bǎ nǐ
de yàoshi dài shàng** 2 他把书放回书架上去(了)。 **tā bǎ shū fàng huí shūjià**

shang qù (le)   3 我不想把我的东西和你的混在一起。 **wǒ bù xiǎng bǎ wǒ de dōngxi hé nǐ de hùn zài yīqǐ**   4 他也把我当作一个朋友。 **tā yě bǎ wǒ dàng zuò yī gè péngyou**   5 他们把我弄火儿了。 **tāmen bǎ wǒ nòng huǒr le**   6 我把她的申请表读了五次/遍。 **wǒ bǎ tā de shēnqǐngbiǎo dú le wǔ cì/biàn**   7 他把信写得很长。 **tā bǎ xìn xiě de hěn cháng**   8 你想把你的包儿/袋子留在这儿吗？ **nǐ xiǎng bǎ nǐ de bāor/dàizi liú zài zhèr ma**

Exercise 1.6   1 爸爸把汽车洗干净了。 **bàba bǎ qìchē xǐ gānjìng le**   2 妈妈把衣服晾出去了。 **māma bǎ yīfu liàng chūqù le**   3 医生把病人医/治好了。 **yīshēng bǎ bìngrén yī/zhì hǎo le**   4 小猫把老鼠抓/逮住了。 **xiǎo māo bǎ lǎoshǔ zhuā/dǎi zhù le**   5 我朋友把饭煮好/熟了。 **wǒ péngyou bǎ fàn zhǔ hǎo/shú le**   6 妹妹把书借 (回) 来了。 **mèimei bǎ shū jiè (huí)lái le**   7 秘书把信寄走了。 **mìshū bǎ xìn jì zǒu le**   8 小男孩把皮鞋擦亮/干净了。 **xiǎo nánhái bǎ píxié cā liàng/gānjìng le**

Unit 2

Exercise 2.1   1 窗户被小孩儿打破了。 **chuānghu bèi xiǎoháir dǎ pò le**   2 钱被她从银行里取了出来。 **qián bèi tā cóng yínháng li qǔ le chūlái**   3 小偷当场被警察抓住了。 **xiǎotōu dāngchǎng bèi jǐngchá zhuā zhù le**   4 汽车被司机修好了。 **qìchē bèi sījī xiū hǎo le**   5 鸡被厨师烤熟了。 **jī bèi chúshī kǎo shú/shóu le**   6 他的头发被理发师剪得太短了。 **tā de tóufa bèi lǐfàshī jiǎn de tài duǎn le**

Exercise 2.2   1 那个苹果被她吃了。 **nà/nèi gè píngguǒ bèi tā chī le** The apple was eaten by her.   2 钥匙被我找到了。 **yàoshi bèi wǒ zhǎo dào le** The key was found by me.   3 我女儿被老师批评了一顿。 **wǒ nǚ'ér bèi lǎoshī pīpíng le yī dùn** My daughter was criticised/told off by the teacher.   4 他被卡车撞倒了。 **tā bèi kǎchē zhuàng dǎo le** He was knocked down by a truck.   5 工人被老板撤了职。 **gōngrén bèi lǎobǎn chè le zhí** The worker was fired by the boss.   6 小偷被关进了监狱。 **xiǎotōu bèi guān jìn le jiānyù** The thief was locked up in prison.

Exercise 2.3   1 我要的书被人借走了。 **wǒ yào de shū bèi rén jiè zǒu le**   2 蛋糕叫小李吃了。 **dàngāo jiào xiǎo lǐ chī le**   3 大家被她说得笑起来了/笑了起来。 **dàjiā bèi tā shuō de xiào qǐlái le/xiào le qǐlái**   4 老鼠让猫给逮住了。 **lǎoshǔ ràng māo gěi dǎi zhù le**   5 她叫自行车给撞倒了。 **tā jiào zìxíngchē gěi zhuàng dǎo le**   6 这个计划让大家给取消了。 **zhè/zhèi gè jìhuà ràng dàjiā gěi qǔxiāo le**   7 她被孙老师当作/成自己的女儿。 **tā bèi sūn lǎoshī dàng zuò/chéng zìjǐ de nǚ'ér**   8 这个问题被老师解释得清清楚楚。 **zhè/zhèi gè wèntí bèi lǎoshī jiěshì de qīngqīng chǔchu**   9 花儿被插在花瓶里了。 **huār bèi chā zài huāpíng li le**   10 行李都让火车给运走了。 **xíngli dōu ràng huǒchē gěi yùn zǒu le**

Exercise 2.4   1 我们的晚饭让猫给吃 (掉) 了。 **wǒmen de wǎnfàn ràng mmāo gěi chī (diào) le**   2 钥匙让司机给忘记 (带来) 了。 **yàoshi ràng sījī gěi wàngjì (dài lái) le**   3 我被老师批评了一顿。 **wǒ bèi lǎoshī pīpíng le yī dùn**   4 那个孩子被公共汽车撞倒了。 **nà/nèi gè háizi bèi gōnggòng qìchē zhuàng dǎo le**   5 我被他当作自己的儿子。 **wǒ bèi tā dàng zuò zìjǐ de érzi**   6 (那扇) 门被警察踢开了。 **(nà/nèi shàn) mén bèi jǐngchá tī kāi le**   7 (那辆) 自行车被小偷弄坏了。 **(nà/nèi liàng) zìxíngchē bèi xiǎotōu nòng huài le**   8 她的书被藏在碗橱后边/背后了。 **tā de shū bèi cáng zài wǎnchú hòubian/bèi hòu le**   9 栅栏被风吹倒了。 **zhàlan bèi fēng chuī dǎo le**   10 我被他气得说不出话来。 **wǒ bèi tā qì de shuō bu chū huà lái**

Unit 3

Exercise 3.1   The direct objects: 1 一只手表 **yī zhī shǒubiǎo**   2 一杯牛奶 **yī bēi niúnǎi**   3 一批文件 **yī pī wénjiàn**   4 一本杂志 **yī běn zázhì**   5 那把 (雨) 伞 **nà/nèi bǎ (yǔ)sǎn**   6 一本书 **yī běn shū**   7 一个秘密 **yī gè mìmì**   8 一些问题 **yīxiē wèntí**   The indirect objects: 1 朋友 **péngyou**   2 同学 **tóngxué**   3 秘书 **mìshū**   4 医生 **yīshēng**   5 他的邻居 **tā de línjū**   6 我 **wǒ**   7 我 **wǒ**   8 老师 **lǎoshī**

Exercise 3.2   1 领事馆发给我一张签证。 **lǐngshìguǎn fā gěi wǒ yī zhāng qiānzhèng**   2 朋友借给我一盘录象带。 **péngyou jiè gěi wǒ yī pán lùxiàngdài**   3 我借了他一把(雨)伞。 **wǒ jiè le tā yī bǎ (yǔ)sǎn**   4 她带给朋友一双鞋。 **tā dài gěi péngyou yī shuāng xié**   5 司机递给我一张票。 **sījī dì gěi wǒ yī zhāng piào**   6 孩子们献给女王一束花。 **háizimen xiàn gěi nǚwáng yī shù huā**

Exercise 3.3   1 寄给 **jì gěi**   2 买给 **mǎi gěi**   3 送给 **sòng gěi**   4 递给 **dì gěi**   5 卖给 **mài gěi**   6 倒给 **dào gěi**   7 租给 **zū gěi**   8 发给 **fā gěi**   9 转给 **zhuǎn gěi**   10 借给 **jiè gěi**

Exercise 3.4   1 请你借给我两块钱。 **qǐng nǐ jiè gěi wǒ liǎng kuài qián**   2 我朋友借了我一件毛衣。 **wǒ péngyou jiè le wǒ yī jiàn máoyī**   3 学生送给老师一个礼物。 **xuésheng sòng gěi lǎoshī yī gè lǐwù**   4 别叫我老张。 **bié jiào wǒ lǎo zhāng**   5 我明天把那支笔还给你。 **wǒ míngtiān bǎ nà/nèi zhī bǐ huán gěi nǐ**   6 我们买什么 (送) 给他呢? **wǒmen mǎi shénme (sòng) gěi tā ne**   7 你有没有把 (那本) 字典/词典交给他? **nǐ yǒu méiyǒu bǎ (nà/nèi běn) zìdiǎn/cídiǎn jiāo gěi tā** or 你把 (那本) 字典/词典交给他了没有? **nǐ bǎ (nà/nèi běn) zìdiǎn/cídiǎn jiāo gěi tā le méiyǒu**   8 我没有把那个秘密告诉他们。 **wǒ méiyǒu bǎ nà/nèi gè mìmì gàosu tāmen**

Unit 4

Exercise 4.1   1 叫 **jiào**   2 不准 **bù zhǔn**/不许 **bùxǔ**/不让 **bù ràng**   3 请 **qǐng**   4 劝 **quàn**   5 要 **yào**/请 **qǐng**   6 禁止 **jìnzhǐ**/不准 **bù zhǔn**/不许 **bùxǔ**   7 劝

quàn   8 催 **cuī**   9 逼 **bī**   10 命令 **mìnglìng**   11 允许 **yǔnxǔ**   12 要 **yào**
13 使 **shǐ**/让 **ràng**/叫 **jiào**   14 吩咐 **fēnfù**   15 使 **shǐ**/让 **ràng**/叫 **jiào**   16 使
shǐ/让 **ràng**/叫 **jiào**

Exercise 4.2   1 父母不许/不准孩子吃巧克力。 **fùmǔ bùxǔ/bù zhǔn háizi
chī qiǎokèlì**   2 这个消息没有使我难过。 **zhè/zhèi gè xiāoxi méiyǒu shǐ wǒ
nánguò**   3 他劝我不要/别买这双鞋。 **tā quàn wǒ bù yào/bié mǎi zhè/zhèi
shuāng xié**   4 经理准我不出席这次会议。 **jīnglǐ zhǔn wǒ bù chūxí zhè/zhèi
cì huìyì** 经理不准我出席这次会议。 **jīnglǐ bù zhǔn wǒ chūxí zhè/zhèi cì
huìyì**   5 她没(有)叫我开灯。 **tā méi(yǒu) jiào wǒ kāi dēng** 她叫我不要/别开
灯。 **tā jiào wǒ bù yào/bié kāi dēng**   6 我不/没(有)让儿子学汉语。 **wǒ bù/
méi(yǒu) ràng érzi xué hànyǔ**

Exercise 4.3   1 有一个小孩曾经在森林里迷了路。 **yǒu yī gè xiǎohái céngjīng
zài sēnlín li mí le lù**   2 这儿有谁认识你？ **zhèr yǒu shéi/shuí rènshi nǐ**   3 今晚
有些朋友到我家来。 **jīn wǎn yǒu xiē péngyou dào wǒ jiā lái**   4 六点钟有一辆
车去伦敦。 **liù diǎn zhōng yǒu yī liàng chē qù lúndūn**   5 有个人在外面等你。
yǒu gè rén zài wàimian děng nǐ or 外面/外边有个人(在)等你。 **wàimian/wàibian
yǒu gè rén (zài) děng nǐ**   6 这儿有谁会讲汉语？ **zhèr yǒu shéi/shuí huì jiǎng
hànyǔ** or 这儿有没有人会讲汉语？ **zhèr yǒu méi yǒu rén huì jiǎng hànyǔ**

Exercise 4.4   1 妈妈叫孩子把衣服穿整齐。 **māma jiào háizi bǎ yīfu chuān
zhěngqí**   2 姐姐催我快起床。 **jiějie cuī wǒ kuài qǐchuáng**   3 弟弟要我帮
(助)他修(理)电脑。 **dìdi yào wǒ bāng(zhù) tā xiū(lǐ) diànnǎo**   4 我不敢劝她不
要抽烟。 **wǒ bù gǎn quàn tā bù yào chōuyān**   5 她不肯让我和/跟她一起去。
tā bù kěn ràng wǒ hé/gēn tā yīqǐ qù   6 老师不允许学生们爬树。 **lǎoshī bù
yǔnxǔ xuéshengmen pá shù**   7 教练命令运动员们在操场上集合。 **jiàoliàn
mìnglìng yùndòngyuánmen zài cāochǎng shang jíhé**   8 哥哥逼我把我最好的
玩具给他。 **gēge bī wǒ bǎ wǒ zuì hǎo de wánjù gěi tā**

Unit 5

Exercise 5.1   1 他打开衣柜拿出一件衬衫给我。 **tā dǎ kāi yīguì ná chū yī
jiàn chènshān gěi wǒ** He opened the wardrobe and took out a shirt/blouse for
me.   2 我买了一束花去医院看望我的朋友。 **wǒ mǎi le yī shù huā qù yīyuàn
kànwàng wǒ de péngyou** I bought a bunch of flowers and went to the hospital
to visit my friend.   3 她戴上眼镜看文件。 **tā dài shàng yǎnjìng kàn wénjiàn**
She put on her glasses and read the document.   4 护士推开门走进病房给病人
打针。 **hùshi tuī kāi mén zǒu jìn bìngfáng gěi bìngrén dǎzhēn** The nurse
pushed open the door, walked into the ward and gave the patient(s) injections/an
injection.   5 学生有几个问题问老师。 **xuésheng yǒu jǐ gè wèntí wèn lǎoshī**
The student had a few questions to ask the teacher.   6 我需要一些钱付房租。
wǒ xūyào yīxiē qián fù fángzū I need some money to pay the rent.

Exercise 5.2   1 坐/乘飞机 **zuò/chéng fēijī**   2 用中文/汉语 **yòng zhōngwén/hànyǔ**   3 用自己的爪子 **yòng zìjǐ de zhuǎzi**   4 坐船 **zuò chuán**   5 站着 **zhàn zhe**   6 骑自行车 **qí zìxíngchē**

Exercise 5.3   1 他坐火车上班去了。 **tā zuò huǒchē shàngbān qù le**   2 我们回家看望奶奶去了。 **wǒmen huí jiā kànwàng nǎinai qù le**   3 他明天出发到西班牙去。 **tā míngtiān chūfā dào xībānyá qù**   4 我的朋友都参加我的生日聚会来了。 **wǒ de péngyou dōu cānjiā wǒ de shēngrì jùhuì lái le**   5 她出门上班去了。 **tā chūmén shàngbān qù le**   6 小刘为我/替我照看孩子来了。 **xiǎo liú wèi wǒ/tì wǒ zhàokàn háizi lái le**

Exercise 5.4   1 不动 **bù dòng**   2 不睡 **bù shuì**   3 不放 **bù fàng**   4 不穿 **bù chuān**   5 不喝 **bù hé**   6 不起来 **bù qǐ lái**

Exercise 5.5   1 我用吸尘器把地毯吸干净了。 **wǒ yòng xīchénqì bǎ dìtǎn xī gānjìng le**   2 我没有机会说英语。 **wǒ méi yǒu jīhuì shuō yīngyǔ**   3 孩子们去电影院买票看电影。 **háizimen qù diànyǐngyuàn mǎi piào kàn diànyǐng**   4 我用白油漆把门漆了一下。 **wǒ yòng bái yóuqī bǎ mén qī le yīxià**   5 船靠码头卸货。 **chuán kào mǎtóu xièhuò**   6 叔叔带着他的孩子到我家来拜年。 **shūshu dài zhe tā de háizi dào wǒ jiā lái bàinián**

Unit 6

Exercise 6.1   1 有 **yǒu**   2 有 **yǒu**   3 都是 **dōu shì**   4 有 **yǒu**   5 都是 **dōu shì**   6 是 **shì**   7 都是 **dōu shì**   8 是 **shì**

Exercise 6.2   1 游着 **yóu zhe**   2 站着 **zhàn zhe**   3 藏着 **cáng zhe**   4 挂着 **guà zhe**   5 放着 **fàng zhe**   6 长着 **zhǎng zhe**   7 亮着 **liàng zhe**   8 拿着 **ná zhe**

Exercise 6.3   1 挤满 **jǐ mǎn**   2 坐满 **zuò mǎn**   3 装满 **zhuāng mǎn**   4 长满 **zhǎng mǎn**   5 充满 **chōng mǎn**   6 塞满 **sāi mǎn**

Exercise 6.4   1 买来 **mǎi lái**   2 飘来 **piāo lái**   3 寄走 **jì zǒu**   4 逃走 **táo zǒu**   5 卖走 **mài zǒu**   6 搬来 **bān lái**

Exercise 6.5   1 树上挂满了梨 (子)。 **shù shang guà mǎn le lí(zi)**   2 海面上飞过一群海鸥。 **hǎimiàn shang fēi guo yī qún hǎi'ōu**   3 沿路都是绿油油的田野。 **yán lù dōu shì lùyóuyóu de tiányě**   4 市场里运来了很多新鲜的蔬菜。 **shìchǎng li yùn lái le hěn duō xīnxiān de shūcài**   5 他的裤子上都是污垢/泥。 **tā de kùzi shang dōu shì wūgòu/ní**   6 车站上挤满了乘客。 **chēzhàn shang jǐ mǎn le chéngkè**   7 上周/星期运走了大量的家具。 **shàng zhōu/xīngqī yùn zǒu le dàliàng de jiājù**   8 瓶子里没有一点儿/一滴酒。 **píngzi li méi yǒu yīdiǎnr/yī dī jiǔ**

Unit 7

Exercise 7.1   Subject–predicate sentences: 1, 5, 7, 10 Topic–comment structures: 2, 3, 4, 6, 8, 9

Exercise 7.2   1 药病人已经吃了。 **yào bìngrén yǐjing chī le** The patient has already taken the medicine.   2 衣服我都晾出去了。 **yīfu wǒ dōu liàng chūqù le** I have put all the washing out to dry.   3 割草机邻居借走了。 **gēcǎojī línjū jiè zǒu le** The neighbour borrowed the lawnmower.   4 那个问题大家讨论过没有？ **nà/nèi gè wèntí dàjiā tǎolùn guo méiyǒu** Has everyone discussed that question?   5 你第二篇文章写好了吗？ **nǐ dì èr piān wénzhāng xiě hǎo le ma** Have you written the second essay?   6 妈妈要的东西爸爸昨天买回来了。 **māma yào de dōngxi bàba zuótiān mǎi huílái le** Father bought yesterday what Mother wanted.

Exercise 7.3   1 积蓄弟弟都存进银行里去了。 **jīxù dìdi dōu cún jìn yínháng li qù le**   2 房间他已经收拾好了。 **fángjiān tā yǐjing shōushi hǎo le**   3 那笔奖金爸爸捐给学校了。 **nà/nèi bǐ jiǎngjīn bàba juān gěi xuéxiào le**   4 这件事我已经告诉他了。 **zhè/zhèi jiàn shì wǒ yǐjing gàosu tā le**   5 昨天买的香蕉他全吃完了。 **zuótiān mǎi de xiāngjiāo tā quán chī wán le**   6 剩下的饭菜妈妈倒在阴沟里了。 **shèngxià de fàncài māma dào zài yīngōu li le**

Exercise 7.4   1 房间我收拾好了。 **fángjiān wǒ shōushi hǎo le**   2 那两封信她寄走了。 **nà/nèi liǎng fēng xìn tā jì zǒu le**   3 饭我煮好了。 **fàn wǒ zhǔ hǎo le**   4 我爸爸的车弟弟借走了。 **wǒ bàba de chē dìdi jiè zǒu le**   5 长城我已经去过两次了。 **chángchéng wǒ yǐjing qù guo liǎng cì le**   6 那盒巧克力妈妈送给了一个朋友。 **nà/nèi hé qiǎokèlì māma sòng gěi le yī gè péngyou** or 那盒巧克力妈妈送给一个朋友了。 **nà/nèi hé qiǎokèlì māma sòng gěi yī gè péngyou le**

Unit 8

Exercise 8.1   1 我会说汉语了。 **wǒ huì shuō hànyǔ le**   2 他不抽烟。 **tā bù chōuyān**   3 树叶黄了。 **shùyè huáng le**   4 商店关门了。 **shāngdiàn guān mén le**   5 天气很冷。 **tiānqì hěn lěng**   6 他不去图书馆了。 **tā bù qù túshūguǎn le**   7 这儿是超级市场了。 **zhèr shì chāojí shìchǎng le**   8 小猫大了。 **xiǎo māo dà le**

Exercise 8.2   1 火车来了。 **huǒchē lái le**   2 我高了。 **wǒ gāo le**   3 (手)表修好了。 **(shǒu) biǎo xiū hǎo le**   4 狗老了。 **gǒu lǎo le**   5 画儿掉下来了。 **huàr diào xiàlái le**   6 钟停了。 **zhōng tíng le**   7 鱼儿死了。 **yúr sǐ le**   8 工作结束了。 **gōngzuò jiéshù le**   9 他醉了。 **tā zuì le**   10 孩子睡着了。 **háizi shuì zháo le**

Exercise 8.3   1 no adjustment necessary   2 我天天喝牛奶。 **wǒ tiāntiān hē niúnǎi**   3 我们快到山顶了。 **wǒmen kuài dào shāndǐng le**   4 哥哥经常喝酒。 **gēge jīcháng hē jiǔ**   5 会议就要结束了。 **huìyì jiù yào jiéshù le**   6 他喜欢跳舞。 **tā xǐhuan tiàowǔ**   7 我每晚都读报。 **wǒ měi wǎn dōu dú bào** 8 新房子快造好了。 **xīn fángzi kuài zào hǎo le**   9 水马上就(要)开了。 **shuǐ mǎshàng jiù (yào) kāi le**   10 弟弟是医生。 **dìdi shì yīshēng**

Exercise 8.4   1 去年这儿的东西很贵，现在便宜多了。 **qùnián zhèr de dōngxi hěn guì | xiànzài piányi duō le**   2 我们走了。 **wǒmen zǒu le**   3 他们上/到哪儿去了？ **tāmen shàng/dào nǎr qù le**   4 我马上就回来。 **wǒ mǎshàng jiù huí lái**   5 我不(再)喜欢吃肉了。 **wǒ bù (zài) xǐhuan chī ròu le**   6 他的头发白了。 **tā de tóufa bái le**   7 她不(住)在这儿了。 **tā bù (zhù) zài zhèr le** 8 要下雪了。 **yào xià xuě le**   9 我没有钱了。 **wǒ méi yǒu qián le**   10 我的中文比以前好一点儿了。 **wǒ de zhōngwén bǐ yǐqián hǎo yīdiǎnr le**

Unit 9

Exercise 9.1   1 对不起！ **duìbuqǐ**   2 没关系！ **méi guānxi**   3 闪电了！ **shǎn diàn le**   4 打雷了！ **dǎ léi le**   5 请在这儿签字！ **qǐng zài zhèr qiānzì** 6 火！/着火了！ **huǒ/zháohuǒ le**   7 一个多么聪明的人！ **yī gè duōme cōngming de rén**   8 请坐！ **qǐng zuò**   9 请安静！ **qǐng ānjìng**   10 不准在此停车！ **bù zhǔn zài cǐ tíng chē**   11 随手关灯！ **suí shǒu guān dēng**   12 别哭(了)！ **bié kū (le)**   13 你的收据！ **nǐ de shōujù**   14 多大的雨哇！ **duō dà de yǔ wā**

Exercise 9.2   1(a) 洗了。 **xǐ le** (b) 没洗。 **méi xǐ**   2(a) 想。 **xiǎng** (b) 不想。 **bù xiǎng**   3(a) 是(的)。 **shì (de)** (b) 不是。 **bù shì**   4(a) 有。 **yǒu** (b) 没有。 **méi yǒu**   5(a) 写。 **xiě** (b) 不写。 **bù xiě**   6(a) 可以。 **kěyǐ** (b) 不可以。 **bù kěyǐ** 7(a) 会了。 **huì le** (b) 还不会。 **hái bù huì**   8(a) 能。 **néng** (b) 对不起，我没空。 **duìbuqǐ | wǒ méi kòng**   9(a) 去过。 **qù guo** (b) 没(有)去过。 **méi(yǒu) qù guo**   10(a) 是的。(在楼上。) **shì de | (zài lóushàng)** (b) 不在楼上(，在楼下)。 **bù zài lóushàng (| zài lóuxià)**

Exercise 9.3   1 Shut the door as you go out!   2 The class is dismissed! 3 Hurry up!   4 Shut up!   5 Go away!/Beat it!   6 Go to bed!   7 Pull! 8 Push!   9 The sun has come out!   10 Be careful!/Careful!

Exercise 9.4   1 那个箱子太重，我不想买。 **nà/nèi gè xiāngzi tài zhòng | wǒ bù xiǎng mǎi**   2 下雨了！ **xià yǔ le**   3 今天星期天/星期日。 **jīntiān xīngqī tiān/xīngqī rì**   4 那些花儿真美丽，我买给你，好吗？ **nà/nèi xiē huār zhēn měilì | wǒ mǎi gěi nǐ | hǎo ma**   5 你去过日本吗？没有。 **nǐ qù guo rìběn ma | méiyǒu**   6 今晚(你)来踢足球吗？来。 **jīn wǎn (nǐ) lái tī zúqiú ma | lái**   7 我们的房子在这张地图上，可是看不见。 **wǒmen de fángzi zài zhè/zhèi zhāng dìtú**

shang | **kěshì kàn bu jiàn**   8 (你) 喜欢这儿吗？(**nǐ**) **xǐhuan zhèr ma**   9 没想到/真想不到在这儿见到你。太巧了！**méi xiǎng dào/zhēn xiǎng bu dào zài zhèr jiàn dào nǐ | tài qiǎo le**   10 多么好听的音乐啊！**duōme hǎotīng de yīnyuè à**   11 你认得那个人吗？不认得。**nǐ rènde nà/nèi gè rén ma | bù rènde**   12 我在找钥匙，但是找不到。**wǒ zài zhǎo yàoshi | dànshì zhǎo bu dào**   13 蓝色的很好看，可是我买不起。**lánsè de hěn hǎokàn | kěshǐ wǒ mǎi bu qǐ**   14 能在这儿抽烟吗？不能。**néng zài zhèr chōuyān ma | bù néng**   15 说中文真容易。**shuō zhōngwén zhēn róngyì**

Unit 10

Exercise 10.1   1 那位运动员不是很健康吗？**nà/nèi wèi yùndòngyuán bù shì hěn jiànkāng ma** Isn't that athlete very healthy?   2 他没有吃过西瓜吗？**tā méiyǒu chī guo xīguā ma** Hasn't he eaten watermelon before?   3 难道那个孩子不懂礼貌吗？**nándào nà/nèi gè háizi bù dǒng lǐmào ma** Isn't the child very polite?   4 我哪儿错了？**wǒ nǎr cuò le** How can I be wrong?   5 他怎么可以说这样的话 (呢)？**tā zénme kěyǐ shuō zhè/zhèi yàng de huà (ne)** How could he say things like that?   6 谁不知道这件事？**shéi/shuí bù zhīdao zhè/zhèi jiàn shì** Who wouldn't know about this?   7 你何不跟他一起去美国呢？**nǐ hébù gēn tā yīqǐ qù méiguó ne** Why don't you go to America with him?   8 你说这件事情不复杂吗？**nǐ shuō zhè/zhèi jiàn shìqíng bù fùzá ma** Don't you think that this matter is really complicated?   9 她干什么生气？**tā gàn shénme shēngqì** Why should she be angry?   10 他难道不是王工程师吗？**tā nándào bù shì wáng gōngchéngshī ma** Isn't he Wang the engineer?

Exercise 10.2   1 Don't you like (eating) chocolate?   2 What's the point of your living in such an old house?   3 Who would buy such an expensive car?   4 What is the use of crying?   5 Why did you do such a dangerous thing?   6 Isn't he happy?   7 Isn't it right to say something like this?   8 Do you think this is complicated?   9 Is there anything cheaper than this?   10 What do you know?

Exercise 10.3   (a)   1 你(真的)不懂吗？**nǐ (zhēn de) bù dǒng ma**   2 你真的每晚都看电视吗？**nǐ zhēn de měi wǎn dōu kàn diànshì ma**   3 你的朋友真的都到了吗？**nǐ de péngyou zhēn de dōu dào le ma**   4 你真的想走吗？**nǐ zhēn de xiǎng zǒu ma**   5 你(真的)不会用筷子吗？**nǐ (zhēn de) bù huì yòng kuàizi ma**   (b)   6 你不是说他们都会说中文吗？**nǐ bù shì shuō tāmen dōu huì shuō zhōngwén ma**   7 你不是看过那个电影吗？**nǐ bù shì kàn guo nà/nèi gè diànyǐng ma**   8 她不是很象她母亲吗？**tā bù shì hěn xiàng tā mǔqīn ma**   9 你星期六不是很忙吗？**nǐ xīngqī liù bù shì hěn máng ma**   10 上海不是中国最大的城市吗？**shànghǎi bù shì zhōngguó zuì dà de chéngshì ma**   (c)   11 你难道把票留在家里了吗？**nǐ nándào bǎ piào liú zài jiā li le ma**

12 难道你还不会写那个中文字吗？ **nándào nǐ hái bù huì xiě nà/nèi gè zhōngwén zì ma** 13 难道他连'谢谢你'也没 (有) 说吗？ **nándào tā lián xièxie nǐ yě méi(yǒu) shuō ma** 14 难道她不吃西红柿吗？ **nándào tā bù chī xīhóng-shì ma** (d) 15 急/忙什么？ **jí/máng shénme** 16 她哪儿能帮助你 (呢)？ **tā nǎr néng bāngzhù nǐ (ne)** 17 他怎么会同意你的观点/意见呢？ **tā zénme huì tóngyì nǐ de guāndiǎn/yìjian ne** 18 她干吗什么也不说呢？ **tā gànmá shénme yě bù shuō ne** 19 谁会买这么贵的东西呢？ **shéi/shuí huì mǎi zhème guì de dōngxi ne** 20 何不坐火车去呢？ **hébù zuò huǒchē qù ne**

Unit 11

Exercise 11.1 1 无论...仍然 (总是)... **wúlùn | réngrán (zhǒngshì)** 2 还是 **háishi** 3 所以 **suǒyǐ**/因此 **yīncǐ** 4 要么/不是...要么/就是... **yàome/ bùshì...yàome/jiùshì** 5 不管/无论...仍 (然)... **bùguǎn/wúlùn | réng(rán)** 6 只有...才... **zhǐyǒu | cái** 7 不仅...连... **bùjǐn | lián** 8 虽然...但是... **suīrán | dànshì** 9 所以 **suǒyǐ** 10 因为...所以... **yīnwèi | suǒyǐ** 11 不然 **bùrán** 12 如果...那么... **rúguǒ | nàme** 13 不过 **bùguò** 14 既然 ...那么... **jìrán | nàme** 15 否则 **fǒuzé**/不然 **bùrán** 16 不过 **bùguò** 17 既然 ...就... **jìrán | jiù** 18 除非...才... **chúfēi | cái** 19 不但/不仅...而且 **bùdàn/bùjǐn/érqiě** 20 但(是) **dàn(shì)**

Exercise 11.2 1 但是没有花园 **dànshì méi yǒu huāyuán** 2 所以我 (上床) 睡觉去了 **suǒyǐ wǒ (shàng chuáng) shuìjiào qù le** 3 因为钥匙不见了/找不到 了 **yīnwèi yàoshi bù jiàn le/zhǎo bu dào le** 4 否则/不然看不到那个电影了 **fǒuzé/bùrán kàn bu dào nà/nèi gè diànyǐng le** 5 但是我仍然很担心 **dànshì wǒ réngrán hěn dānxīn** 6 所以没 (有) 人想游泳 **suǒyǐ méi (yǒu) rén xiǎng yóuyǒng**

Exercise 11.3 1 下雨了，(因此) 你还是呆在家里好。 **xià yǔ le | (yīncǐ) nǐ háishi dāi zài jiā li hǎo** 2 除非你努力学习，不然 (你) 找不到好工作。 **chúfēi nǐ nǔlì xuéxí | bùrán nǐ zhǎo bù dào hǎo gōngzuò** 3 无论你跑得 多快，(你) 也仍然会迟到的。 **wúlùn nǐ pǎo de duō kuài | (nǐ) yě réngrán huì chídào de** 4 只要你诚实，谁都喜欢你。 **zhǐyào nǐ chéngshí | shéi/shuí dōu xǐhuan nǐ** 5 她不是 (在) 哭就是 (在) 捣蛋。 **tā bùshì (zài) kū jiùshì (zài) dǎodàn** 6 今晚我们在家吃饭还是上饭馆？ **jīn wǎn wǒmen zài jiā chīfàn háishi shàng fànguǎn** 7 他虽然去过几次日本，(他) 仍然不会说日语。 **tā suīrán qù guo jǐ cì rìběn | (tā) réngrán bù huì shuō rìyǔ** 8 你去法国还是 (去) 意大利 度假？ **nǐ qǔ fǎguó háishi (qù) yìdàlì dùjià** 9 他们总是谈政治，所以/因此没 (有) 人去找他们。 **tāmen zǒngshì tán zhèngzhì | suǒyǐ/yīncǐ méi (yǒu) rén qù zhǎo tāmen** 10 (如果)天气好的话，我要么去钓鱼，要么去爬山。 **(rúguǒ) tiānqì hǎo de huà | wǒ yàome qù diàoyú | yàome qù páshān**

Unit 12

Exercise 12.1   1 宁愿/宁可...也... **nìngyuàn/nìngkě | yě**   2 虽然...
但是... **suīrán | dànshì**   3 哪怕...也... **nǎpà | yě**   4 与其...不如... **yǔqí
| bùrú**   5 免得/以免 **miǎnde/yǐmiǎn**   6 要是/如果...就... **yàoshi/rúguǒ | jiù**
7 为了/以便 **wèile/yǐbiàn**   8 即使 **jíshǐ**...也 **yě**   9 就 **jiù**   10 虽然...仍然
(还)... **suīrán | réngrán (hái)**   11 如果...就... **rúguǒ | jiù**   12 刚/一...
就... **gāng/yī | jiù**

Exercise 12.2   1 他们一边喝茶一边谈话。 **tāmen yībiān hē chá yībiān
tánhuà**   2 她又会开车，又会骑马。 **tā yòu huì kāichē | yòu huì qí mǎ**
3 她越生气，他就越笑她。 **tā yuè shēngqì | tā jiù yuè xiào tā**   4 你想说什么
就说什么。 **nǐ xiǎng shuō shénme jiù shuō shénme**   5 你去哪儿，我也去
哪儿。 **nǐ qù nǎr | wǒ yě qù nǎr**   6 他一面说，一面向门那儿走去。 **tā yīmiàn
shuō | yīmiàn xiàng mén nàr zǒu qù**   7 谁合适就选谁。 **shéi/shuí héshì jiù
xuǎn shéi/shuí**   8 雪球越滚越大。 **xuě qiú yuè gǔn yuè dà**

Exercise 12.3   1 邻居一开音乐，我就头疼。 **línjū yī kāi yīnyuè | wǒ jiù
tóu téng**   2 她生气的话，我就去道歉。 **tā shēngqì de huà | wǒ jiù qù dàoqiàn**
3 为了让/使大家能听清楚，老师讲课的声音很大。 **wèile ràng/shǐ dàjiā néng
tīng qīngchu | lǎoshī jiǎngkè de shēngyīn hěn dà** or 老师讲课的声音很大，
以便大家能听清楚。 **lǎoshī jiǎngkè de shēngyīn hěn dà | yǐbiàn dàjiā néng
tīng qīngchu**   4 与其上馆子，(倒) 不如自己煮。 **yǔqí shàng guǎnzi | (dào)
bùrú zìjǐ zhǔ**   5 会议开始了，他还没(有)赶到。 **huìyì kāishǐ le | tā hái méi(yǒu)
gǎn dào**   6 只要你努力，就一定能学好汉语。 **zhǐyào nǐ nǔlì | jiù yīdìng néng
xué hǎo hànyǔ**   7 穿上你的靴子，以免在雪地上滑倒。 **chuān shàng nǐ de
xuēzi | yǐmiǎn zài xuědì shang huá dǎo**   8 他能一面弹琴，一面唱歌。 **tā néng
yīmiàn tán qín | yīmiàn chàng gē**   9 外面下着大雪，他却只穿着一件衬衫。
wàimian xià zhe dà xuě | tā què zhǐ chuān zhe yī jiàn chènshān   10 你喜欢
喝什么，我就给你倒什么。 **nǐ xǐhuan hē shénme | wǒ jiù gěi nǐ dào shénme**

Exercise 12.4   1 你一回来就来见我。 **nǐ yī huí lái jiù lái jiàn wǒ**   2 即使你
回来晚了，也要来见我。 **jíshǐ nǐ huí lái wǎn le | yě yào lái jiàn wǒ**   3 我宁愿/
宁可今天回来，也不等到明天才来见你。**wǒ nìngyuàn/nìngkě jīntiān huí lái | yě
bù děng dào míngtiān cái lái jiàn nǐ**   4 只有等我回来，才能来见我。 **zhǐyǒu
děng wǒ huí lái | cái néng lái jiàn nǐ**   5 如果你现在不能回来/回不来，那么晚
点儿才来见我吧。 **rúguǒ nǐ xiànzài bù néng huí lái/huí bu lái | nàme wǎn diǎnr
cái lái jiàn wǒ ba**   6 我马上回来，以免见不着你。 **wǒ mǎshàng huí lái | yǐmiǎn
jiàn bu zháo nǐ**   7 谁今天回来我就见谁。 **shéi/shuí jīntiān huí lái wǒ jiù jiàn
shéi/shuí**   8 你什么时候回来，我就什么时候见你。 **nǐ shénme shíhou huí lái |
wǒ jiù shénme shíhou jiàn nǐ**

Unit 13

Exercise 13.1 1 钢笔和/与/同/跟铅笔 **gāngbǐ hé/yǔ/tóng/gēn qiānbǐ** 2 星期六或 (者) 星期日 **xīngqī liù huò(zhě) xīngqī rì** 3 他们和/与/同/跟我 **tāmen hé/yǔ/tóng/gēn wǒ** 4 无用而且无聊 **wúyòng érqiě wúliáo** 5 简短而明了 **jiǎnduǎn ér míngliáo** 6 你和/与/同/跟我 **nǐ hé/yǔ/tóng/gēn wǒ** 7 不管/无论白天还是黑夜 **bùguǎn/wúlùn báitiān háishi hēiyè** 8 小猫、小狗、小鸡以及各种小动物 **xiǎo māo | xiǎo gǒu | xiǎo jī yǐjí gè zhǒng xiǎo dòngwù** 9 玫瑰、水仙、雏菊和/以及各种各样的花 **méiguì | shuǐxiān | chújú hé/yǐjí gè zhǒng gè yàng de huā** 10 月亮和/与/同/跟星星 **yuèliàng hé/yǔ/tóng/gēn xīngxing** 11 医生或 (者) 工程师 **yīshēng huò(zhě) gōngchéngshī** 12 你或 (者) 他们 **nǐ huò(zhě) tāmen** 13 读和写 **dú hé xiě** 14 坐汽车或者坐火车 **zuò qìchē huòzhě zuò huǒchē**

Exercise 13.2 1 还是 **háishi** 2 而 **ér** 3 而 **ér** 4 不但...而且... **bùdàn | érqiě** 5 以及 **yǐjí** 6 或者 **huòzhě** 7 不管/无论...还是... **bùguǎn/wúlùn | háishi** 8 不管/无论...还是... **bùguǎn/wúlùn | háishi** 9 并且 **bìngqiě** 10 并且 **bìngqiě**

Exercise 13.3 1 她喜欢购买和/并收藏首饰。 **tā xǐhuan gòumǎi hé/bìng shōucáng shǒushi** 2 这间教室明亮而宽敞。 **zhè/zhèi jiān jiàoshì míngliàng ér kuānchang** 3 他擦桌子，我拖地板。 **tā cā zhuōzi | wǒ tuō dìbǎn** 4 你想去巴黎还是纽约旅游？ **nǐ xiǎng qù bālí háishi niǔyuē lǚyóu** 5 请你给我打电话或者发传真。 **qǐng nǐ gěi wǒ dǎ diànhuà huòzhě fā chuánzhēn** 6 我买了电视机，录象机，音响以及各种电器用品。 **wǒ mǎi le diànshìjī | lùxiàngjī | yīnxiǎng yǐjí gè zhǒng diànqì yòngpǐn** 7 这种蛋糕甜而不腻。 **zhè/zhèi zhǒng dàngāo tián ér bù nì** 8 她进了房间，开了电灯。 **tā jìn le fángjiān | kāi le diàndēng** 她进了房间并 (且) 开了电灯。 **tā jìn le fángjiān bìng(qiě) kāi le diàndēng** 9 他不但关心我，而且帮助我。 **tā bùdàn guānxīn wǒ | érqiě bāngzhù wǒ** 10 她要么吃很多，要么一点儿也不吃。 **tā yàome chī hěn duō | yàome yīdiǎnr yě bù chī**

Exercise 13.4 1 桌子上有五本书和三本杂志。 **zhuōzi shang yǒu wǔ běn shū hé sān běn zázhì** 2 学生们都在安安静静地看书或者写东西。 **xuéshengmen dōu zài ān'ānjìngjìng de kànshū huòzhě xiě dōngxi** 3 我们今天踢足球还是打网球？ **wǒmen jīntiān tī zúqiú háishi dǎ wǎngqiú** 4 咱们今天去或者明天去。 **zánmen jīntiān qù huòzhě míngtiān qù** 5 咱们今天去还是明天去？ **zánmen jīntiān qù háishi míngtiān qù** 6 那家/间商店出售毛衣、围巾、袜子以及各种毛织品。 **nà/nèi jiā/jiān shāngdiàn chūshòu máoyī | wéijīn | wàzi yǐjí gè zhǒng máozhīpǐn** 7 委员会讨论并且解决了所有的问题。 **wěiyuánhuì tǎolùn bìngqiě jiějué le suǒyǒu de wèntí** 8 她是一个严厉而慈祥的老师。 **tā shì yī gè yánlì ér cíxiáng de lǎoshī**

Unit 14

Exercise 14.1 1 新朋友 **xīn péngyou** a new friend   2 古老的城市 **gǔlǎo de chéngshì** an ancient city   3 三块蛋糕 **sān kuài dàngāo** three pieces of cake   4 很多人 **hěn duō rén** many people   5 那杯茶 **nà/nèi bēi chá** that cup of tea   6 皮裙子 **pí qúnzi** a leather skirt   7 学习好的孩子 **xuéxí hǎo de háizi** a child who studies well   8 中文老师 **zhōngwén lǎoshī** a chinese teacher   9 这张地图 **zhè/ zhèi zhāng dìtú** this map   10 热牛奶 **rè niúnǎi** hot milk   11 跳舞的男孩 **tiàowǔ de nánhái** the boy who dances   12 我爷爷 **wǒ yéye** my grandpa   13 你的房子 **nǐ de fángzi** your house   14 公司里的秘书 **gōngsī li de mìshū** the secretary of the company   15 木头桌子 **mùtou zhuōzi** a wooden table   16 他们借的书 **tāmen jiè de shū** the books they borrowed   17 干净的街道 **gānjìng de jiēdào** a clean street   18 有趣的游戏 **yǒuqù de yóuxì** an interesting game   19 三岁的儿子 **sān suì de érzi** a three-year-old son   20 英国人 **yīngguó rén** an English person

Exercise 14.2 1 我想买一本新的英文书。 **wǒ xiǎng mǎi yī běn xīn de yīngwén shū** I want to buy a new English book.   2 那是姐姐的一条旧裙子。 **nà shì jiějie de yī tiáo jiù qúnzi** or 那是一条姐姐的旧裙子。 **nà shì yī tiáo jiějie de jiù qúnzi** That is an old skirt of (my) elder sister.   3 那是一辆小李新买的很便宜的汽车。 **nà shì yī liàng xiǎo lǐ xīn mǎi de hěn piányi de qìchē** or 那是小李新买的一辆很便宜的汽车。 **nà shì xiǎo lǐ xīn mǎi de yī liàng hěn piányi de qìchē** That is a cheap car recently bought by Xiao Li.   4 她是一位出色的汉语老师。 **tā shì yī wèi chūsè de hànyǔ lǎoshī** She is an outstanding Chinese-language teacher.   5 湖旁有一对手拉着手，并肩走着的年轻人。 **hú páng yǒu yī duì shǒu lā zhe shǒu | bìngjiān zǒu zhe de niánqīng rén** By the lake there is/was a young couple walking shoulder to shoulder hand in hand.   6 有一只美丽的小鸟在密密的树林里歌唱。 **yǒu yī zhī měilì de xiǎo niǎo zài mìmì de shùlín li gēchàng** or 密密的树林里有一只美丽的小鸟在歌唱。 **mìmì de shùlín li yǒu yī zhī měilì de xiǎo niǎo zài gēchàng** There is/was a beautiful little bird singing in the dense wood.

Exercise 14.3 1 我认识很多中国朋友。 **wǒ rènshi hěn duō zhōngguó péngyou**   2 他的谎言被戳穿了。 **tā de huǎngyán bèi chuōchuān le**   3 利兹是一个有名的城市。 **lìzī shì yī gè yǒumíng de chéngshì**   4 我新买的那本故事书很有趣。 **wǒ xīn mǎi de nà/nèi běn gùshi shū hěn yǒuqù**   5 她是一个很好的大夫。 **tā shì yī gè hěn hǎo de dàifu**   6 这杯热咖啡是我的。 **zhè/zhèi bēi rè kāfēi shì wǒ de**

Exercise 14.4 1 复杂的问题常常/往往很有趣。 **fùzá de wèntí chángcháng/ wǎngwǎng hěn yǒuqù**   2 那些蓝（色）的最好。 **nà/nèi xiē lán(sè) de zuì hǎo**   3 我昨天买的那本书在哪儿？ **wǒ zuótiān mǎi de nà/nèi běn shū zài nǎr**   4 左边的那个女孩是我妹妹，右边的那个是她的朋友。 **zuǒbian de nà/nèi gè nǚhái shì wǒ mèimei | yòubian de nà/nèi gè shì tā de péngyou**   5 那位上星期来帮助你翻译唐诗的中国老教授过去是我的老师。 **nà/nèi wèi shàng xīngqī**

lái bāngzhù nǐ fānyì tángshī de zhōngguó lǎo jiàoshòu guòqù shì wǒ de lǎoshī 6 我不想买这么贵的杂志。 wǒ bù xiǎng mǎi zhème guì de zázhì 7 那辆上午八点开的火车是 (一) 辆快车。 nà/nèi liàng shàngwǔ bā diǎn kāi de huǒchē shì (yī) liàng kuàichē 8 那些中国制造的比这儿制造的好。 nà/nèi xiē zhōngguó zhìzào de bǐ zhèr zhìzào de hǎo

Unit 15

Exercise 15.1 1 我们在公园见面了。 wǒmen zài gōngyuán jiànmiàn le We met (each other) at the park. 2 他吃惊地看着我。 tā chījīng de kàn zhe wǒ He looked/was looking at me with surprise. 3 护士急匆匆地走进病房。 hùshi jícōngcōng de zǒu jìn bìngfáng The nurse came into the ward in a hurry. 4 弟弟在医院工作。 dìdi zài yīyuàn gōngzuò Younger brother works in a hospital. 5 学生常常到图书馆去。 xuésheng chángcháng dào túshūguǎn qù Students often go to the library. 6 妈妈慢慢地会说英语了。 māma mànmàn de huì shuō yīngyǔ le Slowly mother learnt how to speak English. 7 她高高兴兴地走了。 tā gāogāoxìngxìng de zǒu le She left happily. 8 病人整整一天没有吃饭。 bìngrén zhěngzhěng yī tiān méiyǒu chīfàn The patient did not eat the whole day.

Exercise 15.2 1 他显然错了。 tā xiǎnrán cuò le 2 我看电视的时候，偏偏停电了。 wǒ kàn diànshì de shíhou | piānpiān tíng diàn le 3 秘书气得几乎说不出话来。 mìshū qì de jīhū shuō bu chū huà lái 4 我幸亏没 (有) 坐那辆车。 wǒ xìngkuī méi(yǒu) zuò nà/nèi liàng chē 5 我简直不想见她。 wǒ jiǎnzhí bù xiǎng jiàn tā 6 这件事也许是真的。 zhè/zhèi jiàn shì yěxǔ shì zhēn de 7 他总算说出真相。 tā zǒngsuàn shuō chū zhēnxiàng 8 她甚至会驾驶飞机。 tā shènzhì huì jiàshǐ fēijī

Exercise 15.3 1 爸爸六点钟就回家。 bàba liù diǎn zhōng jiù huí jiā 2 他们在礼堂开会。 tāmen zài lǐtáng kāihuì 3 我们上午在花园除草。 wǒmen shàngwǔ zài huāyuán chú cǎo 4 小李今天才写完论文。 xiǎo lǐ jīntiān cái xiě wán lùnwén 5 明天也许会下雪。 míngtiān yěxǔ huì xià xuě 6 我慢慢地喝了一杯茶。 wǒ mànmàn de hē le yī bēi chá 7 她一个人在家里看电视。 tā yī gè rén zài jiā li kàn diànshì 8 那位医生在这个医院工作了三年。 nà/nèi wèi yīshēng zài zhè/zhèi gè yīyuàn gōngzuò le sān nián

Exercise 15.4 1 医生晚上九点钟才到。 yīshēng wǎnshang jiǔ diǎn zhōng cái dào 2 明天我要在图书馆做些研究。 míngtiān wǒ yào zài túshūguǎn zuò xiē yánjiū 3 我五年没去北京了。 wǒ wǔ nián méi qù běijīng le 我没去北京五年了。 wǒ méi qù běijīng wǔ nián le 4 他只买了两本书。 tā zhǐ mǎi le liǎng běn shū 5 因为我说不喜欢她哭，她就偏偏哭起来。 yīnwèi wǒ shuō bù xǐhuan tā kū | tā jiù piānpiān kū qǐlái 6 那些学生甚至会说广州话。 nà/nèi xiē xuésheng shènzhì huì shuō guǎngzhōu huà 7 他清清楚楚地解释了那个问题。 tā qīngqīngchǔchu de jiěshè le nà/nèi gè wèntí 8 我走了。 wǒ zǒu le 9 请 (你) 再说一遍。 qǐng (nǐ) zài shuō yī biàn 10 请 (你) 说得慢一点儿。 qǐng (nǐ) shuō de màn yīdiǎnr 请你慢慢说。 qǐng nǐ mànmàn shuō

Unit 16

Exercise 16.1   1 一条繁忙的马路/街道 **yī tiáo fánmáng de mǎlù/jiēdào**
2 一张旧沙发 **yī zhāng jiù shāfā**   3 一条弯弯曲曲的小路 **yī tiáo wānwān qūqū
de xiǎo lù**   4 我爱看的杂志 **wǒ ài kàn de zázhì**   5 车站那儿的商店 **chēzhàn
nàr de shāngdiàn**   6 我母亲昨天买的外套   **wǒ mǔqīn zuótiān mǎi de
wàitào**   7 山脚下的村庄 **shānjiǎo xià de cūnzhuāng**   8 我骑的自行车 **wǒ qí
de zìxíngchē**   9 一张木头桌子 **yī zhāng mùtou zhuōzi**   10 一个塑料容器
yī gè sùliào róngqì

Exercise 16.2   1 很厚的杂志 **hěn hòu de zázhì** 'a very thick magazine'
2 短裙子 **duǎn qúnzi** 'a short skirt'   3 红色的玫瑰 **hóngsè de méiguì** 'a red rose'
4 我的办公室 **wǒ de bàngōngshì** 'my office'   5 他 (的) 侄女 **tā (de) zhínǚ**
'his niece'   6 当地的图书馆 **dāngdì de túshūguǎn** 'the local library'   7 海上
的轮船 **hǎi shang de lúnchuán** 'ships at sea'   8 旧钟 **jiù zhōng** 'an old
clock'   9 羊毛手套 **yángmáo shǒutào** 'a pair of woollen gloves'   10 聪明的
孩子 **cōngming de háizi** 'a clever child'   11 深深的海洋 **shēnshēn de hǎiyáng**
'a very deep ocean'   12 中文报纸 **zhōngwén bàozhǐ** 'Chinese newspapers'

Exercise 16.3   1 这本书是 (用) 中文写的。   **zhè/zhèi běn shū shì (yòng)
zhōngwén xiě de**   2 那是他的地图。 **nà shì tā de dìtú**   3 这是我的新手表。
zhè shì wǒ de xīn shǒubiǎo   4 这是妈妈讲给我听的故事。 **zhè shì māma jiǎng
gěi wǒ tīng de gùshi**   5 她的书包是新的。 **tā de shūbāo shì xīn de**   6 拳击台
是方的。 **quánjītái shì fāng de**   7 他说的是真的。 **tā shuō de shì zhēn de**
8 这件礼物是我爷爷给的。 **zhè/zhèi jiàn lǐwù shì wǒ yéye gěi de**

Exercise 16.4   1 你给我的礼物 **nǐ gěi wǒ de lǐwù**   2 她喜欢喝的 **tā xǐhuan
hē de**   3 乱七八糟的 **luànqībāzāo de**   4 穿红裙子的 **chuān hóng qúnzi de**
5 你说的 **nǐ shuō de**   6 红的，黄的和蓝的 **hóng de | huáng de hé lán de**

Exercise 16.5   1 地 **de**   2 得 **de**   3 的 **de**   4 地 **de**   5 的 **de**   6 得 **de**
7 得 **de**   8 得 **de**   9 地 **de**   10 得 **de**   11 得 **de**   12 地 **de**

Exercise 16.6   1 我的朋友是一个坚强的人。   **wǒ de péngyou shì yī gè
jiānqiáng de rén**   2 每个学生都写得很好。   **měi gè xuésheng dōu xiě de
hěn hǎo**   3 亚洲的经济发展得很快。 **yàzhōu de jīngjì fāzhǎn de hěn kuài**
4 那位高大的运动员是我弟弟。   **nà/nèi wèi gāodà de yùndòngyuán shì wǒ
dìdi**   5 他开车开得很危险。 **tā kāichē kāi de hěn wēixiǎn**   6 回答问题前你
应该仔细地想想。 **huídá wèntí qián nǐ yīnggāi zǐxì de xiǎngxiǎng**

Exercise 16.7   1 他跑得很快。 **tā pǎo de hěn kuài**   2 我静静地躺下来。 **wǒ
jìngjìng de tǎng xiàlái**   3 昨晚我睡得很好。 **zuó wǎn wǒ shuì de hěn hǎo** or
我昨晚睡得很好。**wǒ zuó wǎn shuì de hěn hǎo**   4 那位经理努力工作。 **nà/nèi
wèi jīnglǐ nǔlì gōngzuò**   5 那位经理显然工作得很努力。   **nà/nèi wèi jīnglǐ**

xiǎnrán gōngzuò de hěn nǔlì 6 那位教师教得很好。 **nà/nèi wèi jiàoshī jiāo de hěn hǎo** 7 那个小女孩穿得很漂亮。 **nà/nèi gè xiǎo nǔhái chuān de hěn piàoliang** 8 那个说话说得很清楚的人是以前没说过话的新老师。 **nà/nèi gè shuōhuà shuō de hěn qīngchu de rén shì yǐqián méi shuō guo huà de xīn lǎoshī** 9 那个静静地坐在后面的人是谁？ **nà/nèi gè jìngjìng de zuò zài hòumian de rén shì shéi/shuí** 10 那些买不到票的人很生气/愤怒，他们都在大声叫嚷。 **nà/nèi xiē mǎi bu dào piào de rén hěn shēngqì/fènnù | tāmen dōu zài dà shēng jiàorǎng**

Unit 17

Exercise 17.1 1 每 **měi** 2 各 **gè**, 各 **gè** 3 每 **měi**, 每 **měi** 4 各 **gè** 5 每 **měi** 6 每 **měi** 7 每 **měi** 8 每 **měi** 9 每 **měi** 10 各 **gè**

Exercise 17.2 1 谁 **shéi/shuí** 2 什么 **shénme** 3 谁 **shéi/shuí** 4 什么 **shénme** 5 哪儿 **nǎr** 6 谁 **shéi/shuí** 7 谁 **shéi/shuí** 8 什么 **shénme** 9 怎么 **zénme** 10 什么 **shénme**

Exercise 17.3 1 哥哥每年夏天都去游泳。 **gēge měi nián xiàtiān dōu qù yóuyǒng** 2 correct 3 每个电影都很惊险。 **měi gè diànyǐng dōu hěn jīngxiǎn** 4 这些字每个写五遍。 **zhè/zhèi xiē zì měi gè xiě wǔ biàn** 5 每个人都需要自由。 **měi gè rén dōu/yě xūyào zìyóu** 6 奶奶吃什么都/也没 (有) 味道。 **nǎinai chī shénme dōu/yě méi(yǒu) wèidao** 7 correct 8 每个地方都有草坪。 **měi gè dìfang dōu yǒu cǎopíng**

Exercise 17.4 1 学校里谁都认识王校长。 **xuéxiào lǐ shéi/shuí dōu rènshi wáng xiàozhǎng** 2 他今天不舒服，什么也不想吃。 **tā jīntiān bù shūfu | shénme yě bù xiǎng chī** 3 谁都说安妮好。 **shéi/shuí dōu shuō ānnī hǎo** 4 哪儿都找过了，钥匙还是没(有)找到。 **nǎr dōu zhǎo guo le | yàoshi háishi méi(yǒu) zhǎo dào** 5 什么都在好起来。 **shénme dōu zài hǎo qǐlái** 6 谁都信任她。 **shéi/shuí dōu xìnrèn tā** 7 她哪儿都/也不想去。 **tā nǎr dōu/yě bù xiǎng qù** 8 什么有汽的饮料他都不喝。 **shénme yǒu qì de yǐnliào tā dōu bù hē** or 他不喝什么有汽的饮料。 **tā bù hē shénme yǒu qì de yǐnliào**

Exercise 17.5 1 北京哪儿都有饭馆。 **běijīng nǎr dōu yǒu fànguǎn** 2 我儿子每两天给我打一次电话。 **wǒ érzi měi liǎng tiān gěi wǒ dǎ yī cì diànhuà** 3 你什么也不必做。 **nǐ shénme yě bùbì zuò** 4 每天五点半，办公室里谁都结束工作。 **měi tiān wǔ diǎn bàn | bàngōngshì li shéi/shuí dōu jiéshù gōngzuò** 5 这张照片里我认不出什么人。 **zhè/zhèi zhāng zhàopiàn li wǒ rèn bu chū shénme rén** or 这张照片里我谁也不认识。 **zhè/zhèi zhāng zhàopiàn li wǒ shéi/shuí yě bù rènshi** 6 他每次开口，我们都要笑。 **tā měi cì kāi kǒu | wǒmen dōu yào xiào** 7 什么时候都行。 **shénme shíhou dōu xíng** 8 这儿哪儿也没有什么小商店了。 **zhèr nǎr yě méi yǒu shénme xiǎo shāngdiàn le**

Unit 18

Exercise 18.1 1 比 **bǐ** 2 比 **bǐ** 3 没有 **méiyǒu** 4 跟 **gēn** 5 跟 **gēn** 6 没有 **méiyǒu** 7 没有 **méiyǒu** 8 比 **bǐ** 9 没有 **méiyǒu** 10 比 **bǐ** 11 跟 **gēn** 12 不跟 **bù gēn**

Exercise 18.2 1 我没有他那么高。 **wǒ méiyǒu tā nàme gāo** or 我比他矮一 厘米。 **wǒ bǐ tā ǎi yī límǐ** or 他比我高一厘米。 **tā bǐ wǒ gāo yī límǐ** 2 这个故 事比那个故事复杂。 **zhè/zhèi gè gùshi bǐ nà/nèi gè gùshi fùzá** 3 他现在认识 的汉字比去年 (认识的) 多。 **tā xiànzài rènshi de hànzì bǐ qùnián (rènshi de) duō** or 他去年认识的汉字没有现在认识的多。 **tā qùnián rènshi de hànzì méiyǒu xiànzài rènshi de duō** 4 这个运动员比那个运动员跑得快。 **zhè/zhèi gè yùndòngyuán bǐ nà/nèi gè yùndòngyuán pǎo de kuài** 5 小李跳舞比我 跳得好。 **xiǎo lǐ tiàowǔ bǐ wǒ tiào de hǎo** or 小李跳舞跳得比我好。 **xiǎo lǐ tiàowǔ tiào de bǐ wǒ hǎo** 6 加拿大比英国大得多。 **jiānádà bǐ yīngguó dà de duō** 7 陈老师教书教得比小王认真。 **chén lǎoshī jiāoshū jiāo de bǐ xiǎo wáng rènzhēn** or 陈老师教书比小王教得认真。 **chén lǎoshī jiāoshū bǐ xiǎo wáng jiāo de rènzhēn** or 小王教书没有陈老师 (教得) (那么) 认真。 **xiǎo wáng jiāoshū méiyǒu chén lǎoshī (jiāo de) (nàme)/rènzhēn** or 小王教书教得没有陈老师 (那么) 认真。 **xiǎo wáng jiāoshū jiāo de méiyǒu chén lǎoshī (nàme)/rènzhēn** 8 这扇门跟那扇 门油漆得一样白。 **zhè/zhèi shàn mén gēn nà/nèi shàn mén yóuqī de yīyàng bái**

Exercise 18.3 1 这条街道比那条更宽。 **zhè/zhèi tiáo jiēdào bǐ nà/nèi tiáo gèng kuān** 2 我写诗比我侄子写得好。 **wǒ xiě shī bǐ wǒ zhízi xiě de hǎo** or 我写诗写得比我侄子好。 **wǒ xiě shī xiě de bǐ wǒ zhízi hǎo** 3 小李对工作 没有你 (对工作) 负责。 **xiǎo lǐ duì gōngzuò méiyǒu nǐ (duì gōngzuò) fùzé** 4 他没有以前那样喜欢串门了。 **tā méiyǒu yǐqián nà/nèi yàng xǐhuan chuànmén le** 5 爸爸跟妈妈一样经常帮助人。 **bàba gēn māma yīyàng jīngcháng bāngzhù rén** 6 伦敦比利兹拥挤得多。 **lúndūn bǐ lìzī yōngjǐ de duō**

Exercise 18.4 1 我认识的人没有你那么多。 **wǒ rènshi de rén méiyǒu nǐ nàme duō** or 我没有你认识的人那么多。 **wǒ méiyǒu nǐ rènshi de rén nàme duō** 2 她弹钢琴比他弹得好。 **tā tán gāngqín bǐ tā tán de hǎo** or 她弹钢琴弹得比 他好。 **tā tán gāngqín tán de bǐ tā hǎo** 3 她的文章比你的长。 **tā de wénzhāng bǐ nǐ de cháng** 4 我的电脑比你的容易出毛病。 **wǒ de diànnǎo bǐ nǐ de róngyì chū máobìng** 5 今年春天没有去年暖和。 **jīnnián chūntiān méiyǒu qùnián nuǎnhuo** 6 他打网球没有你打得好。 **tā dǎ wǎngqiú méiyǒu nǐ dǎ de hǎo** or 他打网球打得没有你好。 **tā dǎ wǎngqiú dǎ de méiyǒu nǐ hǎo** 7 这个跟那个一 样大。 **zhè/zhèi gè gēn nà/nèi gè yīyàng dà** 8 今天这儿的人跟昨天的一样多。 **jīntiān zhèr de rén gēn zuótiān de yīyàng duō** 9 印度的人口仍然没有中国 那么多。 **yìndù de rénkǒu réngrán méiyǒu zhōngguó nàme duō** 10 比这个 漂亮的那个没有这个那么贵。 **bǐ zhè/zhèi gè piàoliang de nà/nèi gè méiyǒu zhè/zhèi gè nàme guì**

Unit 19

Exercise 19.1 1 有经验的老师 **yǒu jīngyàn de lǎoshī** 2 有很多医生 **yǒu hěn duō yīshēng** 3 有雨 **yǒu yǔ** 4 有三个兄弟 **yǒu sān gè xiōngdì** 5 有几家商店 **yǒu jǐ jiā shāngdiàn** 6 有很大的提高 **yǒu hěn dà de tígāo**

Exercise 19.2 1 一年有春，夏，秋，冬四季。 **yī nián yǒu chūn | xià | qiū | dōng sìjì** 2 天气闷热得很，一点风也没有。 **tiānqì mènrè de hěn | yī diǎn fēng yě méi yǒu** 3 我家一共有四口人。 **wǒ jiā yīgòng yǒu sì kǒu rén** 4 昨晚在礼堂有一个舞会。 **zuó wǎn zài lǐtáng yǒu yī gè wǔhuì** 5 那棵小树有一个大人那么高了。 **nà/nèi kē xiǎo shù yǒu yī gè dàrén nàme gāo le** 6 现在有十二点了吧？ **xiànzài yǒu shí èr diǎn le ba** 7 这个人对什么都没有兴趣。 **zhè/zhèi gè rén duì shénme dōu méi yǒu xìngqù** 8 门前有块草坪。 **mén qián yǒu kuài cǎopíng**

Exercise 19.3 1 动物园里动物很多，有的在天上飞，有的在地下跑，有的在水里游。 **dòngwùyuán li dòngwù hěn duō | yǒu de zài tiān shang fēi | yǒu de zài dì xià pǎo | yǒu de zài shuǐ li yóu** 2 河边有不少人，有的在钓鱼，有的在看书，有的在散步，有的在晒太阳。 **hé biān yǒu bù shǎo rén | yǒu de zài diào yú | yǒu de zài kànshū | yǒu de zài sànbù | yǒu de zài shài tàiyáng** 3 妹妹有很多皮鞋，有的是红的，有的是黑的，有的是白的。 **mèimei yǒu hěn duō píxié | yǒu de shì hóng de | yǒu de shì hēi de | yǒu de shì bái de**

Exercise 19.4 1 有趣 **yǒuqù** 2 有可能 **yǒu kěnéng** 3 没有礼貌 **méiyǒu lǐmào** 4 有经验 **yǒu jīngyàn** 5 有胆量 **yǒu dǎnliàng** 6 没有希望 **méiyǒu xīwàng** 7 有钱 **yǒuqián** 8 有权 (力) **yǒu quán(lì)** 9 有办法 **yǒu bànfǎ** 10 有头脑 **yǒu tóunǎo**

Exercise 19.5 1 一年有十二个月。 **yī nián yǒu shí èr gè yuè** 2 市中心有 (一) 座大桥。 **shìzhōngxīn yǒu (yī) zuò dà qiáo** 3 我们图书馆 (里) 的书，有的是英文的，有的是中文的。 **wǒmen túshūguǎn (li) de shū | yǒu de shì yīngwén de | yǒu de shì zhōngwén de** 4 星期三下午有一场足球比赛。 **xīngqī sān xiàwǔ yǒu yī chǎng zúqiú bǐsài** 5 学中文的学生都有了很大的进步。 **xué zhōngwén de xuésheng dōu yǒu le hěn dà de jìnbù** 6 今天的课/讲演很有趣。 **jīntiān de kè/jiǎngyǎn hěn yǒuqù** 7 这儿有电话 (机) 吗？ **zhèr yǒu diànhuà(jī) ma** 8 你问的问题不合理，我没有办法回答。 **nǐ wèn de wèntí bù hélǐ | wǒ méiyǒu bànfǎ huídá**

Unit 20

Exercise 20.1 1 我弟弟是个邮递员。 **wǒ dìdi shì gè yóudìyuán** 2 那个运动员高极了。 **nà/nèi gè yùndòngyuán gāo jí le** 3 下雨了。 **xià yǔ le**

4 这不是 (一架) 电脑。 **zhè bù shì (yī jià) diànnǎo**   5 玫瑰是红的。 **méiguì shì hóng de**   6 他们不是工程师。 **tāmen bù shì gōngchéngshī**   7 桌子上有个果盆。 **zhuōzi shang yǒu gè guǒpén**   8 鱼缸里的鱼不是热带鱼。 **yúgāng li de yú bù shì rèdài yú**   9 他是一个医生。 **tā shì yī gè yīshēng**   10 这个会议非常重要。 **zhè/zhèi gè huìyì fēicháng zhòngyào**   11 那个湖很深。 **nà/nèi gè hú hěn shēn**   12 时间到了。 **shíjiān dào le**   13 晚了。 **wǎn le**   14 那儿有条狗。 **nàr yǒu tiáo gǒu**

Exercise 20.2   In the following sentences, 是 **shì** may be omitted: 1, 3, 5

Exercise 20.3   1 他是前年来的英国。 **tā shì qiánnián lái de yīngguó** or 他是前年来英国的。 **tā shì qiánnián lái yīngguó de**   2 体操比赛是在体育馆举行的。 **tǐcāo bǐsài shì zài tǐyùguǎn jǔxíng de**   3 学生是骑自行车去的学校。 **xuésheng shì qí zìxíngchē qù de xuéxiào**   4 是护士给病人喂的药。 **shì hùshi gěi bìngrén wèi de yào**   5 是他告诉我这个秘密的。 **shì tā gàosu wǒ zhè/zhèi gè mìmì de**   6 这双鞋是比那双鞋漂亮。 **zhè/zhèi shuāng xié shì bǐ nà/nèi shuāng xié piàoliang**   7 她是愿意做我的朋友的。 **tā shì yuànyì zuò wǒ de péngyou de**   8 我是不喜欢游泳的。 **wǒ shì bù xǐhuan yóuyǒng de**   9 他是卖的旧书。 **tā shì mài de jiù shū**   10 中国人是用筷子吃饭的。 **zhōngguó rén shì yòng kuàizi chīfàn de**   11 她是三年前学的打字。 **tā shì sān nián qián xué de dǎzì**   12 是闹钟把我闹醒的。 **shì nàozhōng bǎ wǒ nào xǐng de**

Exercise 20.4   1 你妹妹是不是喜欢看科学幻想小说？ **nǐ mèimei shì bu shì xǐhuan kàn kēxué huànxiǎng xiǎoshuō**   2 他是不是能用筷子搛菜？ **tā shì bu shì néng yòng kuàizi jiān cài**   3 这件事是不是很重要？ **zhè/zhèi jiàn shì shì bù shì hěn zhòngyào**   4 吃完饭，他是不是帮你洗碗？ **chī wán fàn | tā shì bu shì bāng nǐ xǐ wǎn**   5 爸爸前天是不是把篱笆修好了？ **bàba qiántiān shì bu shì bǎ líba xiū hǎo le**   6 妈妈昨晚是不是用烤炉烤的鸡。 **māma zuó wǎn shì bù shì yòng kǎolú kǎo de jī**

Exercise 20.5   1 这个地方/这儿以前是个电影院，但是现在是个俱乐部 (了)。 **zhè/zhèi gè dìfang/zhèr yǐqián shì gè diànyǐngyuàn | dànshì xiànzài shì gè jùlèbù (le)**   2 我们不是坐火车来的。 **wǒmen bù shì zuò huǒchē lái de**   3 那件毛衣是很好看，可是我买不起。 **nà/nèi jiàn máoyī shì hěn hǎokàn | kěshì wǒ mǎi bu qǐ**   4 他买的那辆车是红的。 **tā mǎi de nà/nèi liàng chē shì hóng de**   5 明天星期五。 **míngtiān xīngqī wǔ**   6 我太太今年三十岁。 **wǒ tàitai jīnnián sān shí suì**   7 那个手表你是在香港买的吗？ **nà/nèi gè shǒubiǎo nǐ shì zài xiānggǎng mǎi de ma**   8 他们是星期六来看我们，不是星期五。 **tāmen shì xīngqī liù lái kàn wǒmen | bù shì xīngqī wǔ**   9 我是一九九零年上的大学，他却是一九九二年才上的大学。 **wǒ shì yī jiǔ jiǔ líng nián shàng de dàxué | tā què shì yī jiǔ jiǔ èr nián cái shàng de dàxué**   10 今晚吃饭的钱/今晚的饭钱是你付还是我付？ **jīn wǎn chīfàn de qián/jīn wǎn de fànqián shì nǐ fù háishì wǒ fù**

Unit 21

Exercise 21.1 1 correct   2 我采了一些蘑菇。**wǒ cǎi le yīxiē mógu**   3 他去看牙医了。**tā qù kàn yáyī le**   4 他侄女常常给他写信。**tā zhínǚ chángcháng gěi tā xiě xìn**   5 她来参加舞会。**tā lái cānjiā wǔhuì**   6 我从没吃过龙虾。**wǒ cóng méi chī guo lóngxiā**   7 他用扫帚扫地。**tā yòng sàozhou sǎo dì**   8 我骑自行车旅行。**wǒ qí zìxíngchē lǚxíng**   9 correct   10 correct   11 我过去爱看小说。**wǒ guòqù ài kàn xiǎoshuō**   12 他准备买电脑。**tā zhǔnbèi mǎi diànnǎo**   13 会计数了数钱。**kuàijì shǔ le shǔ qián**   14 老师看了一下手表。**lǎoshī kàn le yīxià shǒubiǎo**   15 correct

Exercise 21.2 1 湿了 **shī le**   2 黄了 **huáng le**   3 少了 **shǎo le**   4 准备好了 **zhǔnbèi hǎo le**   5 撬开了 **qiào kāi le**   6 锁好了 **suǒ hǎo le**   7 开了 **kāi le**   8 打破了 **dǎ pò le**   9 好了 **hǎo le**   10 老了 **lǎo le**   11 病了 **bìng le**   12 圆了 **yuán le**   13 坏了 **huài le**   14 枯萎了/谢了 **kūwěi le/xiè le**   15 寄走了 **jì zǒu le**   16 扫干净了 **sǎo gānjìng le**   17 都到了 **dōu dào le**   18 结束了 **jiéshù le**   19 修好了 **xiū hǎo le**   20 弄脏了 **nòng zāng le**

Exercise 21.3 1 我写了两封信（了）。**wǒ xiě le liǎng fēng xìn (le)**   2 我朋友买了今天的报纸。**wǒ péngyou mǎi le jīntiān de bàozhǐ**   3 今天上午病人吃了点药。**jīntiān shàngwǔ bìngrén chī le diǎn yào**   4 玻璃窗破了。**bōlichuāng pò le**   5 他高了三公分（了）。**tā gāo le sān gōngfēn (le)**   6 电视机修好了。**diànshìjī xiū hǎo le**   7 学生毕业了。**xuésheng bìyè le**   8 我们参观了博物馆。**wǒmen cānguān le bówùguǎn**   9 我学了三年中文。**wǒ xué le sān nián zhōngwén**   10 我学了三年中文了。**wǒ xué le sān nián zhōngwén le**   11 我们今天下午走。**wǒmen jīntiān xiàwǔ zǒu**   12 我不喝啤酒了。**wǒ bù hē píjiú le**

Exercise 21.4 It had gone dark, the sun had set and the little birds had returned to their nests.

The moon had risen. From the lakes came a breeze and the surrounding trees rustled.

At this moment, Father came home.

He came through the door, wiped his shoes on the doormat, took off his hat, hung up his coat, turned around and kissed me, and then went into the kitchen.

Mother had already prepared the meal for him. Father sat down, took a sip of the tea, and smiled at my mother. Then he picked up his knife and fork and started to devour the food ravenously.

In a while, Father finished his meal and returned to the living room. He called me to his side and asked: 'Have you finished your homework? Do you want to watch television?' I nodded. He went over and switched on the television. By now, Mother had finished washing the dishes and wiping the table. She came out of the kitchen and sat down to watch television with us.

Unit 22

Exercise 22.1   1 过 **guo**, 了 **le**   2 着 **zhe**, 着 **zhe**   3 (正) 在 (**zhèng**) **zài**   4 着 **zhe**   5 着 **zhe**   6 着 **zhe**, 了 **le**   7 着 **zhe**   8 过 **guo**   9 过 **guo**, 了 **le**   10 (正) 在 (**zhèng**)**zài**, 着 **zhe**   11 (正) 在 (**zhèng**)**zài**   12 (正) 在 (**zhèng**)**zài**, (正) 在 (**zhèng**)**zài**, 呢 **ne**

Exercise 22.2   1 汽车沿着大路疾驶。 **qìchē yán zhe dà lù jíshǐ**   2 学生们在打篮球。 **xuéshengmen zài dǎ lánqiú**   3 奶奶戴着一顶帽子。 **nǎinai dài zhe yī dǐng màozi**   4 她说着说着笑了起来。 **tā shuō zhe shuō zhe xiào le qǐlái**   5 我去过那个古堡。 **wǒ qù guo nà/nèi gè gǔbǎo**   6 经理从来没有跟我们生过气。 **jīnglǐ cónglái méi(yǒu) gēn wǒmen shēng guo qì**   7 这回爸爸没穿牛仔裤。 **zhè/zhèi huí bàba méi chuān niúzǎikù**   8 我没有学过化学。 **wǒ méi(yǒu) xué guo huàxué**   9 她买了很多激光唱片。 **tā mǎi le hěn duō jīguāng chàngpiàn**   10 我在缝衣服。 **wǒ zài féng yīfu**

Exercise 22.3   1 这个运动员高着呢。 **zhè/zhèi gè yùndòngyuán gāo zhe ne**   2 我心里急着呢。 **wǒ xīnli jí zhe ne**   3 我们的老师严着呢。 **wǒmen de lǎoshī yán zhe ne**   4 他的朋友多着呢。 **tā de péngyou duō zhe ne**   5 那道题目难着呢。 **nà/nèi dào tímù nán zhe ne**   6 这件事怪着呢。 **zhè/zhèi jiàn shì guài zhe ne**

Exercise 22.4   1 你看过京剧吗/没有？ **nǐ kàn guo jīngjù ma/méiyou**   2 他们在那儿坐着等律师来。 **tāmen zài nàr zuò zhe děng lǜshī lái**   3 外面有人在抽雪茄烟。 **wàimian yǒu rén zài chōu xuějiāyān**   4 她笑着走了进来。 **tā xiào zhe zǒu le jìnlái**   5 墙上贴着几张政治标语。 **qiáng shang tiē zhe jǐ zhāng zhèngzhì biāoyǔ**   6 他跑着跑着腿都酸了。 **tā pǎo zhe pǎo zhe tuǐ dōu suān le**   7 我从来没有这么快乐过。 **wǒ cónglái méi(yǒu) zhème kuàilè guo**   8 我 (从前) 做/当过新闻记者。 **wǒ (cóngqián) zuò/dāng guo xīnwén jìzhě**   9 我去看他时/去看他的时候，他正在看电视。 **wǒ qù kàn tā shí/qù kàn tā de shíhou | tā (zhèng)zài kàn diànshì**   10 那个人在做/干什么？ **nà/nèi gè rén zài zuò/gàn shénme**

Unit 23

Exercise 23.1   1 来着 **lái zhe**   2 罢了 **bà le**   3 来着 **lái zhe**   4 嘛 **ma**   5 呗 **bei**   6 罢了 **bà le**   7 呗 **bei**   8 嘛 **ma**   9 来着 **lái zhe**   10 罢了 **bà le**

Exercise 23.2   1 这个问题么，很复杂。 **zhè/zhèi gè wèntí me | hěn fùzá**   2 你饿了么，就先吃。 **nǐ è le me | jiù xiān chī**   3 去看电影吧，没钱；待在家里吧，无聊。 **qù kàn diànyǐng ba | méi qián | dāi zài jiā li ba | wúliáo**   4 坐飞机吧，危险；坐轮船吧，太慢。 **zuò fēijī ba | wēixiǎn | zuò lúnchuán ba | tài màn**   5 他当领导吧，不行。 **tā dāng lǐngdǎo ba | bù xíng**   6 让我去么，我就去。 **ràng wǒ qù me | wǒ jiù qù**

Exercise 23.3   1 你要走就走吧，我也没有办法。 **nǐ yào zǒu jiù zǒu ba | wǒ yě méi(yǒu) bànfǎ**   2 碎就碎了吧，再买一个新的呗。 **suì jiù suì le ba | zài mǎi yī gè xīn de bei**   3 他当然会做，他是数学家嘛。 **tā dāngrán huì zuò | tā shì shùxuéjiā ma**   4 这次考得不好，以后努力呗。 **zhè/zhèi cì kǎo de bù hǎo | yǐhòu nǔlì bei**   5 那很容易嘛。 **nà hěn róngyì ma**   6 这个人么，我记不起来了。 **zhè/zhèi gè rén me | wǒ jì bu qǐlái le**

Exercise 23.4   1 你说什么来着？ **nǐ shuō shénme lái zhe**   2 我只是想问个问题嘛/罢了。 **wǒ zhǐshì xiǎng wèn gè wèntí ma/bà le**   3 说我赢了吧，太骄傲；说没赢吧，不是真的。 **shuō wǒ yíng le ba | tài jiāo'ào | shuō méi yíng ba | bù shì zhēn de**   4 你不愿跟我说话么，我就不再来了。 **nǐ bù yuàn gēn wǒ shuōhuà me | wǒ jiù bù zài lái le**   5 说这个贵么，是贵；总之你买不起。 **shuō zhè/zhèi gè guì me | shì guì | zǒngzhī nǐ mǎi bu qǐ**   6 他是这个公司的经理呗！ **tā shì zhè/zhèi gè gōngsī de jīnglǐ bei**   7 我只想使你高兴罢了。 **wǒ zhǐ xiǎng shǐ nǐ gāoxìng bà le**   8 他中文说得很好嘛！ **tā zhōngwén shuō de hěn hǎo ma**

Unit 24

Exercise 24.1   1 你的玩具熊呢？ **nǐ de wánjùxióng ne**   2 笔在这儿，纸呢？ **bǐ zài zhèr | zhǐ ne**   3 我晚上十点钟睡觉，你呢？ **wǒ wǎnshang shí diǎn zhōng shuìjiào | nǐ ne**   4 我的眼镜呢？ **wǒ de yǎnjìng ne**   5 你在做实验，他们呢？ **nǐ zài zuò shíyàn | tāmen ne**   6 你侄儿呢？ **nǐ zhír ne**

Exercise 24.2   1 Your elder sister can cook, how about you?   2 Do you intend to go into town or go home?   3 May I sit here?   4 Brother, where is my notebook?   5 The new director is at a meeting.   6 The railway station is far from here.   7 Where has my wallet gone?   8 Why aren't you doing it yourself?   9 I won't bother myself about him.   10 No wonder they are inviting me to dinner!   11 Mother doesn't know anything about this yet.   12 Everything is ready.

Exercise   24.3   1 今晚你去电影院呢，还是去朋友家？ **jīn wǎn nǐ qù diànyǐngyuàn ne | háishi qù péngyou jiā**   2 她是医生呢，还是护士？ **tā shì yīshēng ne | háishi hùshi**   3 你看小说呢，还是听音乐？ **nǐ kàn xiǎoshuō ne | háishi tīng yīnyuè**   4 他骑车去呢，还是开车去？ **tā qí chē qù ne | háishi kāichē qù**   5 孩子们在花园里玩儿呢，还是在街上玩儿？ **háizimen zài huāyuán li wánr ne | háishi zài jiē shang wánr**   6 你想养猫呢，还是想养狗？ **nǐ xiǎng yǎng māo ne | háishi xiǎng yǎng gǒu**

Exercise 24.4   1 你想去哪儿吃晚饭呢？ **nǐ xiǎng qù nǎr chī wǎnfàn ne**   2 看！小猫在喝牛奶呢！ **kàn | xiǎo māo zài hē niúnǎi ne**   3 爷爷也在读报呢！ **yéye yě zài dúbào ne**   4 八十岁的老人在海里游泳呢！ **bā shí suì de lǎorén zài hǎi li yóuyǒng ne**   5 你的衣服怎么湿了呢？ **nǐ de yīfu zénme shī le ne**

6 你想买什么呢？ **nǐ xiǎng mǎi shénme ne**   7 那个孩子在画画儿呢！**nà/nèi gè háizi zài huà huàr ne**   8 她在写什么呢？**tā zài xiě shénme ne**   9 这辆火车去不去伦敦呢？**zhè/zhèi liàng huǒchē qù bù qù lúndūn ne**   10 你究竟想不想看这本小说呢？**nǐ jiūjìng xiǎng bù xiǎng kàn zhè/zhèi běn xiǎoshuō ne**

Unit 25

Exercise 25.1   1 喔喔喔地 **wōwōwō de**   2 扑通 **pūtōng**   3 劈里啪啦的 **pīlipālā de**   4 哗哗地 **huāhuā de**   5 嘭嘭地 **pēngpēng de**   6 淅沥淅沥地 **xīlì xīlì de**   7 隆隆的 **lónglóng de**   8 嘡哐 **kuānglāng**

Exercise 25.2   1 唉 **ài**   2 嘿 **hēi**   3 嗯 **ng**   4 嗬 **hē**   5 哦 **ò**   6 呸 **pēi**   7 哼 **hng**   8 哎呀 **āiyā**   9 唉 **ài**   10 哼 **hng**

Exercise 25.3   1 first tone   2 second tone   3 second tone   4 third tone   5 fourth tone   6 fourth tone   7 third tone   8 first tone

Exercise 25.4   1 她扑通一声掉进了湖里。 **tā pūtōng yī shēng diào jìn le hú li**   2 我可以听到大厅里的旧钟在滴答滴答地走着。 **wǒ kěyǐ tīng dào dàtīng li de jiù zhōng zài dīdā dīdā de zǒu zhe**   3 哦，现在我明白她是什么意思了。 **ò｜xiànzài wǒ míngbái tā shì shénme yìsi le**   4 嘿，那件蓝毛衣真漂亮。 **hēi｜nà/nèi jiàn lán máoyī zhēn piàoliang**   5 唉，下雨了。 **ài｜xià yǔ le** 6 嗬，爸爸回来了。 **hē｜bàba huí lái le**